T H E
SOCIALLY RESPONSIVE
PORTFOLIO

BALANCING
POLITICS & PROFITS

IN INSTITUTIONAL
MONEY
MANAGEMENT

JAMES MELTON

MATTHEW KEENAN

PROBUS PUBLISHING COMPANY
Chicago, Illinois
Cambridge, England

© 1994, Probus Publishing Company

This publication is designed to provide accurate and authoritative information in regard to the subject matter covered. It is sold with the understanding that the author and the publisher are not engaged in rendering legal, accounting, or other professional service.

ISBN 1-55738-501-7

Printed in the United States of America

BB

1 2 3 4 5 6 7 8 9 0

To Sarah L. Snow
—JM

To Patricia Daniel Keenan
—MK

Contents

List of Figures
and Tables

Acknowledgments

The authors are appreciative of the many people who shared with us their experiences, insights, research, and writings and who were otherwise so helpful and gracious to us during the preparation of this book:

Alton Bathrick, Christie Baxter, Kevin Bean, David Berge, Dianne Bratcher, Francis Brody, Remi Browne, Richard Chimberg, Raymond Codey, Kalyn Culler Cohen, Michael Crosby, Donna Dean, Darren DeVore, Amy Domini, Mark Dowie, Gilbert Gaul, Joel Getzendanner, Wendy Grover, Valerie Heinonen, Stanley Karson, Richard Knight, Brad Krevor, Jack Litzenberg, Carolyn Mathiasen, William McAlpin, Sean McManus, Meredith Miller, Marcy Murningham, Kirsten Moy, Jeremy Nowak, Wayne Owens, Jean Pogge, Trex Proffitt, Allyson Randolph, Judy Samuelson, David Sand, Tom Seel, John Simon, Andy Smith, Timothy Smith, Judy Samuelson, Joan Shapiro, Mitchell Sviridoff, Jeanne Tang, Pamela Tate, Darle Tilly, Martin Paul Trimble, Michael Troutman, Mark Tulay, Stephen Viederman, Dennis White, Steve Williams, Dan Wingerd, and Louis Winnick.

We are also grateful to Peter Kinder for his advice and suggestions in the preparation of the manuscript and to the staff at Probus Publishing for their patience and assistance.

Introduction

Profit is today a fighting word. Profits are the lifeblood of the economic system, the magic elixir upon which progress and all good things depend ultimately. But one man's lifeblood is another man's cancer.

— Paul A. Samuelson
Economist

Throughout the centuries, poets, scholars, and philosophers have given money an almost anthropomorphic dimension. It is greedy, it is generous. It is the grantor of freedom, or its taker; a source of power, and a source of enslavement. It is good, it is evil. The poetic and philosophical debate about the true nature of wealth, money, and investment capital is as old as civilization itself. The fact is, however, that wealth, in and of itself, has no power, and certainly no personality of its own. Our money is only what we choose to make of it.

It is also the most powerful tool we have for shaping the future. How our society, and others decide to harness investment capital will go a long way toward determining how rich, free, and peaceful the world will be tomorrow. Such decisions will also have an impact on how polluted and resource-depleted that world becomes. Like it or not, all investment decisions are social investment decisions to some degree.

Over the past two decades, investors have begun to take that responsibility to heart. According to the Social Investment Forum, it is likely that, in the United States alone, $775 billion is invested utilizing some kind of social or ethical restrictions applied (see Table 1). As Peter Kinder, a consultant and writer on ethical investing puts it: "What has changed over the years? Everything. [Responsive investing] has grown from a kind of hippy-dippy operation to become something with a high degree of professionalism, with an increasingly institutional outlook; it's become more than an industry that's growing. It's an industry that's mature."

The growth of socially responsive investing has been attributed to a number of things, such as a general rise in social—especially environmental—consciousness, the apparent success of the South African divestment movement, and the coming of age of the socially concerned baby boom generation. Clearly, one of the most important factors has been the emergence of large, wealthy, sophisticated institutional investors that service immense and diverse constituencies. As their portfolios have become larger, the ability of pension funds, endowments, foundations, and other institutions to get the attention of corporate America has grown enormously.

The constituencies of these institutions represent a cross-section of the American public. Pension funds represent public, union, and other workers.

TABLE 1   The Growth of Institutional Investors

	1992	1976
Total tax-exempt plan sponsors*	38,322	6,154
Total asset size	$3.03 trillion	$324 billion
Corporate plan sponsors	33,799	3,733
Asset size	$1.53 trillion	$155 billion
Largest: AT&T	$45.7 billion	$679 million
Public plan sponsors	1,175	454
Asset size	$1.06 trillion	$115 billion
Largest: CalPERS	$68 billion	$7.7 billion
Union plan sponsors	1,581	817
Asset size	$216 billion	$15 billion
Largest: Teamsters Western Conf.	$12.1 billion	$1.3 billion
Foundations	1,439	666
Asset size	$118 billion	$24 billion
Largest: Ford Foundation	$6.1 billion	$2.5 billion
University endowments	828	454
Asset size	$109 billion	$15 billion
Largest: Harvard University	$5.1 billion	$1.25 billion

* With more than $1 million in assets.

Source: "From Carter to Clinton: The Pension Market Explodes," *Plan Sponsor,* April 1993.

Endowments are invested for the benefit of students, professors, and hospitals. Foundations invest money for the benefit of charities and nonprofit organizations.

Institutional investors in the United States, particularly pension funds, represent a vast store of wealth unparalleled in history. The total value of U.S. pension funds with over $1 million in assets is now about $3 trillion, including over $1 trillion in public sector funds, $216 billion in union funds, and over $1.5 trillion in corporate funds. Endowments with more than $1 million total another $109 billion. Foundations over $1 million total $118 billion.[1]

Most of the money invested with social restrictions attached consists of the assets of large institutions that have rules against investing in companies doing business in South Africa. But, even as South Africa restrictions melt away in response to the African National Congress' recent call for an end to sanctions, the movement of socially responsive investing will remain deeply ingrained. The South Africa issue has ignited among investors concern for human rights everywhere, from Northern Ireland to Burma to Central America and Mexico. In addition, investors—large, powerful institutions among them—are demanding better environmental performance, more accountability and a higher degree of good corporate citizenship from the companies they invest in.

Thanks to the global economy, and the emergence of large, powerful institutional investors, people all over the world are connected to one another by an invisible web of capital. The investment of money connects New York public employees to the plight of homosexuals in the South, college endowments to the struggle of blacks in South Africa, and food industry workers to the lives of political prisoners forced to work in Chinese factories, through their equity holdings in global corporations.

Of course, these ethical and social considerations stray significantly from the traditional role of the fiduciary. Trustees and money managers of foundations, endowments, and certainly pension funds have been understandably reluctant to invest using any criteria other than strict economic and financial considerations. But the reality is that social responsibility is becoming an integral part of investing an institutional portfolio. Social and ethical investment concerns have moved from beyond the radar screen to among the most important policy considerations faced by the guardians of institutional assets.

Even the South Africa issue shows no signs of going away. Investors that once called for companies to divest under the apartheid regime are now working to ensure that foreign investors follow strict ethical codes of conduct.

The reasons that institutions need to concern themselves with the impact of their investments are more than just political, although politics certainly plays a role. These days, social and economic considerations very often overlap. Nowhere is that more obvious than in the case of environmental performance, where a poor record can cost a corporation millions or hundreds of millions of dollars in fines, litigation, and clean-up costs. But its is also true that issues like equal employment, product safety, and community relations can have a measurable impact on a company's bottom line.

The primary aim of this book to provide aid and assistance to the trustees and officials of institutions who must decide when and how their organization's investment portfolio can be made to reflect the social and ethical concerns of its constituency. It is also hoped that it will provide guidance for pension beneficiaries, communities, public officials, activists, and others interested in socially responsive investing.

The authors have divided *The Socially Responsive Portfolio* into two sections. The first section outlines some of the most important issues faced by institutional investors. The second, longer section, outlines ways that specific kinds of institutions have dealt with the issues that confront them.

Discussed in the first chapter are seven broad issues that have attracted a great deal of attention in recent years: economically targeted investing; environmentalism; affirmative action; oppressive regimes; proxy activism; so-called "sin" investments; and the opportunities for the growth of responsive investing presented by the rise of defined contribution retirement plans.

Economically targeted investing, or ETI, is the practice of directing investment capital, especially pension money, into investments that seek to provide "spin-off" benefits to the local community while at the same time paying a competitive return. Among pension fund officials, few issues are more controversial, or have more serious long-term implications. This section deals with the growth of ETI, its origins, and the elements of sound ETI policy that can protect pension assets from unsafe and unwise investments.

Environmentalism is said to be on the verge of replacing South Africa as the most talked-about responsive investing issue. Institutions have shown interest for both ethical and economic reasons. As the effect of the Exxon Valdez oil spill proved, environmental behavior can and does affect the profitability of a company. To deal with this issue, some institutions have, with limited success, promoted a code of conduct called the CERES Principles (for the Coalition for Environmentally Responsive Economies) as a benchmark for corporate conduct.

Led by public pension funds, more institutions are hiring women- and minority-owned money management firms to manage a portion of their assets. This trend has increased opportunities for women and minorities in fund management, but such firms still manage only a tiny fraction of institutional assets. In addition, institutions have dealt with the issue of affirmative action by filing proxy resolutions at companies asking them to report on their equal opportunity policies or, in the case of banks, their community reinvestment performance.

Despite the apparent success of anti-apartheid forces in South Africa, the issue of oppressive regimes is likely to gain prominence in years to come. Already, institutions have filed proxy resolutions opposing investments in military-led Burma, and the purchase of Chinese goods that might be made with prison labor. In addition, investors concerned with South Africa seem poised to keep a watchful eye on business practices there as Western investors re-enter the country.

The issue of investing in "sin" industries, namely tobacco, alcohol, and gambling, has long been part of the agenda of religious organizations, many of whom have avoided the stocks of such companies for decades. But in recent years, the fight against the tobacco industry has been joined by college and hospital endowment funds that have sold off their holdings in tobacco companies. Success has been mixed, but anti-smoking activists intend to continue to put the issue before institutional investors.

Some "socially responsible" investment options have begun to surface in 401(k) and other defined contribution plans across the country. As retirement programs begin to look more like menus, employers will increasingly need to decide whether socially screened options belong on the bill of fare.

The second section of the book deals with eight categories of institutional investors and how some of them have dealt with the political and social aspects of managing their portfolios.

At public pensions, interest in economically targeted investing is growing fast, even though many fund officials are deeply suspicious of this trend. Several examples of ETI programs around the country are presented. In addition, we outline the issues of proxy activism, women- and minority-owned money managers, and the pitfalls suffered of Minnesota's ban on investing in sin stocks.

Among foundations some major philanthropic organizations have used their investment portfolio to complement grant programs through so-called program-related investing. While still a minor part of foundation assets, such investments are gaining attention as a cost-effective way to meet the social mandate of these institutions.

Union involvement in responsive investing has been limited, but, in some cases, successful. For example, during an otherwise disastrous era for real estate investing, funds designed to let union pension funds invest in union-built properties have been top performers. In addition, unions have begun to flex their economic muscles as proxy activists on issues like corporate governance and the alleged use of prison labor to produce Chinese exports.

The insurance industry has been praised for investing a lot of money in ways designed to promote lofty social goals. But others criticize the industry's responsive investment efforts as self-serving and ineffective. Chapter 5 explains why some critics say the industry's efforts don't go far enough, while others say they go too far.

Meanwhile, on the nation's campuses, student efforts to force college endowments to divest from South Africa showed amazing success in the beginning, but slowed to a crawl as the movement fell victim to its own success and events in South Africa pointed to an end to apartheid. Since then, no investment issue has so mobilized student activists.

Religious organizations have, for many years, sponsored the lion's share of proxy resolutions dealing with social issues. In addition, they have been active in various kinds community development investing. Chapter 7 discusses the kinds of issues churches have pursued—and will pursue—on the proxy statements and gives several examples of the community investment programs initiated by various denominations.

So-called "good guy" lenders—community development banks, community development credit unions, and community development loan funds—have been able to make high-risk loans without high loan losses. But not all good-guy lending is done by these institutions. Chapter 10 also explains how two mainstream banks have made a difference by changing their lending policies.

Finally, several examples are given of institutional money managers that offer various kinds of socially responsive investment products.

As one might guess, each section of this book could have been a book by itself. Our purpose, however, has been to provide an overview of the major social and political issues that affect institutional portfolios and to present some of the ways in which institutions have dealt with them. In this way, we hope to alleviate the sense of isolation felt by trustees and investment officials when such issues arise at their institutions.

We hope that *The Socially Responsive Portfolio* will contribute to a greater understanding of socially responsive investing among institutions and that it will contribute to the ongoing debate about when and where institutional investors can use their vast investment portfolios to make the world a better place.

NOTE

1. *Directory of Pension Funds and their Investment Managers* (Charlottesville, Virginia, Money Market Directories Inc., 1992), p. XV.

1

Current Issues in Socially Responsive Investing

ECONOMICALLY TARGETED INVESTING: THAT'S WHERE THE MONEY IS

One of the stories most repeated at pension fund conferences is about Willie Sutton, the notorious bank robber. When asked why he robbed banks, Sutton replied: "Because that's where the money is." In today's cash-starved public sector, the nation's $1 trillion in public sector pension fund assets presents more than one of the world's largest stores of investment capital, it presents the only game in town.

While pension fund officials are justifiably reluctant to utilize that vast pile of cash for any purpose other than paying benefits to retirees, funds in more states and communities are attempting to make those assets work harder by steering a small part of their capital away from traditional asset classes and into economically targeted investments, or ETIs. There is no generally accepted definition of ETIs, however, the definition used by the Institute for Fiduciary Education (IFE) best captures the aim of pension funds when they set up such programs:

> An economically targeted investment (or ETI) is an investment designed
> to produce a competitive rate of return commensurate with risk as well as
> to create collateral economic benefits for a targeted geographic area,
> group of people, or sector of the economy.[1]

Targeted investments take a number of forms. In some cases, pension funds make direct investments in local companies or allocate a part of their resources to venture capital investments aimed at local and/or minority- and women-owned businesses. However, the bulk of targeted investing programs are devoted to affordable housing, either by providing low-interest mortgages to home buyers or financing the construction of low- and moderate-priced apartments and single-family homes. In all cases, pension funds that make targeted investments seek to earn a return that is equal to that which could be earned from other kinds of investments at a comparable risk.

While there is still little agreement on what constitutes an ETI, and when it is appropriate to make such investments, pension officials universally agree that such investments must be designed to meet the fiduciary require-ments of the fund. In many cases, ETIs utilize federal or other kinds of gov-ernment guarantees and provide mechanisms for regular oversight by the pen-sion fund's board of trustees. Some generally accepted elements of a good targeted investing policy will be dealt with later in this chapter.

Pension funds have invested an enormous sum in ETIs, but it represents only a tiny portion of the entire mass of pension fund assets. According to a recent survey by the IFE, U.S. pension funds had invested at least $19.8 bil-lion in 95 separate economically targeted investments as of 1992. Of that

FIGURE 1-1   Distribution of ETI Assets 1992

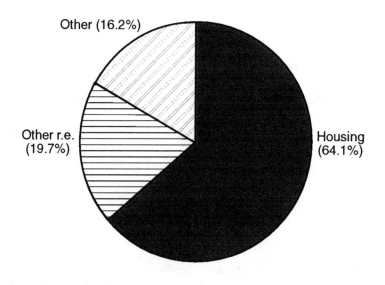

Other (16.2%)

Other r.e. (19.7%)

Housing (64.1%)

Source: Institute for Fiduciary Education.

amount, $12.7 billion was invested in housing and another $3.9 billion was in other kinds of real estate investments. Other kinds of targeted investments included small business loans, venture capital, commercial mortgages, certificates of deposits, and private placements (see Figures 1-1 and 1-2).[2] The IFE's results were based on responses from 119 large U.S. pension funds; of that group, 46 reported that they had targeted investing programs. A similar study released by the IFE in 1989 found $7.1 billion invested in 78 such programs by 41 funds.[3]

Proponents of such investments argue that pension funds—particularly public sector funds—are uniquely qualified to make profitable and socially beneficial investments in their community. Because of the local orientation of such funds, it is argued, they should be able to find and exploit areas for investment that are ignored by traditional investors because of inertia, racism, different time horizons, or simply a lack of imagination. By filling such

FIGURE 1-2   ETI Programs Nationwide 1989 and 1992

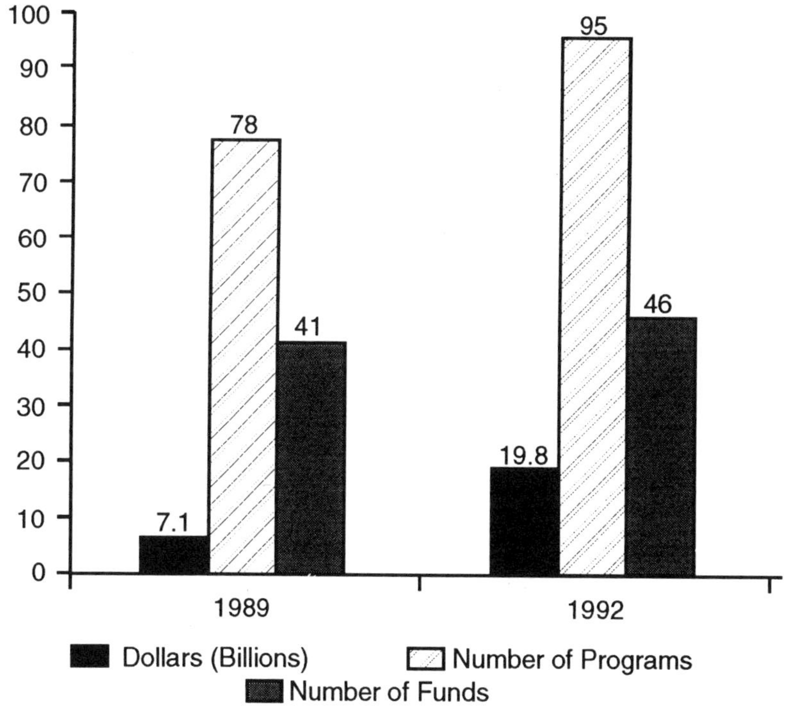

Source: Institute for Fiduciary Education.

"capital gaps," proponents claim ETIs can make money for the pension fund while also creating jobs and renewing long-neglected communities. In short, the idea is to "do well by doing good."

As New York City Finance Commissioner Carol O'Cleireacain, a long-time proponent of ETI put it:

> State-of-the-art ETI does not put positive social and economic externali-
> ties ahead of a pension fund's fiduciary obligations. Rather, the search
> for positive externalities has become an investment screen for savvy
> pension fund trustees seeking to rectify market inefficiencies, and, in the
> process, to reap above-market returns.[4]

In other words, as they search for ways to provide spin-off economic benefits from their investment activities, pension funds are likely to uncover—and benefit from—opportunities otherwise missed by more traditional investors. Indeed, many pension funds have been successful in making targeted investments work. New York City's five pension funds claim to earn more on their ETIs than on their general bond portfolios.

In the IFE study, 46 percent of the funds with targeted investment programs said their ETIs met expectations and 16 percent said the investments exceeded expectations. Another 14 percent said the investment failed to meet the benchmark, while 22 percent said the investments were "too new to make a meaningful assessment of their financial performance." Among the 26 targeted investments for which performance data was provided, the average annual rate of return was 9.82 percent (see Figure 1-3).[5]

But, as the IFE study and numerous pension plan officials are quick to point out, targeted investing remains controversial. Many public pension fund officials are deeply suspicious of targeted investing, fearing that the trend is nothing more than an attempt by politicians to subsidize social policy goals by short-changing retired public employees. Critics say that most targeted investments are inappropriate for pension funds because they are too risky, provide a lower risk-adjusted return than can be earned elsewhere, or both.

The IFE found that "the most frequent reason expressed by retirement systems for not investing in ETIs was the belief that doing so conflicted with the pension system's fiduciary duty." Other reasons for objecting to ETIs include the idea that "geographic concentration conflicts with their objective of greater diversification," a belief that such investments provide poor returns, and concern that "external demands for ETIs would infringe on the fund's independence."

Because of such concerns, pension funds have frequently resisted even light-handed attempts to push them into making targeted investments. For example, in 1991, opposition from state pension funds helped to defeat a bill

FIGURE 1-3   Performance of ETIs among Funds with Targeted Investments

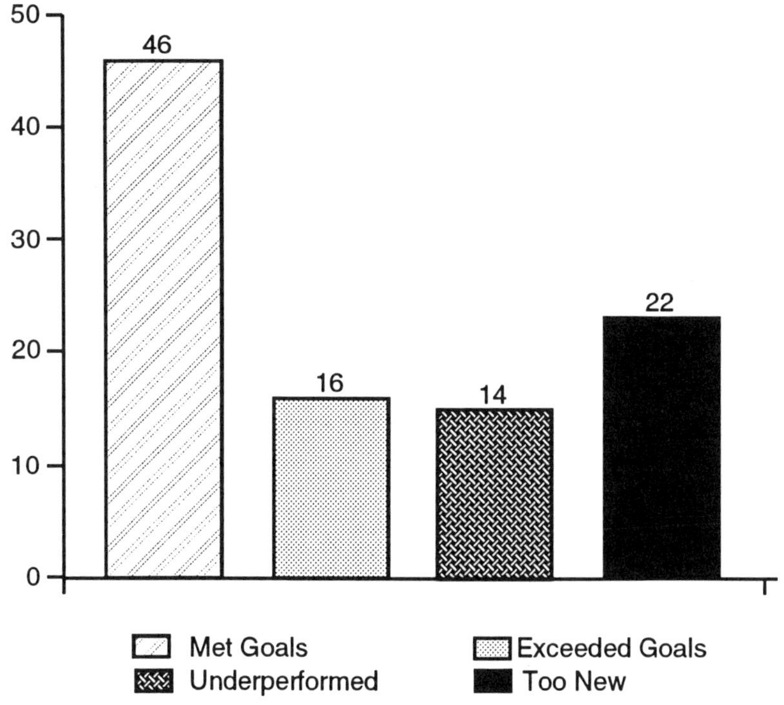

Met Goals   Exceeded Goals
Underperformed   Too New

Source: Institute for Fiduciary Education.

that would have specifically authorized, but not required, the funds to invest a portion of their assets in small business and venture capital in the state. "You cannot legislate fiduciary concerns," said James P. Hadley Jr., director of the Louisiana Teachers' Retirement System, Baton Rouge.[6]

A few high-profile failures have added ammunition to the argument against ETIs. Probably the best-known flop has been the targeted investment program of the nearly $5 billion Kansas Public Employees' Retirement System. In 1991, the fund revealed enormous losses from its program to invest in a series of private placements and partnerships to assist businesses in the state. As of February 1993, the Kansas fund had written off about $138 million in losses, and estimates of the fund's losses (which had yet to be fully calculated) were running as high as $238 million. (The losses prompted the Kansas Legislature to pass a series of reforms in early 1993. Among other things, the new rules give pension fund trustees more oversight responsibility and limit investments in real estate and private placements.)[7]

Another well-publicized failure is the State of Connecticut Trust Fund's $25 million investment in CF Holdings, formerly the firearms division of Colt Industries. When the state pension fund stepped in, it heralded the move as a creative way to save local jobs, but the operation fell into bankruptcy in 1992.

ETI opponents point out that neither investment program would have been made if the pension systems involved had stuck to their knitting and declined to make their investment portfolios an instrument for social policy. Targeted investment advocates counter that any investment can turn sour and that pension funds sometimes face serious losses even when they stick to more traditional assets, like stocks and bonds.

Are ETIs Mainstream Investments?

Given the publicity that targeted investing has received in recent years, one might think that it is an idea that is sweeping like a firestorm through the pension fund community; one might predict that it is only a matter of time before ETIs take their place with equities, U.S. Treasury and corporate debt, and cash as a part of the investment portfolio of virtually all funds. Or, an observer might as easily predict that all this ETI nonsense is nothing but the social policy "flavor of the month," and that pension funds will quickly forget about the idea as state and local governments slowly begin to balance their budgets and capital sources like banks and insurance companies return to health.

At this point reports of the death of ETI, or of its acceptance into the mainstream of investment policy, are both greatly exaggerated. While most signals indicate that targeted investing may be here to stay, the evidence also indicates that the pension fund community as a whole is ambivalent about the idea.

The Institute for Fiduciary Education study found that the number of ETI programs and the amount of money invested in them continues to rise. However, the same study found that the number of pension funds starting targeted investing in recent years only slightly exceeds the number that have quit. Thirteen, or almost 32 percent of the 41 funds that reported ETIs in the institute's first study in 1989 had eliminated the programs by 1992.

Reasons for the attrition were varied. For example, some funds had made ETIs for only a limited period and did not replace the programs when the original investment matured. Some funds were not satisfied with investment returns, while others simply lost interest when ETI proponents left the board of trustees.

Furthermore, as many of the supporters of targeted investing concede, ETIs, unlike traditional stocks and bonds, cannot be incorporated into the portfolio of every pension fund. In some cases, funds may not have the staff to adequately manage an ETI portfolio and, in others, the asset base may simply be too small to risk moving beyond traditional asset classes.

Another problem with participation by small funds is that, even if they do find a way to make a targeted investment, the "collateral economic benefits" may be too small to greatly affect the local economy. An additional $100 million in funding for affordable housing in a particular state, county, or municipality may be enough to provide shelter for hundreds of families; but a $10 million commitment may prove to be little more than a symbolic effort. In general, the smaller the pension fund, the fewer opportunities there are to make safe, effective ETIs.

Thus, it is not surprising that, among the funds surveyed by the IFE, targeted investments were made most frequently by the largest public pension funds, many of which have large internal staffs and, thus, more ability to oversee these investments. Pension funds reporting targeted investing programs averaged $11 billion in assets, compared with an average of $4.6 billion in assets for funds without ETIs.

Among the 139 funds in the IFE's survey universe, 60 percent of those with assets over $5 billion reported having ETI programs, while only 31 percent of those with assets over $1 billion had such programs. Likewise, targeted investments were twice as likely to be found in the portfolio of state pension funds than in the generally smaller municipal or county funds.

Elements of Good ETI Policy

As any money manager will say, the first three rules of investing are: (1) preserve capital; (2) preserve capital; and (3) preserve capital. But when a pension fund is considering making economically targeted investments, fiduciary responsibility requires moving far beyond the basics. An acceptable ETI must not only protect the retirement assets of the fund, it must provide a rate of return comparable to that of other, more traditional investments with similar levels of risk.

An investment that simply "makes money" may appear sound, but pension fund trustees are short-changing the fund's beneficiaries if they purposely forgo opportunities to make a larger return elsewhere within similar risk parameters. In the long-run, every percentage point in lost returns can translate into millions—even tens or hundreds of millions—of dollars in lost revenue to the fund. The result is that governments must pour more tax dollars into the pension fund or provide fewer benefits to retirees. In short, the positive spin-off benefits of poorly constructed ETIs can easily be overwhelmed by the detrimental effects of an irresponsible investment policy.

Keen to avoid the pitfalls of low returns and high risk, most pension funds require that their ETIs adhere to at least a loose set of written investment guidelines. According to the IFE study, 80 percent of funds with targeted investments have policies that "spell out—to one degree or another—the kinds of investments allowed." Also, "63 percent of funds reported setting out the financial performance they expect from their ETI."

The stringency of these written policies varies greatly from fund to fund. However, a consensus appears to be emerging on at least the broad outlines of good ETI policy. Stated simply, the guiding principles are that good ETI programs will: seek a market rate of return, provide for regular oversight of targeted investments, seek to provide capital that otherwise would not be available, and utilize guarantees whenever possible to limit the investment risk.

Furthermore, most pension fund officials agree, ETIs should be voluntary. Attempts by Congress and state legislatures to mandate targeted investing will face strong opposition from fund officials because by and large, pension funds perform better when investment concerns, not politics, drive asset allocation policy.

In 1991, an advisory panel convened to recommend an ETI policy for the Massachusetts State Teachers and Employees Retirement System (MASTERS), and it created a set of criteria that sum up many of the generally accepted ideas concerning good ETI management.

The panel recommended "targeted investments must offer a potential return at least equal to the return offered by other investments with similar risk." As the report stated:

> Subsidizing certain mortgages or commercial loans may be justified in terms of economic return to the State. However, the State should bear the cost of the subsidy directly, not hide it in MASTERS. For instance, MASTERS could make loans below market rates, provided the state concurrently paid MASTERS an amount equal to the value of the subsidy. This would provide MASTERS with a market rate of return, quantify the cost of the subsidy to the taxpayer and properly distinguish between the cost of pension benefits and the cost of loan subsidies.[8]

The panel said targeted investment by the pension fund must "fill a capital gap," by providing capital that otherwise would not be available. "A targeted investment program will contribute little to the State economy if the investment simply displaces funds that would be provided by other sources," the panel pointed out.

Next, the panel said, the program should "minimize local credit risk" by utilizing federal, state, or corporate guarantees and insurance whenever possible. For example, ETIs could take the form of loans insured by the Small Business Administration, Fair Housing Administration, or "quasi-governmental guarantees" such as those provided by the Federal National Mortgage Association.

In addition, the panel asserted that all targeted investments should be made in full compliance with state law and that any targeted investment program ought to be "structured to minimize staff involvement, particularly in situations that require direct experience, investment analysis and judgment." The panel went on to suggest that the pension fund hire two additional people to oversee the ETI program on a full-time basis and suggested several specific targeted investment programs for consideration. (Many of the panel's suggestions were later adopted by Boston-based MASTERS. For a description of the fund's ETI program, see Chapter 2.)

The criteria established by the Massachusetts report closely parallels the three rules set out by New York state's Governor's Task Force on Pension Fund Investment in its 1990 report entitled "Competitive Plus: Economically Targeted Investments by Pension Funds." The task force states:

> First, the two key legal precepts of pension fund investing—the duty of prudence and the exclusive benefit rule—should not be modified, abrogated, or ignored for the sake of achieving higher levels of ETIs.
>
> Second, pension funds should not undertake investments which produce concessionary rates of return for the funds in order to promote social goals or achieve economic development goals. A concessionary investment is one with a low rate of return unjustified by a suitably low level of risk or a high risk investment without suitably high returns.
>
> Third, the participation of pension funds in ETI programs . . . should be voluntary, not mandatory. There is no legal basis . . . for mandating specific ETI programs. Investment decisions are each fund's to make.[9]

The findings of the governor's task force eventually led to the creation of an intermediary called Excelsior Capital Corp. The quasi-public body designed to make investment in the state has raised about $250 million from public and private pension funds for investments in affordable mortgages and financing for medium-sized companies in the state.[10]

Yet another variation on the theme is offered by the State of Connecticut Trust Funds, which recently expanded its ETI program. It adopted a policy that says that, in addition to seeking a market rate of return and attempting to fill capital gaps, the fund will avoid competing with existing state programs and treat ETIs as a separate asset class. The policy also gives the state treasurer (who is the sole trustee of the state pension fund) the ability to select investments "with the advice and counsel" of the pension consultant retained by the fund.

What Is the Role of the Legislature?

In most cases, pension fund officials will argue that it is they, and not state legislatures or Congress, who should take a leading role in deciding when and where ETIs should be made. Generally, pension funds resist any legislative attempts to dictate, or even recommend, investment policy guidelines.

On the other hand, it is clear that, without the creation of various state and federal guarantees, many targeted investment programs would not be viable. Clearly, there is much that the federal, state, and local governments can do to encourage targeted investing, short of dictating investment policy through legislative action. Along those lines, the Washington, D.C.–based Center for Policy Alternatives (CPA) suggests numerous ways that state governments can and should take steps to facilitate and nurture (though not require) targeted investments by their public sector pension funds.

In a report released in 1992, CPA recommends that, where investment restrictions placed on funds inhibit ETIs, those rules should be changed. For example, the CPA suggests that states eliminate so-called "legal lists" of allowable investments, replacing the lists with "prudent person" standards that give pension funds greater flexibility in selecting investment options.

The center also suggests that legislators help to identify and target capital gaps that might be filled using ETIs and create financial intermediaries, or "community capital builders," to help pension funds make investments which, otherwise, might be too small to consider. The report states:

> To make relatively small loans or capital investments pension funds need a broker—a financial intermediary—to overcome the diseconomies of scale . . . First, an intermediary reduces transaction costs . . . second, [it] reduces risk by analyzing investment opportunities and monitoring performance . . . Third, an intermediary leverages additional external risk reduction tools, by taking advantage of loan guarantee programs and securing other credit enhancements.[11]

CPA advocates the establishment of more "appropriate risk reduction mechanisms," such as state or private insurance pools and loan guarantees, to make ETIs more attractive to pension funds, such as those administered by New York State's Rehabilitation Mortgage Insurance Corp. and the State of New York Mortgage Association.

By early 1993, some states were considering legislation that would urge their pension funds to invest a part of their assets in ETI.[12] As will be discussed in Chapter 2, the federal government is also becoming interested in finding ways to use pension capital to meet various kinds of capital shortages, particularly to provide financing for infrastructure projects. One option under consideration is the creation of a national investment fund—a sort of super intermediary—of pooled investment capital from pension funds and other sources for such projects. Investors would be repaid with revenue from tolls, fees, and an increased gasoline tax.

ENVIRONMENTALISM
AND THE CERES PRINCIPLES

In 1993, two occurrences suggest that environmentalism may emerge as the most important issue among socially motivated investors. First, shareholders filed more proxy resolutions dealing with environmental issues than any other topic—replacing South Africa as the issue most commonly addressed in such resolutions. And second, the Boston-based Coalition for Environmentally Responsible Economies (CERES) persuaded Sun Co., the Philadelphia-based oil giant, to become the first major U.S. corporation to become a signatory to the CERES Principles, the organization's code of conduct for corporate environmental behavior.

Whether these events signal an epochal change in the social investment movement toward a period of "green" issues dominating the agenda, it is clear that the environmental performance of companies is likely to receive a great deal of attention from shareholders in years to come. The reasoning is two-fold: first, environmental awareness has become deeply ingrained in the psyche of the American public; and second, large shareholders have discovered that poor environmental policies of a corporation can have a large, negative impact on profitability over the long term.

The second consideration, in particular, has caught the attention of some of the country's largest public sector pension funds. Supporters of resolutions dealing with the CERES Principles include New York City Employees Retirement System—which has been the only public fund so far to actually sponsor CERES-related resolutions—the California Public Employees Retirement System, and the California State Teachers and Employees' Retirement System.

In addition, several religious organizations have sponsored shareholder resolutions dealing with environmental performance, including numerous resolutions calling on companies to adhere to the CERES Principles. According to information compiled by the Interfaith Center on Corporate Responsibility (ICCR), more than 50 shareholder resolutions dealing with the CERES Principles were filed in 1993, most of which asked corporations to become signatories to the code of conduct.

In addition, the 1993 proxy season saw a number of environmental shareholder resolutions dealing with specific, single issues. Among the environmental issues dealt with were requests for several utilities to report on efforts to help their customers conserve energy and requests for reports from companies to detail their efforts to reduce emissions and minimize other environmental risks.

CERES and its Principles

CERES is a nonprofit coalition of environmental organizations, trustees of major public sector pension funds, social investment organizations, and religious groups. Members include the National Wildlife Federation, the Sierra Club, the comptroller and finance commissioner of New York City, the controller of the state of California, U.S. Trust Co., the Interfaith Center for Corporate Resposibility (ICCR), and the Presbyterian Church, USA.

Formed in the wake of the giant Exxon Valdez oil spill, the coalition introduced its CERES Principles—then known as the Valdez Principles—in 1989. The 10-point code calls on signatory companies to reduce the release of environmentally damaging substances; strive to "make sustainable use of renewable resources" and conserve those that are non renewable; conserve energy; strive to minimize health and safety risks to employees and the communities in which they operate; and to eliminate, to the extent possible, the creation and sale of environmentally unsafe goods and services.

The code of conduct also contains clauses that commit signatories to "promptly and responsibly" correct any environmental mishaps, inform the public of any potential danger to safety or the environment, ensure that the chief executive and board of directors remain informed and involved in environmental issues, and conduct an annual audit of the company's adherence to the CERES Principles, called the CERES Report. In order to pay for the cost of maintaining its oversight function, the CERES organization assesses a sliding scale fee to its signatories based on their annual gross revenues. (For the full text of the CERES Principles, see Appendix 1.)

During the first few years of the CERES campaign, large corporations generally resisted the code of conduct. Numerous small companies, social investment organizations, and nonprofit groups, most of whom were not in highly polluting industries, signed on to the principles. However, the nation's largest manufacturers and service companies—the real targets of the code—refused to sign up, citing concerns that compliance would be too costly and that signatory status might expose corporations to potential legal liabilities.

However, in 1992, largely as a result of its negotiations with Sun Co. and other large corporations, CERES issued a revised version of the principles. While retaining the essence of the code, CERES adopted new wording that addressed many of the concerns of corporate lawyers and agreed to change the name, thus eliminating the embarrassing reference to the oil industry's greatest ecological disaster. In addition, the coalition changed its reporting procedures to make compliance with the code less costly and burdensome for signatories.

In February 1993, Sun Co. became the first large U.S. corporation to become a CERES signatory by adopting a version of the CERES principles specially designed to fit in with its operations.

Among the adaptations, the wording of the first principle was changed to say that Sun will "reduce our overall emissions to the environment (air, water and land) with special emphasis on toxic substances." The original wording of the principles states that signatories will "reduce and make continual progress toward eliminating the release of any substance that may cause environmental damage to the air, water, or the earth and its inhabitants." The change is subtle, but it allowed Sun to pledge to reduce its overall emissions without making a specific pledge to help eliminate the pollutants created when gasoline, its major product, is burned.[13]

In a testimony to the power of small margins of support for proxy resolutions dealing with social issues, Sun Co. reached its agreement with CERES despite the fact that its investors had solidly rejected a shareholder proposal asking the company to adopt the code. The measure, which was voted on in 1992, was defeated by margin of 94 percent to 6 percent.

At the time, the jubilant leadership of the CERES coalition predicted that other large corporations would soon follow Sun Co. to become signatories to the code. As of August 1993, no other major corporations had joined Sun Co. in endorsing the code of conduct, but CERES officials and coalition members continued to maintain a dialogue with numerous large companies.

In May 1993, Dow Chemical and eight other corporations[14] announced their own set of voluntary environmental reporting guidelines, the Public Environment Reporting Initiative (PERI). "They (CERES) just didn't come together, and we felt it was more important that we have something" that informed the public about the companies' performance and progress on environmental reporting, Dennis M. Heydanek, director of environment and issues management said.

In contrast to CERES, PERI has no single set of reporting guidelines; each company will control what it reveals and how the information will be presented. PERI's co-signers are a "very loose coalition of companies, very truly an [ad hoc] group," Heydanek said. The ICCR viewed the guidelines skeptically. In a 1993 report, it said:

> Companies are finding that working with outsiders and responding
> directly to their concerns raises their credibility far more effectively
> than fending off the public with elaborate publicity and glossy self-
> promotion. Forward-thinking companies are acknowledging that
> the next challenge lies in verification: how can the public know that

corporation's actual environmental conduct supports their claims of environmental excellence. Concerned investors want to know the real facts. . . .[15]

The continued growth in the number of environmental shareholder resolutions at a time when the number of South Africa resolutions are diminishing leads some to the conclusion that "green" issues are poised to become the shareholder activist movement's "next South Africa." That is to say that environmentalism could, as the issue of South Africa did, become the issue that unites socially motivated shareholders and which motivates many of them to remain interested in utilizing their proxy voting rights for social ends.

There are some problems with comparing environmentalism to the South Africa cause. For one thing, while determining whether a company has operations in South Africa can often be accomplished with certainty, determining what is good environmental behavior is a subjective process. For example, an "environmentally correct" mining company could, for some, be a firm that minimizes pollution and conscientiously reclaims the land after it ceases operations in an area. For others, it may be an oxymoron.

On the other hand, the sheer importance of these issues—both for the Earth and for the profitability of corporate America—suggests that environmental accountability and performance will continue to occupy shareholders for some time to come. Therefore, whether environmentalism replaces South Africa as the most important focus of socially motivated shareholder activism, it is safe to predict the influence of ecological awareness will continue to be felt in boardrooms across the country.

AFFIRMATIVE ACTION

Institutional investors, by their nature, serve a broad and ethnically diverse constituency. Foundations, for example, often aim their philanthropic work toward helping economically disadvantaged, minority communities and/or women with small children. Pension funds invest assets on behalf of workers whose cultural, ethnic, and religious backgrounds are as diverse as the United States itself. In many cases, particularly in the public sector, the majority of a pension fund's participants are women or minorities.

Given this diversity, some have found it unfair that the bulk of these institutions' assets are invested by firms controlled by white men. Furthermore, such assets are sometimes invested in the securities of companies that have shown a questionable commitment to affirmative action and equal employment opportunities.

In order to rectify the situation, institutional investors have addressed affirmative action on two fronts: shareholder resolutions aimed at improving opportunities for women and minorities at public corporations; and the appointment of women- and minority-owned money management firms, brokerage firms, and other service providers.

In the 1993 proxy season, as in past years, a number of corporations faced shareholder resolutions asking them to make reports to shareholders on their affirmative action goals as well as their equal opportunity policies and performance. The language of the resolutions varied from company to company, but one resolution typical of those corporations faced in 1992 and 1993 was filed with Sears, Roebuck & Co., Chicago, by two Catholic religious organizations. The resolution called for a report containing:

1. A chart identifying our company employees according to their sex and race in each of the nine major EEO [Equal Employment Opportunity] Commission–defined job categories. . . .
2. A summary description of Affirmative Action Programs to improve performance, especially in job categories where women and minorities are under utilized and a description of major problems in meeting the company goals and objectives in this area.
3. A description of any communications or steps taken with company franchises, merchandise suppliers, and service providers to encourage positive action on these issues.
4. A description of our policy and progress to prevent sexual harassment in the workplace.[16]

It is important to note that the Securities and Exchange Commission, which has typically allowed shareholders to file shareholder resolutions related to affirmative action and equal opportunity, has recently changed its policy. In 1993, the commission allowed Bentonville, Ark.–based Wal-Mart Stores to exclude a similar resolution, also filed on the grounds that the issues addressed fall into the category of "ordinary business." However, that decision was later overturned in federal court (see the section "No More Wall Street Walk" later in this chapter).

During the 1993 proxy season, several resolutions asked companies to improve the diversity of their boards of directors and/or top management. Other resolutions called on banks to provide detailed information about their compliance with the Community Reinvestment Act, a federal law that requires banks to make loans in areas where they receive deposits. Yet another resolution called on the Federal Home Loan Mortgage Corp.

to report on its efforts to finance multi-family housing in large urban areas.[17]

In addition to the affirmative action-oriented shareholder resolutions, institutional investors have, in recent years, moved to increase the amount of their assets managed by women- and minority-owned money management firms—often referred to as "emerging managers."

According to information compiled by Port Chester, NY–based Nelson Publications and the National Investment Managers Association,[18] a Washington, D.C.–based trade association, the amount of money managed by emerging firms had grown to almost $47 billion by 1992, up from $23.5 billion in 1987. Of that amount, the largest portion—44 percent—came from corporate pension funds, and 29 percent came from public pension funds. Another 10 percent was from union pension funds and the remainder came from foundations, endowment funds, and associations. In addition, the number of women- and minority-owned money management firms grew by 66 percent between 1987 and 1992.[19]

A survey by Greenwich Associates, a benefits consulting firm,[20] found that public sector pension funds are more likely than other kinds of institutions to hire emerging money managers. The Greenwich survey found that 26 percent of the 313 public pension funds surveyed said they used minority-owned money management firms to invest a portion of their assets in 1993. Another 10 percent of the public sector funds stated that they plan to hire minority firms in the future. The support was highest among the 84 state-wide pension funds in the survey; 31 percent of such funds used minority firms and 12 percent planned to hire them. Among the 218 municipal funds, 24 percent used minority firms and 10 percent had plans to use them.

Public pension systems that utilize minority- and women-owned money managers include such large systems as those of the State of California, the state and city of New York, and the states of Connecticut, Illinois, and Louisiana. Large, multi-billion dollar public pension systems like these are probably the most fertile market for emerging managers, but such firms have also been employed by smaller funds, including the pension systems of the Virgin Islands and the City of San Diego.

Greenwich found a far lower level of support for minority managers among corporate pension funds and endowments and foundations. Of the 284 corporate funds, 8 percent used minority firms to manage a portion of their assets and another 2 percent planned to use them. Of the 172 foundations and endowments surveyed, 7 percent employed emerging firms, while another 3 percent said they planned to employ them. Among Greenwich's total universe of 769 fund sponsors, 15 percent reported use of minority managers and 6 percent had plans to hire such firms.

One example of a corporate pension fund that has aggressively hired women- and minority-owned firms is the fund of Chicago-based Ameritech Corp. In December 1992, the telephone company announced a plan to hire up to 20 women- and minority-owned money managers to invest up to $200 million in domestic stocks. To accomplish this, Ameritech retained RCB Trust, Stamford, Conn., to act as a "manager of managers," overseeing the firms.

Another way institutional investors can promote affirmative action is to encourage their existing money management firms to utilize brokerage firms or other service providers owned by women or minorities. Both public and corporate pension funds often adopt such policies, although, in most cases, money managers are not actually required to hire such firms, if they can receive better or less expensive service elsewhere.

Such a policy was recently adopted at Burbank, Calif.–based Walt Disney Co. In July 1993, the company's pension fund circulated a list of 23 recommended women- and minority-owned brokerages to its money managers. According to one press report, Disney also plans to hire women and minority money managers to invest part of its pension fund. The new policy was adopted as part of a larger corporate policy to promote business opportunities for women- and minority-owned enterprises in general.[21]

OPPRESSIVE REGIMES

Well aware of the global influence of major U.S. corporations, institutional investors have for over 20 years used their influence to persuade companies to work to change political oppression and injustice in the countries in which they operate. Starting with the first South Africa–related shareholder resolution in 1971, such investors have called for, and won, the withdrawal of numerous U.S. companies from that country. In recent years, the attention of socially motivated investors has spread to other parts of the world as well, most notably Northern Ireland, China, and Myanmar (also called Burma). However, unlike the case of South Africa, other shareholder campaigns dealing with oppressive regimes have concentrated on promoting ethical business practices overseas, rather than divestment.

Many observers of socially responsible investing believe that the issue of worldwide human rights will continue to be an increasingly important issue as the economy continues to grow more globalized and institutional investors continue to make investments in more countries. It may seem far-fetched that a group of shareholders from, say, Kansas can have much impact on labor practices as far away as China. But one only has to observe the success of South Africa divestment to realize the power of collective efforts by American corporations and their investors.

In the case of certain institutions—public sector pension funds in particular—officials will debate whether it is proper for investment policy to become embroiled in issues that may seem to be matters of foreign policy. However, as institutional investors become a more important force in the U.S. economy, they become a more powerful force in the world economy as well. Therefore, the opportunities for institutional shareholders to be heard and to make a difference in the fight against political and economic oppression are likely to increase in the years ahead.

South African Divestment

Talk to many fund managers about socially responsible investing and the first issue to come to their minds will be South Africa. It was, after all, the controversy surrounding the involvement of U.S. corporations in South Africa which, for all intents and purposes, spawned the social shareholder activism movement. And, among institutional investors, no other single social issue has been debated more fiercely or has had a bigger impact on investment policy over the past decade.

In the early days of the anti-apartheid movement in the United Stated, activists concentrated on promoting and enforcing a code of conduct called the Sullivan Principles (now called the Statement of Principles), developed in 1977 by Rev. Leon H. Sullivan, a Philadelphia minister and a member of the board of directors of General Motors. Under the Statement of Principles program, corporations doing business in South Africa are invited to become formal signatories to the code, and compliance is monitored by third parties.

The Statement of Principles, which was designed to eliminate apartheid from the work place, have been largely denounced by the anti-apartheid groups since the middle of the 1980s, when most of them began calling for sanctions and divestment to replace the "constructive engagement" policy embodied in Statement of Principles. In 1987, Rev. Sullivan, "frustrated by the lack of progress toward equality and the end of apartheid, renounced the principles himself" and began to endorse sanctions and divestment.[22]

While a precise tally of South Africa–screened assets is not available, observers believe that of the estimated $775 billion in U.S. capital invested based on social investment criteria,[23] the lion's share is totally or partially divested from South Africa. If anecdotal evidence is any indication, South African divestment is by far the most common social investment restriction placed on institutional assets in the United States.

During the 1980s—a time when pension funds were beginning to cast off a variety of other kinds of investment restrictions—a large number of public pension funds adopted, or were forced to adopt, rules against investing in companies with South African ties. By 1992, 20 states, 14 counties, 70 cities, and the Virgin Islands had laws on the books that mandated "total or partial divestment policies" restricting investments in South Africa–related companies, according to the Investor Responsibility Research Center (IRRC), Washington, D.C. Including those jurisdictions, a total of 27 states, 105 cities, and 32 counties and municipalities had "some type of South Africa restrictions on their banking, investment, and procurement practices."[24]

Total divestment, as defined by the IRRC, means that fund managers are required to sell off "all holdings in South Africa–related companies." Partial divestment means that holdings in South Africa–related companies are sold unless the companies meet "certain minimum standards" that vary by jurisdiction. In some cases, for example, localities are allowed to invest in companies that are signatories to the Statement of Principles.

Other kinds of sanctions include restrictions on using banks that make loans in South Africa and selective contracting laws that prohibit the purchase of goods and services from companies that do business in South Africa.[25]

Despite the fact that President Bush lifted federal trading sanctions against South Africa in July 1991, the vast majority of the local divestment laws passed in the late 1970s and 1980s remained in place until late 1993.

Never popular among money managers and pension fund officials charged with implementing divestment, these state and local investment restrictions—along with a large number of shareholder resolutions and laws largely forbidding state and local governments from purchasing goods and services from South Africa–related companies or making deposits in banks that do business there—are, nonetheless, credited with helping to create an exodus of U.S. corporations from that country during the 1980s.

As of August 1992, the number of U.S. companies with direct investment ties or employees in South Africa stood at 109, according to IRRC data. The number is up slightly from the 104 identified a year earlier, but still a considerable reduction compared with 1984, when almost 300 U.S. companies maintained equity ties there (see Figure 1-4).[26]

It is impossible to quantify exactly how much credit the divestment movement can take for the fact that South Africa finally seems on an irreversible path toward majority rule. It is possible, after all, that, without the withdrawal of Western investors, the system of apartheid might have fallen under the weight of its own oppressive nature. But those at the forefront of the fight against apartheid have consistently cited foreign economic sanctions and divestment as major forces for hastening the decline of statutory apartheid and for bringing the South African government to the bargaining table with the African National Congress (ANC).

FIGURE 1-4   Companies with Equity Ties to South Africa

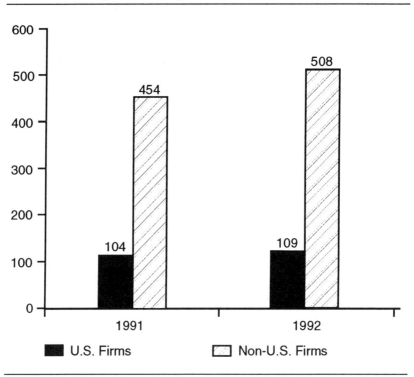

Source: Investor Responsibility Research Center.

Speaking to a conference organized by Social Investment Forum, Walter (Max) Sisulu, chief economist for the ANC said:

> There is no doubt that our struggle would not have reached such an advanced stage without the moral, spiritual, and material support of yourselves and men and women of conscience everywhere.
>
> Sanctions, particularly financial and economic sanctions, were instrumental in bringing the apartheid regime to the negotiating table. It is sanctions that will keep the regime seated at the negotiating table until a new political and socio-economic dispensation is finally hammered out.[27]

But, even if the divestment movement does deserve much credit for the success of groups like the ANC, some studies suggest that, effective or not, divestment has cost institutional investors possibly billions of dollars in lost investment opportunities over the years. For this reason, state and local pension fund officials have very often opposed divestment, arguing that such restrictions violate fiduciary duty because limitations that shrink the investment universe of a portfolio almost inevitably reduce long-term investment returns.

Evidence that divestment reduces the long-term return of a portfolio comes from a comparison of the unrestricted and South Africa–free versions of two frequently used stock indexes. According to data supplied by San Francisco–based Wells Fargo Nikko, the world's largest manager of indexed portfolios, the five-year annualized return for the South Africa–free Standard & Poor's 500 stock index was 13.84 percent for the period ended June 30, 1993. By contrast, the entire S&P 500 returned an annualized 14.19 percent during the same five-year period (see Figure 1-5).

FIGURE 1-5   Index Returns—Periods Ended June 30, 1993

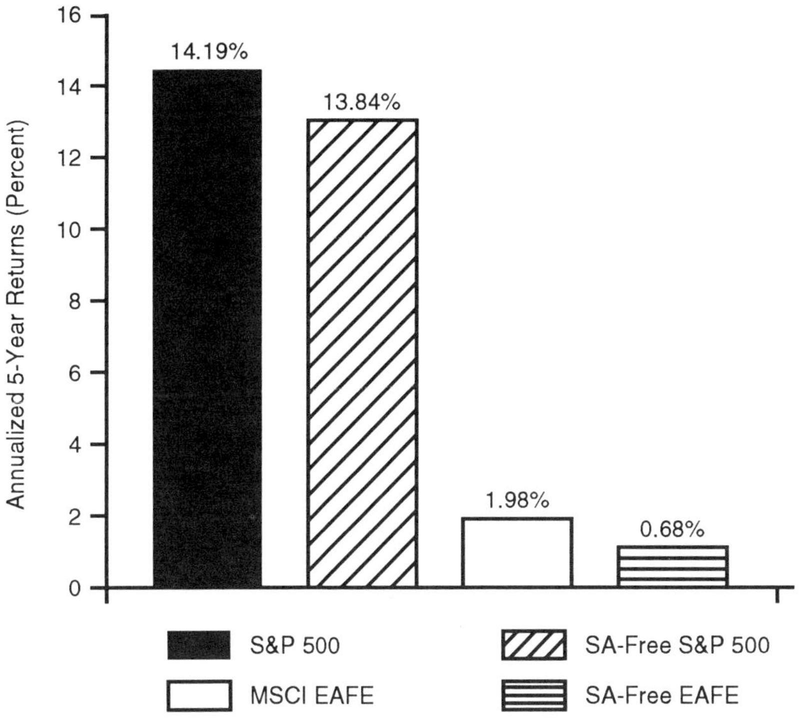

Source: Wells Fargo Nikko and Morgan Stanley.

Likewise, the five-year annualized return for the South Africa–free portion of the Morgan Stanley Europe Australia Far East (EAFE) index returned an annualized 0.68 percent for the five years ended June 30, 1993, compared with 1.98 percent for the entire EAFE index, according to Morgan Stanley.

Of course, actively managed portfolios perform differently than passive stock indexes. Money managers that specialize in socially responsible investing counter that some firms use the existence of South Africa restrictions as an excuse for poor performance and add that it is impossible to accurately tell, in hindsight, what any money manager would or would not have done at any given time in the absence of social restrictions.

What is clear, however, is that officials of most major pension funds that operate under South Africa restrictions would like to see those restrictions lifted.

Roland Machold, executive director of the New Jersey Division of Investment and an outspoken critic of South African divestment, has complained that the restrictions slowed the state pension fund's entry into non-U.S. securities markets because of the problems the state has had in researching the South African ties of foreign companies. In addition, he said, the New Jersey statute restricts the state pension fund from investing in about 20 percent of the U.S. equity market.

A study commissioned by the California Public Employees' Retirement System, the nation's largest public sector pension fund with $74 billion in assets, estimates that the fund would have earned an additional $600 million in investment returns from 1987–1990 had the state-imposed South Africa investment restrictions never been imposed.[28] On numerous occasions, officials of the fund have stated publicly that they are anxious to see the restrictions repealed by the state legislature.

The New Era

Just before press time, the African National Congress, having reached an agreement for the creation of a transitional government and the country's first multi-racial elections, called for an end to sanctions and reinvestment by foreign investors. This announcement led numerous jurisdictions to begin lifting their divestment rules.

Prior to the ANC's call, only two jurisdictions—the state of Oregon and Fairfax County, Va.—had reversed their divestment policies. Most state and local restrictions remained in place because officials chose to follow the lead of South African activists—principally ANC—rather than the federal government, on this issue. It is widely believed, however, that virtually all of the state and local divestment policies will now be repealed.

However, pension officials should not expect that the South Africa issue will simply disappear as a policy consideration after a new South African government takes over. On the contrary, the end of apartheid may actually serve to intensify the debate over the role of U.S. corporations and other foreign investors in South Africa's economy. Much of the anti-apartheid movement is set to shift gears toward advocating not only an end to divestment and sanctions, but also an active campaign of Western *investment* in the reformed South Africa, based on codes of conduct aimed at redressing the injustices of the apartheid era. Such thinking is strongly encouraged by the ANC, which, in anticipation of eventually taking power, has already begun courting, and laying the ground rules for, new foreign investment in South Africa.

In his speech in Boston, the ANC's Max Sisulu pointed out that, just as economic sanctions were vital to the ANC's efforts to end apartheid, an infusion of fresh Western investment dollars will be invaluable to its efforts to build a democratic country. Toward that end, he called on investors to "begin the process of serious preparations to enter the new non-racial and non-sexist democratic South Africa."

After his speech, Sisulu said that the ANC had already begun talks with foreign governments as well as representatives of the European Community, the International Monetary Fund, the World Bank, corporations, and institutional investors worldwide to discuss ways to attract foreign investment once a new government has taken power in South Africa.

It is unlikely that pension funds, given their strict fiduciary rules and justifiable aversion to risk, will soon make direct investments in South Africa or will become major investors in the handful of mutual funds currently being set up to invest in that country. However, it is expected that, once a majority-dominated government takes power, a lot of investment capital will become available to that country as Western corporations, freed from the stigma of doing business in a so-called "pariah nation," begin setting up operations there.

Therefore, even if pension funds do not invest directly in South African enterprises, they can continue to exert influence over the development of South Africa in their capacity as shareholders of most large, multinational corporations. Just as they were asked to apply pressure on companies to move operations out of South Africa, pension funds are likely to be called upon to help promote ethical business practices there as Western corporations return.

Furthermore, human rights, religious, and social investment organizations began years ago to think about ways to ensure that foreign investment is used as a positive political and social force after the end of apartheid. For example, the National Council of Churches has long made it clear that, in its opinion, the fight for economic justice in South Africa does not end with the establishment of majority rule.

A conference sponsored by the council issued a "call to action" on October 27, 1991. The council called for a continuation of "local sanctions and selective purchasing laws" as well as actions to encourage U.S. companies to leave that country. However, the conference statement also made clear that its participants expect U.S corporations to actively participate in rebuilding South Africa and southern Africa in the aftermath of apartheid. The council statement said the churches would continue to work for justice in South Africa by:

+ Encouraging U.S. companies to work with the Southern African Development Coordinating Council and other African countries on economic development;

+ Affirming the Rustenberg Declaration's[29] call for "acts of restitution in the fields of health care, psychological healing, education, housing, employment, economic infrastructure, and especially land ownership;"

+ Holding U.S, corporations to high standards of conduct and accountability. . . once power has been transferred to an Interim Government of National Unity which invites foreign companies to reinvest in South Africa;

+ [And] exploring with our South African partners positive investment alternatives and economic development models that are empowering and sustainable.

However, while the council's goal of using economic pressure and ethical business practices to help to create a just and sustainable economy in a post-apartheid South Africa is laudable, deciding what constitutes "high standards of conduct" will no doubt become a matter of fierce debate in the years to come. So far, there is no generally accepted code of conduct for corporations, such as the Statement of Principles, to serve as a benchmark for judging corporate behavior after the start of majority rule.

Undoubtedly, what looks like economic expansion to some, may look like environmental catastrophe or economic exploitation to others. And measures intended to create "economic empowerment," "sustainability," and to redistribute land could offend the free market sensibilities of some investors.

In the complicated times ahead, investors will have to let their conscience be their guide and, likely, will have to agree to disagree about certain points. As has been the case with the anti-apartheid movement, most ethically motivated investors will take guidance from the statements made by freedom-seeking institutions within South Africa, such as the ANC and the South

African Council of Churches, and will engage in an ongoing dialogue with those organizations.

In one attempt to provide such guidance, South African and international religious leaders met at Broederstroom, South Africa in February 1992, at a conference convened by the South African Council of Churches, Southern African Catholic Bishops Conference, the Institute for Contextual Theology, and the Kagiso Trust. The conference statement, while far short of a detailed code of corporate conduct, spells out some basic principles for dealing with foreign investment after the end of international sanctions.

"Foreign investments," the statement says, "must be regarded with caution" and therefore, "control measures" need to be in place to ensure that such activity enhances "a life-sustaining economy." Such control measures should combat poverty, enhance democratic participation, redress the injustices of apartheid, enhance access to vital resources, make companies accountable to their workers and others, encourage self-sufficiency and local initiatives, and protect the environment.

Furthermore, the statement sets out what the churches consider to be the components of ethical economic activity. They are:

✦ Affirmative action to assist blacks and other "disadvantaged groups," including women.

✦ Measures "to redress rural/urban imbalances."

✦ An obligation for companies "to respect the rights of their workers," especially the right to unionize.

✦ An obligation for companies to address the needs of communities in which they operate and to consult with those communities.

✦ A responsibility for companies to invest in ways that address the most urgent needs and social priorities, such as creation of maximum employment and housing."

✦ The protection of the environment.

In addition, the South African Council of Churches (SACC), in accordance with several other South African organizations, in July 1993 issued a 10-point business code of conduct that in many respects echoes the conference statement from Broederstroom. In its statement, the council stated that it hopes that the document will form the basis of foreign investment policies of a new government and "in the interim . . . apply to companies doing business in South Africa." (See Appendix 2 for full text.)

While SACC's statement was not intended to be an invitation for corporations to begin ending their investment embargo against South Africa, its timing did reflect reality. Unwilling to stand on the sidelines and wait for the ANC's blessing before investing, numerous companies from the U.S. and other Western countries had already re-entered the country, mainly through indirect ties such as licensing and franchise agreements.

The number of U.S. companies with such "non-equity" ties to South Africa grew to 256 as of late 1992, up from 178 in 1990.[30] Corporations based outside the U.S., which were generally much slower to divest from South Africa than their American counterparts, have been more willing to make direct equity investments there. As of late 1992, 508 non-U.S. companies held direct equity ties to the country, up from 454 a year earlier.[31]

Northern Ireland and the MacBride Principles

Unlike those working for an end to the apartheid regime in South Africa, activists concerned with ensuring equal employment opportunities for Northern Ireland's Roman Catholic population have not called on companies to cease operations there. Taking their cue from the early days of the South Africa movement, a coalition of Irish organizations, religious institutions, and public sector pension funds has instead concentrated its efforts on promoting a code of conduct for U.S. companies doing business in Northern Ireland.

Inspired by the Statement of Principles for companies doing business in South Africa, the MacBride Principles lay out nine rules designed to put an end to religious discrimination against Catholic workers and job applicants in Northern Ireland. They include making a commitment to increasing the representation of religious minorities on the work force, protecting the safety of Catholic workers, banning "provocative" emblems such as British Union Jacks from the workplace, and a commitment to see that religious bias is eliminated from the recruitment, training, and promotion of workers (see Table 1-1 on pages 34 and 35).

The MacBride Principles were launched in 1984 by the Washington, D.C.–based Irish National Caucus (INC), which developed the code to address what it perceived as the weakness of British anti-discrimination laws in Northern Ireland. The principles are named for the late Sean MacBride, who served as the organization's liaison in Ireland from 1979 until his death in 1988.

To promote acceptance of the code by U.S. corporations and government bodies, the INC and its allies have concentrated on three fronts.

First, shareholder resolutions are filed annually asking corporations doing business in Northern Ireland to sign a code of conduct. According to the Interfaith Center for Corporate Responsibility, 12 such resolutions were filed in the 1993 proxy season. Another nine proposals asked companies to report on their equal opportunity practices in Northern Ireland.[32] In 1992, MacBride shareholder proposals fared well with investors, scoring an average of 12.5 percent of the vote, an average gain of two percent compared with the previous year.

While no mechanism exists for companies to formally become signatories to the MacBride Principles, 25 U.S. corporations targeted for shareholder proposals have agreed to implement the MacBride code to the extent possible under British law in exchange for withdrawal of the resolutions (see Table 1-2 on page 36).

Second, activists promote the passage of state and local laws that forbid signing contracts or investing in Northern Ireland employers that have not signed the code. According to the IRRC, 14 states and 14 municipalities incorporated the MacBride Principles into their purchasing and/or investment policies as of July 1993.

So far, only one state, Connecticut, mandates divestment of Northern Ireland–related companies that do not comply with the MacBride Principles. On the local level, similar laws are on the books in Boston, Burlington, Vermont, Minneapolis, New Haven, and Philadelphia. A law in Baltimore forbids new investments in companies that have not agreed to comply with the code.[33]

In addition, MacBride supporters have lobbied Congress—so far unsuccessfully—for passage of a federal law that would forbid U.S.-based companies from importing products they make in Northern Ireland unless those companies are in compliance with the MacBride Principles. Several bills have been introduced over the past few years, but so far, Congress has failed to act on them, despite the fact that the INC counts numerous members of congress and senators as "friends" of the organization.

China

In recent years, union pension funds and others have used shareholder action to call attention to political repression and the alleged use of prison labor in the People's Republic of China.

In the first such action the Amalgamated Clothing and Textile Workers Union (ACTWU), New York, proposed a shareholder resolution in 1991 that would have asked Chicago-based Sears, Roebuck & Co. to certify that none of the goods it imports from China are made by prisoners. The resolution was later withdrawn after the giant retailer agreed to a procedure for making such certifications.

Under its agreement with the union, Sears circulated a statement to all of its Chinese suppliers outlining its policy against buying prison-made goods and incorporating language prohibiting the use of prison labor into all contracts with those suppliers. Sears also agreed to maintain a list of manufactur-

TABLE 1-1   The MacBride Principles

The nine-point MacBride Principles, issued by the Irish National Caucus, Washington, D.C., in 1984, commit companies to meeting nine specific goals aimed at eliminating job discrimination against Roman Catholics in Northern Ireland. The following is the full text of the MacBride Principles, including amplifications issued by Sean MacBride in 1986 (in italics).

1. Increasing the representation of individuals from under-represented religious groups in the work force, including managerial, supervisory administrative, clerical and technical jobs.

A workforce that is severely unbalanced may indicate prima facie that full equality of opportunity is not being afforded all segments of the community in Northern Ireland. Each signatory to the MacBride Principles must make every reasonable lawful effort to increase the representation of under-represented religious groups at all levels of its operations in Northern Ireland.

2. Adequate security for the protection of minority employees both at the work place and while travelling to and from work.

While total security can be guaranteed nowhere today in Northern Ireland, each signatory to the MacBride Principles must make reasonable good faith efforts to protect workers from intimidation and physical abuse at the work place. Signatories must also make reasonable good faith efforts to ensure that applicants are not deterred from seeking employment because of fear for their personal safety at the work place or while traveling to and from work.

3. The banning of all provocative religious or political emblems from the work place.

Each signatory to the MacBride Principles must make reasonable good faith efforts to prevent the display of sectarian emblems at their plants in Northern Ireland.

4. All job openings should be advertised publicly and special recruitment efforts made to attract applicants from under-represented religious groups.

Signatories to the MacBride Principles must exert special efforts to attract employment applications from the sectarian community that is substantially under-represented in the workforce. This should not be construed to imply a diminution of opportunity for other applicants.

5. Layoff, recall and remination procedures should not in practice favor a particular religious group.

Each Signatory to the MacBride Principles must make reasonable good faith efforts to ensure that layoff, recall and termination procedures do not penalize a particular religious group disproportionately. Layoff and termination practices that involve seniority

Continued

can result in discrimination against a particular religious group if the bulk of employees with greatest seniority are disproportionately from another religious group.

6. The abolition of job reservations, apprenticeship restrictions and differential employment criteria which discriminate on the basis of religion.

Signatories to the MacBride Principles must make reasonable good faith efforts to abolish all differential employment criteria whose effect is discrimination on the basis of religion. For example, job reservations and apprenticeship regulations that favor relatives of current or former employees can, in practice, promote religious discrimination if the company's workforce has historically been disproportionately drawn from another religious group.

7. The development of training programs that will prepare substantial numbers of current minority employees for skilled jobs, including the expansion of existing programs and the creation of new programs to train, upgrade and improve the skills of minority employees.

This does not imply that such programs should not be open to all members of the workforce equally.

8. The establishment of procedures to assess, identify and actively recruit minority employees with potential for further advancement.

This section does not imply that such procedures should not apply to all employees equally.

9. The appointment of a senior management staff member to oversee the company's affirmative action efforts and the setting up of timetables to carry out affirmative action principles.

In addition to the above, each signatory to the MacBride Principles is required to report annually to an independent monitoring agency on its progress in the implementation of these Principles.

Source: Irish National Caucus, Washington, D.C.

---

ing sites used by suppliers and to periodically visit those sites to ensure that no inmate labor is being employed.[34]

It is important to note that ACTWU never accused Sears of knowingly buying goods made with prison labor, which would have been a violation of federal law. ACTWU, concerned that many U.S. retailers may be unwittingly purchasing prison-made goods, chose to start its shareholder campaign with Sears because of the company's prominent position in the retailing industry, union officials said.

In another case of shareholder action related to China, the Food and Allied Service Trades (FAST) Department of the American Federation of

TABLE 1-2 Corporate Supporters of the MacBride Principles

*No formal mechanism exists for companies to become signatories to the
MacBride Principles. However, in response to shareholder proposals since 1986,
25 corporations agreed to abide by the code to the extent legally possible. Of
those companies, 23 still have operations in Northern Ireland. Those corporations
are:*

Alexander & Alexander Services	Nacco Industries
AM International	International Business Machines
American Home Products	Nynex Corp.
American Telephone & Telegraph	Oneida
Avery Dennison	Pitney Bowes
BCE Corp./Northern Telecom	Procter & Gamble
Data General	Sara Lee*
Digital Equipment	Sunoco
DuPont	Teleflex
Federal Express*	Texaco
Fruit of the Loom	Unisys Corp.
GATX Corp.	VF Corp.
Honeywell	

* No longer has operations in Northern Ireland.

Source: Irish National Caucus.

Labor-Congress of Industrial Organizations, Washington, D.C., conducted an
independent proxy solicitation in 1992 of the shareholders of Wal-Mart
Stores. The resolution asked the retailer to certify that it, too, was not buying
goods made with forced labor in China. The solicitation received about 25
million votes, or about 5 percent of the total, according to the union.

In response to a shareholder resolution filed by Boston-based Franklin
Research & Development Corp., a manager of socially screened investment
portfolios, Wal-Mart signed an agreement to set standards designed to ensure
that its suppliers meet various ethical standards.

Similar to agreements already signed by Levi Strauss and Reebok, the
set of standards contains clauses requiring suppliers to comply with all
applicable laws, fairly compensate their workers "consistent with prevailing
local standards," "maintain reasonable employee work hours in compliance
with local standards" and laws, and refrain from the use of forced or child
labor in the manufacture of their products. In addition, the standards contain
clauses that require suppliers to maintain "a safe, clean, healthy, and productive" work environment, find ways to improve environmental conduct, and
buy as many materials and components as possible in the United States.

The standards also lay out a procedure for the regular inspection and certification of Wal-Mart's suppliers.

Myanmar

Another example of shareholder influence to protest political oppression is the action by some institutional investors to influence companies doing business in Myanmar (also known as Burma), where the military government still refuses to recognize the results of free elections in 1990.

After losing in a landslide to the National League for Democracy, Myanmar's government arrested numerous opponents, including National League leader Aung San Suu Kyi, who was awarded the 1991 Nobel Peace Prize, and 43 elected legislators from several political parties. Since then, the government has been accused of numerous human rights abuses, including the imprisonment of over 500,000 people in barbed-wire internment camps.

While the situation in Myanmar has received only a fraction of the attention paid to South Africa and Northern Ireland over the years, the beginnings of an investor and corporate backlash against human rights abuses there has begun to surface in the United States and Canada.

San Francisco–based Levi Strauss & Co. has decided to suspend operations in Myanmar, citing human rights and political repression there. And, in May 1992, Petro Canada, in response to the requests by religious groups affiliated with the Task Force on Churches and Corporate Responsibility, agreed to "review its policy of political neutrality in Myanmar and to revise its social responsibility statement to include ethical standards for doing business overseas."[35]

During the 1993 proxy season, at least two Myanmar-related proxy resolutions sponsored by religious organizations were filed with companies based in the United States, according to the Interfaith Center on Corporate Responsibility.

A resolution filed with Chicago-based Amoco Corp. asked the company (one of about 14 foreign oil companies operating in the country) to make a "comprehensive report on its operations and future plans in Burma" and make that report available to all shareholders. Sponsors of the resolution were the Detroit Province of the Society of Jesus (Jesuits), the Dominican Sisters of the Sick Poor, and the Loretto Literary and Benevolent Institution.

The second resolution, filed with Purchase, N.Y.–based PepsiCo, called for the company and its subsidiaries to "terminate forthwith their investments and operations in Burma until political prisoners are released and political power is transferred to the democratically elected government of Burma." The PepsiCo measure was sponsored by the Detroit Jesuits and the Missionary Oblates of Mary Immaculate.[36]

"SIN" INVESTMENTS

In the beginning, there were the Ten Commandants. Then the Seven Deadly Sins. Now, among social investors, the list of sins has narrowed to the Big Three: tobacco, alcohol, and gambling.

For nearly eight decades, a small group of investors, primarily religious institutions and their followers, in a desire to match their Christian principles with their investment policy, have avoided this group of industries. This philosophy—indeed, the very roots of modern social investing—dates to the Social Gospel movement of the early 1900s.

Adherents of the Social Gospel reasoned that "sin, or evil, was not theological but sociological . . . and that the way to suppress it was for the good men to take action in the place where it arose and prospered." It was not enough, then, for individuals to profess faith and renounce individual sins; they had to work for the collective eradication of sin. A "burning desire to bring the ethics of the church down to the factory, the street, and the market place" led the more moderate followers of the Social Gospel—the mainline Protestant denominations—to bar alcohol and tobacco holdings from their investment portfolios, thus keeping them free of the wages of sin.[37]

Since then, they have been largely alone, their investment policies standing out from the prevailing ethos of the marketplace. Occasionally in the early decades, they were joined by others: the first socially screened mutual fund, the Boston-based Pioneer Fund, was established in 1928 for evangelical Protestants who did not wish to invest in alcohol, cigarettes, and cigars; the Foursquare Fund, launched by Christian Scientists in 1962, excluded investments in liquor and tobacco, as well as drug companies;[38] and Earlham College, a small, Quaker-affiliated school in Richmond, Indiana, officially proscribed investments in sin stocks in the 1950s. More recently, other medical and religious investors have divested themselves.

Still, sin-free investors are largely preaching to the choir. Relatively few institutional investors have changed their strategies since the days when smoking and drinking were made to look fun, glamorous, and daring (as in "The Wild One" and "The Thin Man") and celebrity endorsers such as Ronald Reagan extolled the health benefits of lighting up. That could change. In an era of 12-step programs, Surgeon General's reports, and Mothers Against Drunk Driving, tobacco and alcohol consumption is declining and, with the Clinton administration considering sharp increases in sin taxes, the profitability of these industries is being squeezed. Of the Big Three, only gambling is making gains—and its stability is suspect.

"I think as the value of the stocks goes down, institutions with a history of social investing [on other issues] will sell," said Gregory N. Connolly, a leading anti-tobacco activist. Rather than attribute the divestment to the anti-sin-stock activists, "they'll say the stock doesn't look that good." In the current climate, the strategy of avoiding sin may not just be politically correct but also financially smart.

Tobacco and Alcohol

In 1604, after Sir Walter Raleigh brought tobacco from North America to England, King James I remarked that smoking was "a custome lothsome to the eye, hatefull to the nose, haremfull to the braine, daungerous to the Lungs, and in the black sinking fume thereof, neerest resembling the horrible Stigian smoak of the pit that is bottomlesse."[39]

It took the colonies longer to catch on. But U.S. researchers in the last 40 years have built an overwhelming scientific case confirming what James suspected. In 1953, scientists at Memorial Sloan-Kettering Cancer Center in New York painted tobacco tars on the backs of mice and produced tumors. Since then, more than 50,000 studies have linked smoking to cancer, respiratory illness, and cardiovascular disease; they include the 1964 Surgeon General's report calling smoking a health hazard and the January 1993 report by the Environmental Protection Agency that concluded secondhand smoke poses especially serious risks for indoor workers and children. According to the Centers for Disease Control and Prevention, 434,000 people died from smoking-related causes in 1988.[40]

In light of that evidence, anti-smoking activist Brad S. Krevor said institutions ought to examine whether their ethics match their bottom lines. Hospitals and charities should not "reap dividends from the purveyors of sickness and death;" universities should refrain from exploiting the young, the less-educated, minorities, and Third World nations when tobacco companies use bogus scholarship to support their claims of safety; and insurers and state and local governments, so familiar with the health costs associated with smoking, should act in their own, and society's, best interests by dropping the stock.[41]

Institutions that share his moral outrage are left with two choices: challenge the Big Six tobacco corporations[42] directly, through shareholder resolutions and dialogue, or divest. Both have been tried. Neither has been resoundingly successful, although each campaign, by its own measure, can claim some victories.

The proxy voting effort began after Michael Crosby of the Midwest Province of Capuchin Franciscans, a Roman Catholic order of brothers, returned from a trip to Latin America in 1979. During his tour, he saw huge marketing campaigns by U.S. tobacco companies in Nicaragua and El Salvador. A two-pack-a-day smoker of Pall Malls and Lucky Strikes in his teenage years, he empathized with the Latin American people, whom he said were not truly free to make a decision not to smoke.

In 1980, the Midwestern province, a member of the Interfaith Center for Corporate Responsibility, introduced a resolution demanding that Philip Morris and R.J. Reynolds (the predecessor of RJR Nabisco) report on their marketing and sales in Asia, Africa, and Latin America, growing markets for cigarette makers faced with a shrinking customer base at home. The resolutions failed to get enough support to be reconsidered. In 1987, the Capuchins filed a similar resolution with Philip Morris, which agreed to the request before it came up at its annual meeting and the proposal was withdrawn.[43]

In 1988, with a resolution that even anti-smoking allies call naive, the Capuchins and ICCR asked tobacco companies to form health evaluation committees that would have put them out of business. If those panels were unable to present persuasive evidence that smoking was not a leading cause of death, the resolutions stated, the companies would have been forced to immediately stop marketing and advertising. And they would have been required to be completely smoke-free within four years. The Securities and Exchange Commission ruled the resolutions infringed on the corporations' ordinary business and ordered them withdrawn.[44]

In 1989 and 1990, the ICCR Tobacco Interest Group allied itself with Connolly, a dentist and director of the Office of Non-Smoking and Health for the Massachusetts Department of Health, and John Slade, an addictions specialist with the St. Peter's Medical Center in New Brunswick, New Jersey. Together, they crafted resolutions calling on tobacco companies and their suppliers to get out of the business by the year 2000. Though initially rejected by the SEC, the resolutions were later allowed to proceed. The resolutions failed to get wide support, but their inclusion on proxy ballots was hailed as a breakthrough by anti-smoking forces.[45]

Most resolutions since then have targeted the marketing and advertising practices of tobacco companies. The 17 resolutions introduced in 1993 included two asking Loews Group and Philip Morris to put surgeon general-style warning labels on all merchandise, including promotional T-shirts. Two others call on RJR Nabisco and American Brands to evaluate ad campaigns they say entice children (RJR's Old Joe cartoon character, which promotes Camels) and poor and black consumers (American Brands' promotion of discount-brand cigarettes) to smoke.[46]

And increasingly they target companies with limited relationships to tobacco. Beginning in 1990, Aetna Life & Casualty has been asked to account for its ownership of tobacco stocks while it issues policies insuring against smoking-related disease, premature death, and property losses. (In

1993, the same questions were also asked of American Brands, parent of Franklin Life Insurance, and Loews, which owns CNA Insurance.) Other resolutions asked pharmacies to stop selling cigarettes and call on McDonald's and PepsiCo, owner of KFC, Pizza Hut, and Taco Bell, to prohibit smoking in their facilities.[47]

Crosby and his allies have won from less than 2 percent of shareholders' votes to just under 9 percent over 13 years. He said that they consider themselves successful if they can persuade a corporation to accept its demands, as Philip Morris did in 1987, or if a resolution gets enough votes to be reconsidered.

"What we're doing as investors is just what we can do to see that our investments get a good return as the companies are weaned way from smoking," said Crosby, who advises 25 Midwestern members of the ICCR. He pointed out that smoking in the United States is on the decline and unit sales of tobacco products is dropping by 2 to 3 percent a year. With federal health officials pushing for a smoke-free society by the turn of the century, he said, "we believe that it is not in the best interest of the companies" to rely on tobacco revenue "and we as investors do not want to be left high and dry when that day comes."

While religious investors were sponsoring resolutions, anti-smoking activists used a strategy that worked for the South Africa movement: divestment. One of the leading groups is the Tobacco Divestment Project. A shoestring operation with a $15,000 annual budget (compared with an estimated $16 million for the Tobacco Institute, a trade association, and millions more for the Council on Tobacco Research),[48] the project is aligned with the Tobacco Control Resource Center in Boston. The parent organization, formerly the Clean Indoor Air Educational Foundation, is headed by lawyer Richard A. Daynard, who once represented the family of Rose Cipollone in its suit against the Liggett Group.[49]

Krevor, executive director of the Tobacco Divestment Project, said his group hopes to break institutions from their addiction to tobacco profits.

"There is a central lie to which the tobacco industry is committed. That lie is that tobacco smoking is a freely chosen adult behavior. It is not freely chosen. It is a compulsion. It is an addiction," said Krevor, who smoked for 18 years and now teaches smoking-cessation classes. And, he said, many institutions are as hooked on tobacco as smokers. "One shouldn't profit from tobacco addiction, and we call upon hospitals, universities and philanthropies to show some leadership."

Shortly after the Tobacco Divestment Project was formed in 1990, Harvard University president Derek Bok wrote to three members of a committee of public health students, informing them the school had quietly divested its tobacco holdings the previous year. (Those assets amounted to $58 million, or 1.2 percent of an endowment then worth $4.7 billion.) Bok wrote that the university did not want to be linked "with companies engaged in significant sales of products that create a substantial and unjustified risk to other human beings." Although the university chose to tell only a small campus group rather than make a general announcement to the news media, it was the clearest gesture against tobacco investment by a major institution.[50]

Since then, the divestment movement has had mixed success. Johns Hopkins University in Baltimore, City University of New York, Wayne State University in Detroit, New England Deaconess Hospital in Boston, the Presbyterian Church U.S.A., and Unitarian Universalist Association gave up a total of more than $15 million in tobacco holdings in 1990 and 1991. But Cornell University, Yale University, and the California State Employees Retirement System, among others, declined to put up smoke screens. Cornell opted to evaluate its tobacco investments on a case-by-case basis, as it does with South Africa. Yale, whose investment advisory committee chairman called divestment a "hollow gesture," recommended close monitoring of the industry's advertising and marketing records. And CalPERS refused in 1991 to drop more than $300 million in tobacco-related stocks, saying it would place no further restrictions on investment.[51]

Public pension funds have generally been unsupportive of anti-tobacco forces. The Cambridge, Massachusetts, Retirement System has guidelines against tobacco investing, although not a strict prohibition, and the New York City Employees Retirement System has co-sponsored proxy resolutions on tobacco advertising with ICCR members. But they are exceptions. Most public funds fear a diminished return. They could point to the $8 billion Minnesota State Board of Investment, which recently dropped its prohibitions against sin stocks. Since the early 1970s, the board prevented its managers from investing in any company that takes in more than 50 percent of revenue from tobacco or alcohol. The trustees came to believe the policy cost them $150 million and estimate they will sacrifice $185 million in return over five years if the restrictions remain in place as it expands its international holdings.[52]

Likewise, BARRA, a Berkeley, California, investment consulting firm, found that stocks from the three sin industries outperformed the Standard & Poor's 500 from 1980 to 1991. Tobacco offered an "exceptional return," 8.4 percent above the S&P benchmark, while liquor and gambling exceeded the mark by 5.8 percent and 1.9 percent, respectively.[53]

Tobacco industry analysts say both shareholder resolutions and divestment have had a negligible impact on companies. Divestment, in fact, may have the unintended consequence of making tobacco stocks, already undervalued by about 25 percent because of fear of higher taxes or litigation, even more of a bargain for other investors.[54] "I am tempted to say that 99 percent of it is not the campaign against the stocks because most institutions have not paid attention to it," said Roy Burry, beverage and tobacco analyst for Kidder Peabody.

Furthermore, activists cannot persuade the largest shareholders to give up stocks that, in the case of Philip Morris, almost double the return of the S&P 500. "Performance of tobacco stocks has been terrific, so institutions can't stay away from it or they will look silly because they will be giving up income," Burry said. Christopher Luck, senior consultant with BARRA, said social restrictions put managers "behind the eight ball."[55]

But Crosby, of the Capuchins, insisted the anti-tobacco movement will be to the 1990s what the South Africa campaign was to the 1970s and 1980s. "I mean, it's in the papers continually. The economic impact, the health-related impact and the human impact of all the deaths. So I think it's just going to increase."

As for alcohol—perhaps because it can be used in moderation without adverse health problems, perhaps because it is used by a larger segment of the population—it has not become as significant an investment issue as smoking. A few institutions, among them the W.K. Kellogg Foundation and the College Retirement Equity Fund's Social Choice Account, prohibit alcohol from their portfolios.

Only one alcohol-related shareholder resolution was introduced in the 1993 proxy season, according to the Investor Responsibility Resource Center. Sponsored by John Slade, it would have required Philip Morris, owner of Miller Brewing Co., the nation's second-largest beer maker, to adhere to and promote the federal government definition of moderate drinking. The corporation challenged the resolution and it was withdrawn. Slade's resolutions on the company's advertising won just over 3 percent of the vote in 1991 and 1992, the latter not strong enough to qualify it for an automatic rehearing.

"I think it is easier to outline in a few words what the issue is with tobacco," Slade said. "With alcohol, you have to put a few qualifiers on the issue."

Gambling

During the 1993 National Basketball Association playoffs, when the Chicago Bulls' Michael Jordan was the subject of a book detailing hundreds of thousands of dollars in gambling debts and was spotted in Atlantic City losing thousands more, league commissioner David Stern said, "We don't think we should be regulating whether a player can go to a casino and engage in an activity that is not only legal, but is actually encouraged by virtually all state governments." Stern said society's message is: " 'Go to casinos. Go to Indian reservations for gambling. Go to riverboats. Bet lots. Gambling is good. It supports higher education, lower education, senior citizens, you name it.' As the states rush headlong into attempts to raise new money, there seems to be a national campaign encouraging gambling."[56]

The restrictions on gambling in the United States for most of this century, and the relatively small number of public corporations directly involved in the industry, have made this sin a moot issue for most institutions.

That was before legitimate gambling surged to the fore, to wide popular appeal. From the 1900s to the mid-1970s, gambling in the United States was confined to Las Vegas' glitzy Strip and a handful of other cities in Nevada, and a few state lottery games, starting with New Hampshire's in 1969. No publicly traded corporations were involved in the game. After the state of New Jersey allowed casino gambling in Atlantic City, however, the lid was off the box.

Since the 1980s, cash-poor state governments reluctant to raise sales or income taxes have been seeking out politically painless sources of revenue. Their solution: tax greed. Peter Kinder said, "Every politician is looking to gambling to cure the deficits." New state-run lottery games, from instant scratch tickets to computer terminal keno to sports betting, and state-sanctioned riverboat gambling have fit the bill. At the same time, Indian tribes in 19 states from Connecticut to Minnesota have used the Indian Gaming Regulatory Act of 1988 to circumvent state regulations and open full-scale casinos on their lands. The sites rake in $6 billion a year for once-destitute tribes, and many more are planning gambling ventures.[57]

A large and prosperous new industry has sprung up around gambling. Casinos, suppliers, and computer hardware and software makers are getting in on the action. Circus Circus Enterprises has impressed investors with its double-digit returns. And several new companies are challenging such established corporations as Caesar's World and MGM Grand, and were expected to pull in $500 million to $100 million each in 1992–93, their first year of operation. At this writing, Wall Street is bidding up the stock of such companies as President Riverboat Casinos, whose vessels ply the Mississippi coast, and more established ones like GTECH, a cutting-edge lottery computer company with government contracts from its home state of Rhode Island to Australia and Eastern Europe.[58]

The gambling industry is extremely volatile, however. Ask Michael Jordan. Clearly, social investors like churches will stay away from it. So will foundations that work to alleviate poverty—and seek to protect gamblers who, disproportionately, unlike Jordan, are poor. But plenty of conventional institutional investors already own gambling stocks and bonds. They're no doubt attracted by the bright lights of an industry based on the premise that the house always wins. Inevitably, there will be a shaking-out process in which weaker companies will fold. Waiting that out may make a virtue of necessity.

NO MORE WALL STREET WALK: SHAREHOLDER ACTIVISM AS A SOCIAL INVESTING TOOL

If an individual investor doesn't like the social record of a company, the best approach often is to take "the Wall Street walk." That is, sell the stock and use the proceeds to invest in a company in which management follows a code of ethics the investor feels comfortable with.

In some cases, investors choose to stick with a company and attempt to use their influence as an active investor to change it from within. This type of activity, sometimes called activist investing, social (as opposed to "ethical") investing, or relationship investing, takes a variety of forms, including letter-writing campaigns, face-to-face meetings with management, and the sponsorship of resolutions to be included on a company's annual proxy ballot.

Proxy resolutions, which can be sponsored by shareholders or management, often are used to address issues, ranging from ordinary and uncontroversial "housekeeping" measures (such as minor changes in bylaws, or operations), to the creation of new classes of stock or the election of an entirely new slate of corporate directors. And, as social activists discovered more than twenty years ago, such resolutions can also be used to call attention to a company's poor environmental record, its bad labor relations, or its involvement in countries with oppressive regimes, among other things. In recent years, more shareholders—particularly religious organizations and public sector pension funds—have effectively utilized their access to proxy ballots to make themselves heard on a wide variety of social issues.

According to information provided by the Interfaith Center on Corporate Responsibility (ICCR), a New York group that coordinates shareholder activism by religious groups, 220 socially motivated shareholder resolutions were filed at 155 corporations in 1993 (see Figure 1-6). The resolutions dealt with a wide variety of issues including the environment; business operations in South Africa, Northern Ireland, and Myanmar; equal employment opportunity; executive compensation; the international debt crisis; drug pricing; infant formula; weapons manufacturing; tobacco; and the Mexican border (maquiladora) operations of U.S. companies.

Sponsors of the resolutions included many of the nearly 250 ICCR-affiliated Christian religious organizations, public sector pension funds, unions, environmental groups, and individuals. In addition, some resolutions were filed by socially motivated financial services companies: Calvert Social Investment Fund, Bethesda, Maryland; Franklin Research and Development,

FIGURE 1-6   Social Issues Proxy Resolutions 1991–1993

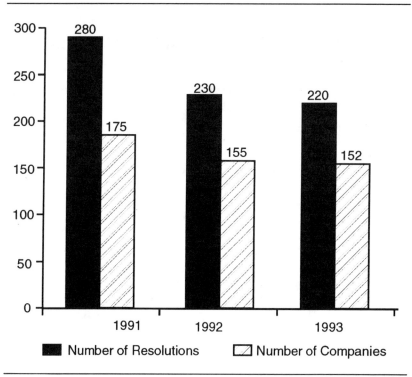

Source: Interfaith Center on Corporate Responsibility.

Boston; Progressive Securities, Eugene, Oregon; and United States Trust of Boston.[59]

Companies facing proposed social issue shareholder resolutions in 1993 represented a wide range of industries, from retailing (Sears, Roebuck & Co., Kmart Corp., and Wal-Mart Corp.) to banking (Citicorp, Chemical Bank, and Sun Trust banks, among others), to high technology (Texas Instruments and International Business Machines).

While proxy resolutions dealing with social issues rarely garner more than a small fraction of the votes cast by shareholders, this kind of activism has proved to be a remarkably successful method for changing corporate behavior. Proxy campaigns by shareholders—some of whom own a relatively small number of shares—have helped persuade corporations to improve their environmental performance, end economic ties to South Africa, pledge · nondiscrimination against Roman Catholics in Northern Ireland, and investigate charges that some Chinese goods are made with prison labor, among other things.

Other shareholder campaigns have led to important reform in the governance of corporations, such as the adoption of confidential proxy voting, the nomination and election of more outside corporate directors, and the elimination of anti-takeover defenses such as "poison pill" anti-takeover measures that, some shareholders say, can discourage legitimate suitors from bidding on companies and can, therefore, depress the value of their stock holdings.

Led by public pension funds (most notably, the California Public Employees' Retirement System), members of the United Shareholders Association (USA), and the Council of Institutional Investors, investors have been speaking up and being heard by the management of some of the nation's largest corporations.

Effectiveness of Social Issue Resolutions

As Timothy Smith, executive director of the ICCR, writes, socially motivated shareholder action dates back to 1970.

> [In that year] the Project on Corporate Responsibility had broken ground and challenged General Motors with a series of shareholder resolutions on such issues as putting women and minorities on the board, the environment, corporate governance, and non-discrimination in employment. A new era of corporate accountability had been born. Over the next twenty years, [socially motivated] shareholder resolutions grew from a small handful to more than 350 sponsored in 1991.[60]

In 1971, the Episcopal Church filed the first of many hundreds of social proxy resolutions to be sponsored by religious organizations, again at General Motors. The church asked the auto maker to adopt a set of guidelines designed to ensure equal employment opportunities for blacks at the company's South African operations. From that point forward, religious organizations have been by far the most active filers of social proxy resolutions; in recent years, however, it has become much more common for other types of institutions— notably public sector and union pension funds—to file such resolutions.

For reasons to be explained later, the number of social proxy resolutions decreased significantly after 1991. But the proposals continue to be a widely used and powerful tool for influencing corporate behavior.

Since they first started to appear, no social issue proxy resolution has received the majority—or anywhere near the majority—of the votes cast by shareholders. The fact is that most shareholders either don't vote or they vote with management. When social issues resolutions come to a vote, management virtually always opposes them. Thus, the sponsors of such proposals often count themselves lucky if they can gather enough votes to reintroduce the resolution the following year. (To be reintroduced, a shareholder resolution needs to gain at least three percent of the vote the first time it appears on the ballot, six percent the second time around, and 10 percent thereafter, according to Securities and Exchange Commission rules.)

So, why do shareholders continue to sponsor the resolutions? Despite the seemingly minuscule vote counts, such resolutions are often effective because they can generate adverse publicity for the company or because they can be used by activists to open a dialogue with management over an issue that might otherwise be ignored. And, given the overwhelming tendency of shareholders to vote in favor of management, even a 3–5 percent dissenting vote can be enough to get the executive suite to take notice, especially if some important institutional investors join in.

While no social issue resolutions and relatively few corporate governance resolutions sponsored by shareholders have ever received a majority of votes cast, a number of such proposals filed in recent years were able to receive considerably more than the number of votes needed to be reintroduced. In his book, *Good Money: A Guide to Profitable Social Investing in the 1990s,* Ritchie P. Lowry points out:

> By 1988, some shareholder proxies had begun receiving a significant portion of the votes cast at annual meetings. A proposal for confidential voting procedures received one-third of all the votes cast at Phelps Dodge, more than 20 percent at Honeywell, and more than 19 percent at Lockheed. At CBI Industries, a proposal to sign a statement of fair employment at the company's South African operations received 23 percent of all votes cast.[61]

And quite often, the resolution itself is just one part of a larger campaign to change a corporation's behavior. As the ICCR's Timothy Smith points out, such resolutions are often used along with other pressure, ranging from "gentle persuasion" to "media outreach, demonstrations, boycotts, and legal actions."[62]

Thus, even while they have little chance of winning majority support of shareholders, sponsors of such resolutions are often able to persuade corporations to make the policy changes. In many cases, activists have found that they can reach agreements with a corporation on certain issues before the proxy statement is printed, allowing them to withdraw their resolutions before they are even voted on by shareholders. Some examples:

+ In 1992, Amalgamated Clothing and Textile Workers Union withdrew a shareholder resolution aimed at Sears, Roebuck & Co.

after the company agreed to take steps to insure that none of the goods it imports from China are made with prison labor (see p. 33).[63]

✦ In 1993, Sun Co. became the first major (i.e. Fortune 500) company to sign the CERES Principles (formerly the Valdez Principles), an environmental code of conduct developed by the Coalition for Environmentally Responsible Economies. The company had been the target of shareholder proposals asking it to sign the code filed by ICCR coalition members American Baptist Home Mission Society and the Sisters of St. Francis of Philadelphia, along with the New York City Employees' Retirement System (see p. 17).

✦ Also in 1993, members of the ICCR coalition announced that it had reached agreements with pharmaceutical makers Johnson & Johnson, Eli Lilly, Pfizer, Schering Plough, and Syntex, under which the companies will publish reports on their drug pricing policies.[64]

Among the most well-known, and most successful, campaigns of the shareholder activism movement has been its role in persuading a large number of companies to end their business ties to South Africa or sign the Statement of Principles (formerly the Sullivan Principles), a code of conduct aimed at providing equal employment opportunities to that nation's black majority.

Until 1993, more shareholder resolutions were filed regarding South Africa than any other social issue, and the results were tangible. This pressure from shareholders—combined with a campaign of stock divestment and selective contracting to exclude South Africa–connected companies from state and local government contracts—resulted in almost 200 companies selling their South African operations between 1984 and 1991.[65]

This kind of economic pressure from corporations and other kinds of economic sanctions imposed by the world community have largely influenced the South African government to negotiate with the African National Congress and other groups fighting for majority rule in that country.

Therefore, while proxy activists seem unlikely to overcome the tendency of most shareholders to vote with management or decline to vote on resolutions dealing with social issues, they can and have changed corporate behavior. Such resolutions, when combined with a campaign to publicly expose the perceived "wrongdoing" of a corporation, can bring results, provided that the demands of the activists are reasonable and that the organizations involved are open to frank negotiations and compromise with the corporations involved.

Despite some resistance from the Securities and Exchange Commission (see below), there is strong evidence that, even as the South Africa issue begins to fade from shareholder resolutions, access to the proxy statements of public corporations will continue to be an important tool for shareholders concerned with the ethical performance of the companies they own.

Trends in Shareholder Activism

By the 1993 proxy season, in response to political change in South Africa and shareholder sentiments, the nature of South Africa–related shareholder resolutions underwent a subtle shift. In the past, the resolutions had asked corporations to divest from the country; the resolutions filed in late 1992 for consideration in 1993 generally asked companies to refrain from expanding their operations there.[66]

The change in emphasis is not surprising. In the preceding year support for South African divestment resolutions had, after several years of steadily increasing support, begun to fall off as many investors began to anticipate the end of apartheid. The average level of support for South Africa–related shareholder resolutions in 1992 dropped to less than 10 percent of votes cast, compared with about 13 percent in 1991, according to data supplied by the Investor Responsibility Research Center (IRRC), Washington, D.C.

For the first time, no such proposal received more than 20 percent of the vote. Among 62 resolutions tracked by the IRRC, the highest vote was recorded at Texas Instruments, where a proposal asking the company to cut its economic ties to South Africa received 17.2 percent of the vote.

At the time, Carolyn Mathiasen, director of the IRRC's social issues service, told *Responsive Investing News* that the outcome of the South Africa resolutions was greatly influenced by timing. Most of the votes were held in the spring, shortly after the South African government's successful referendum on holding talks to end apartheid, but before those talks broke down. Mathiasen said that much of the drop-off in support occurred among small, individual investors and that the IRRC was unable to identify an institutional investor that had changed its position.

However, while 1992 was a bad year for South Africa resolutions, it was arguably the best year ever for a range of other shareholder resolutions dealing with social and corporate governance issues (see Figure 1-7).

Of the 165 social issue resolutions tracked by the IRRC, only five received less than 3 percent of the votes cast—the lowest percentage of very

FIGURE 1-7   Percent of 1992 Proxy Resolutions that Could Be Reintroduced

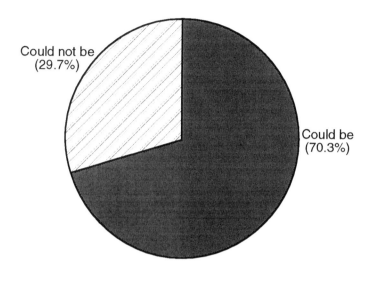

Could not be (29.7%)

Could be (70.3%)

Source: Interfaith Center on Corporate Responsibility.

low votes since the group began compiling data in 1973. In all, 116 of the proposals received enough support to be reintroduced the following year. Among the better performers in 1992 were shareholder resolutions dealing with the CERES environmental principles. All but one of the 30 CERES resolutions tracked by IRRC received enough votes to be reintroduced.

Good showings were also scored for resolutions asking companies with operations in Northern Ireland to adhere to the MacBride Principles, a code of conduct designed to insure equal employment opportunities for Roman Catholics in the province. Those proposals scored an average of 12.5 percent of the vote, an average gain of two percent compared with the previous year.

Corporate governance proposals fared especially well in 1992. For the first time, the Securities and Exchange Commission allowed shareholders to vote on proxy resolutions dealing with executive pay, and the 13 resolutions filed on the issue garnered an average of 22.2 percent of the vote, according to the IRRC.[67] In the same year, resolutions calling for confidential proxy voting averaged almost 38 percent, a 2.6 percent increase from 1991. Proposals calling for the annual election of directors received an average of 32.6 percent of votes cast, while anti-poison pill proposals received 42.5 percent support on average.

In another piece of corporate governance activism, the Washington, D.C.–based Council of Institutional Investors, which coordinates shareholder activism among pension funds, initiated a "just vote no" in a 1992 campaign to encourage investors to vote against the slate of directors offered by underperforming companies.

By the 1993 proxy season, new rules requiring increased disclosure of executive pay and allowing large shareholders to discuss proxy activity more freely encouraged a large number of shareholders to take bold stands on corporate governance. For example, Boston-based Fidelity Investments announced that it would, for the first time, begin voting against the boards of directors of certain companies. And, following on the high vote tallies for such resolutions in 1992, numerous resolutions were filed dealing with executive compensation and the composition of corporate boards.

In many cases, merely the threat of a shareholder vote was enough to get results. In 1993, most corporate governance resolutions filed at 50 companies targeted by the United Shareholders Association were withdrawn after companies reached agreements with the filers. In addition, the California Public Employees Retirement System, which targeted 12 companies for action, and the Teachers Insurance and Annuity Association–College Retirement Equities Fund, which targeted 10 companies, were both able to reach agreements in most cases.[68]

Among the corporate governance successes enjoyed by shareholders in 1993 was a proposal to remove a poison pill anti-takeover defense at Hartmarx Corp., a Chicago-based clothing retailer. The shareholder resolution, sponsored by a member of the USA coalition, received 80.5 percent of the vote, the largest margin of success ever recorded for such a proposal. Other shareholder proposals receiving large votes included a proposal asking Houston-based Southdown Inc. to allow shareholders to vote on future "golden parachute" severance agreements with executives (79.8 percent of the votes cast) and a resolution asking Dime Savings Bank, New York, to adopt confidential proxy voting (71 percent).[69]

Among socially motivated shareholder resolutions, the 1993 season marked a continued decline in the importance of South Africa–related resolutions. For the first time, environmental resolutions out-numbered South Africa resolutions, historically the most common type of social issue resolution. The majority of the environmental resolutions dealt with the CERES Principles, while others asked for reports on ozone depletion, chemical emissions, and environmentally damaging accidents.[70]

Securities and Exchange Commission Gets Tough

Despite their effectiveness—or because of it—social issue–oriented proxy resolutions began to look like an endangered species in the 1992 proxy season. In that year, the SEC began holding such resolutions to much more rigid standards when deciding which resolutions can lawfully be excluded from proxy ballots by corporations and which must be included.

As SEC Commissioner Richard Y. Roberts told *Responsive Investing News*, the staff of the commission began "scrutinizing social and political proxy issues more closely than in the past" because many of the social resolutions were deemed to lack a strong connection to the business interests of the companies involved, or dealt with matters of ordinary business that are not appropriate for the shareholder ballot. Commissioner Roberts, who is credited with helping to persuade the SEC staff to adopt a more hard-line approach to such socially motivated proxy resolutions, has been an outspoken critic of those who would use the proxy ballot as a soapbox for political and social causes. In a speech before the New York Chapter of the American Society of Corporate Secretaries in October 1991, Roberts said the commission should adopt a policy of excluding proposals that "promote social or political causes" or, at the very least, should raise the threshold of support necessary for the measures to be reintroduced.

Later, Roberts told *Responsive Investing News* that, in his opinion, the sponsors of all shareholder resolutions should be able to demonstrate that their proposal is strongly connected to the business interests of the company involved. "I'm not interested necessarily in eliminating the ability of shareholders to offer resolutions in the social or political arena," he said, "just so long as there is a strong nexus with the economic interests of the company." He cited resolutions on environmental performance as one example where economic and social concerns may often intersect, but added that his views on proxy matters were strictly his own and that he was not attempting to speak for the commission as a whole.[71]

The SEC's change in philosophy is evident in its decisions on numerous socially motivated resolutions filed for the 1993 proxy season.

For example, the commission ruled excludable a shareholder resolution asking Cracker Barrel Old Country Store to make a pledge of nondiscrimination against homosexuals. Another proposal receiving the thumbs-down from the commission requested that Wal-Mart Stores disclose data on its equal employment opportunity and affirmative action record. In both cases the commission, which had previously allowed shareholders to include resolutions on some employment-related issues, had decided to reverse its policy by ruling that the resolutions were matters of "ordinary business," and excludable under SEC rules.

In his decision on the Cracker Barrel case, SEC Special Counsel William H. Carter conceded that exceptions had been made in the past for employment proposals dealing with social policy concerns. However, the commission decided it was time to change its approach because "the line between includable and excludable employment related proposals based on social policy considerations has become increasingly difficult to draw," the decision said. The SEC staff, therefore, "determined that the fact that a shareholder proposal concerning a company's employment policies and practices for the general work force is tied to a social issue will no longer be viewed as removing the proposal from ordinary business operations."

The resolution at Cracker Barrel, sponsored by the New York City Employees' Retirement System (NYCERS), was filed because in early 1991, the company made headlines by announcing a policy against employing homosexuals and dismissing several employees thought to be gay or lesbian. The company later softened its position, but none of the fired employees were allowed to return to their jobs.

The Wal-Mart resolution was sponsored by the Amalgamated Clothing and Textile Workers Union (ACTWU), Progressive Securities, and a group of ICCR-affiliated religious groups concerned about the company's equal opportunity record.

Other resolutions omitted by the SEC in 1993 included those asking Unisys Corp. and United Technologies Corp. to comply with the MacBride Principles, along with resolutions dealing with smoke-free restaurants and bank lending practices in urban areas, according to the ICCR.

As might be expected, the SEC's recent hard line on social proxy resolutions has provoked a strong reaction from sponsors of those resolutions, who have, with some success, waged a campaign of litigation and public pressure to reverse the SEC's policy. Some recent examples:

+ In April 1993, Judge Kimba Wood, with the U.S. District Court for Southern New York, granted the request of ACTWU and its allies to overturn the SEC's decision in the Wal-Mart case. Judge Wood enjoined the retailer from excluding the resolution from its proxy ballot, finding that the subject of the proposal did not, in her opinion, constitute ordinary business.[72]

+ In March 1993, the NYCERS, in conjunction with the Women's Division of the Board of Global Ministries of the United Methodist Church and United States Trust Co. sued the SEC to challenge its decision in the Cracker Barrel case. As of press time, the Cracker Barrel case was still in litigation.

+ In 1992, the NYCERS successfully sued Dole Foods after the SEC had allowed the company to exclude a resolution dealing with national health care—the first proposal ever filed on the issue, according to NYCERS.

The resolution, which asked the company to report on how each of three major national health care proposals would affect the company and its competitiveness, received 6 percent of the votes cast at Dole's annual meeting—a slim margin of support, but twice the amount needed to be reintroduced. At the time, a NYCERS spokeswoman said the pension fund would consider bringing back the proposal at the next annual meeting and would consider filing similar resolutions at other companies.[73]

In addition, activist investors—particularly the ICCR and the New York pension funds—have launched a campaign of letters, press releases, lobbying, and public testimony aimed at putting public pressure on the commission.

In a statement issued in March 1993, the ICCR said that, in addition to participating in court action against Wal-Mart and Cracker Barrel, the coalition was "leading a campaign to challenge the SEC's negative interpretation of proxy rules." As of that time, the ICCR claims, "conscientious institutional and individual investors [had] contacted the SEC in approximately 5,000 protest phone calls, letters and cards."

Proxy resolutions are a potent weapon in the arsenal of the social investment movement because they enable institutional investors to affect change in corporate behavior, when divestment is not practical or is undesirable. Fiduciaries are also drawn into shareholder activism because of rules that require them to take responsibility for understanding proxies and considering them carefully. Proxy resolutions are filed by pension funds, religious institutions, unions, and others to address operating procedures, corporate governance, and company policies on a wide variety of social issues.

While the motivation is often to improve the moral behavior of companies, the resolutions are also filed to increase long-term profitability. A small percentage of the votes cast can have a profound impact on corporate policy. In the past decade, such proxy resolutions have helped: change the situation in South Africa; improve the environment; decrease discrimination; and make corporations more accountable to shareholders and communities. While the effects of proxy resolutions have been strong, the process has not been smooth sailing. The SEC has recently allowed companies to exclude a growing number of socially motivated resolutions, resulting in a decrease in the number of resolutions filed. The outcome of the ongoing conflict between the commission and shareholder activists will have an enormous impact on the future of the social investment movement in the United States.

THE GROWTH OF DEFINED CONTRIBUTION PLANS: AN OPPORTUNITY FOR SOCIAL INVESTING

The growth of 401(k) plans and other retirement funds in which employees contribute money and/or direct the investment of their assets provides a significant opportunity for the growth of socially responsible investing. This is because, with the growth of these so-called defined contribution plans, retirement plans are beginning to look more and more like menus, and employees are being given greater flexibility to decide what types of investments they want to "order" for themselves, depending on their own financial situation, tolerance for risk, and, at least potentially, social criteria.

Thus, while employees formerly depended on their employers to invest their retirement money and then to make good on the company's promise to pay benefits, workers are now given a greater responsibility for making both financial contributions and the tough investment choices that will determine the amount of benefits they will receive. It is not unusual for a company 401(k) plan or other defined contribution plan to contain several options, allowing workers to allocate assets among stocks, bonds, cash, company stock, international investments, and, in some cases, even portfolios invested with social considerations in mind.

Pension officials who may be understandably reluctant to impose social investment criteria on the assets of a traditional pension plan have shown a greater willingness to offer "socially responsible" options, such as one or more of the numerous social investment mutual funds now available to participants of defined contribution plans. By providing such options, officials of retirement programs are able to address the social concerns of certain members while, at the same time, allowing other members to invest their assets in a more traditional manner.

Such socially screened investment options are most common among non-profit organizations—particularly religious organizations and those with progressive political or social agendas—and, in some cases, public sector retirement systems. Some recent examples of retirement plans giving participants the option of investing in socially screened vehicles include:

♦ The giant College Retirement Equities Fund (CREF), which introduced its Social Choice Account in 1990. The account avoids investing in corporations that have economic ties to South Africa, do not adhere to the MacBride Principles in Northern Ireland, produce nuclear energy, derive a significant portion of their revenue from weapons production, and which produce or market alcoholic beverages or tobacco products. In 1992, the Social Choice Account added restriction on investing in companies with poor environmental records.

CREF, along with its sister organization, the Teachers Insurance and Annuity Association, which invests in fixed income instruments, offers investment funds to employees of more than 4,700 colleges, universities, and related nonprofit educational institutions. Combined assets total about $125 billion.

✦ The New Mexico Public Employees Retirement Association which, in 1991, added the socially screened Dreyfus Third Century Fund, a growth-oriented equity mutual fund, to the options available to investors in its deferred compensation plan. The fund, which was added alongside a new international equity option, was added at the request of plan participants.

✦ Evangelical Lutheran Church of America, which offers participants in its pension program the choice of equity, bond, and balanced (mixed equity and bond) investment options with varying degrees of social screening.

The church's three Social Purpose Funds offer pension plan members the chance to invest their money in portfolios that avoid companies that are screened for a variety of social issues. These portfolios avoid companies doing business in South Africa, those that produce alcoholic beverages, tobacco, pornography, or gambling opportunities, or contribute to the creation of weapons of mass destruction. The Social Choice funds also avoid investing in companies that engage in unfair labor practices or which have exceptionally bad environmental records.

The church also offers three investment funds that are screened solely for South Africa–related companies. Three others are virtually unscreened except for a provision that requires them to avoid South Africa–related companies whenever those securities can be replaced with investments of similar risk and return characteristics.[74]

Socially motivated investment options have had some success in attracting assets from pension fund participants. However, a progressive social agenda is not enough to persuade employees to invest their retirement money. Socially responsible investments, like investments in general, need to be safe, adequately diversified, and provide a rate of return that fairly compensates investors for whatever risks they are taking. The experience of one retirement system shows that employees can be every bit as concerned with issues like diversification and prudence as investment professionals.

In the spring of 1993, an option that gave participants of the Los Angeles County Employees Retirement Association's defined contribution plan a chance to invest assets in the county received a disappointing response. The Los Angeles County Investment Fund, which was to be used to help the county avoid the immediate layoff of thousands of workers and cutbacks in services, raised only $19.7 million of the $200 million officials had predicted. The lackluster response was received despite the fact that the investment would have paid employees a half point more interest than another fixed income option offered by the defined contribution plan.[75]

At the time the investment option was closed to new investors, county officials declined to speculate on why the fund was unable to raise the $200 million expected. However, one plausible explanation might be that the investment, which was not diversified and not subject to federal insurance, was perceived as riskier than other fixed-income investments available.

Corporate retirement systems have been generally slow to adopt social investment options. However, the sheer growth of defined contribution plans among corporations, along with a trend toward increasing the number of options available to participants, offers a sizable, if so far largely untapped, opportunity for social investment advocates.

According to information from the Employee Benefits Research Institute (EBRI), the amount of money available in so-called defined contribution plans for the private sector stood at $911 billion at the end of 1992, compared with $1.57 trillion in traditional defined benefit pension funds. However, if current growth predictions hold, EBRI predicts, the assets of defined contribution plans will swell to $5.75 trillion by 2002, slightly exceeding the assets projected for traditional pension plans.[76]

Partly in response to such rapid growth and partly as a result of voluntary government guidelines that call on companies to add investment options to such plans, numerous sponsors of defined contribution plans are in the process of adding new investment options for employees. According to a study of investment management trends conducted by Greenwich Associates, Greenwich, Connecticut, 23 percent of the 534 companies surveyed in 1992 planned to add new options to their defined contribution plans.[77]

Most of these added investment options will have nothing to do with social investing—the emphasis will be on giving employees a greater chance to do things like invest in overseas companies and move more assets into stocks and out of fixed-income instruments. But, as the nation's deferred compensation plans add investment options, this will clearly create a greater opportunity for sellers of socially responsible investment products to break into this marketplace. This is particularly true if employees, like those of the state of New Mexico, continue *asking* their employers to add socially responsible choices to these plans.

Socially responsible investing may not be for everyone, but, with defined contribution plans becoming more popular among employers, a compelling case can be made for adding it to the investment menu.

NOTES

1. Taken from a draft copy of *Economically Targeted Investment: A Reference for Public Pension Funds.* Institute for Fiduciary Education, 1993.
2. Ibid.
3. It is important to note, however, that a comparison between the two IFE studies may overstate the growth of ETIs since the later study is based on responses from 119 funds, compared with 99 in the original study.
4. Carol O'Cleireacain, "No ETI Trade Off," *Pensions & Investments,* March 22, 1992, p. 14.
5. As the study points out, however: "These returns include results from a few ETIs made in the early 1980s, when interest rates hit historic highs. Returns on comparable investments today would be substantially lower."
6. "LA Lawmakers Reject Targeted Investing Bill; Create New Actuarial Body." *Responsive Investing News,* Aug. 8, 1992, p. 1.
7. Christine Philip, "Kansas Takes Up Reforms," *Pensions & Investments,* Feb. 22, 1992, p. 32.
8. Massachusetts State Treasurer's Office, *Economically Targeted Investments: Massachusetts State Teachers' and Employees' Retirement System,* 1991, p. 4.
9. New York State Industrial Cooperation Council, *Competitive Plus: Economically Targeted Investments by Pension Funds,* 1990, p. 4.
10. Joel Chernoff, "Excelsior Pool Nabs Corporate Funds," *Pensions & Investments,* Feb. 22, 1992, p. 32.
11. Richard Ferlauto, Robert Stumberg, and Robin Sampson, *State Policy Support for Targeted Pension Fund Investment,* Center for Policy Alternatives, 1992, p. 9.
12. Joel Chernoff, "State Pension Funds Tugged Toward ETIs," *Pensions & Investments,* Feb. 22, 1992, p. 4.
13. Matthew L. Wald, "Corporate Green Warrior, Sun Oil Takes Environmental Pledge," *New York Times,* Feb. 11, 1993, p. D5.
14. Other companies joining PERI were: Amoco, duPont, IBM, Northern Telecom, Phillips Petroleum, Polaroid, Rockwell International and United Technologies.
15. "ICCR Action Plans: July 1993–June 1994," Interfaith Center for Corporate Responsibility, July 1993, p. 19.
16. *Church Proxy Resolutions,* Interfaith Center on Corporate Responsibility, 1993, p. 31.
17. Ibid., pp. 32–38.
18. As of the summer of 1993, representatives of NIMA and the National Association of Securities Professionals, an Atlanta-based organization of female and minority investment executives, were in the process of working out a plan to merge the two organizations. The proposed merger had not yet been formally approved by the membership of the two organizations at press time.

19. "New Directory Reveals Growth of Female, Minority Money Managers," *Responsive Investing News,* May 11, 1992, p. 5.
20. *Big Job Gets Bigger: Investment Management 1993,* Greenwich Associates, 1993, p. 89.
21. *P&I Daily,* July 28, 1993; see also "Disney May Seek Woman- and Minority-Owned Money Managers," *Money Management Letter,* August 14, 1993, p. 10.
22. Myra Alperson, Alice Tepper Marlin, Jonathan Schorsch, and Rosalyn Will, *The Better World Investment Guide* (New York: Prentice Hall Press, 1991), p. 27.
23. Estimate provided by the Social Investment Forum, Washington, D.C.
24. William F. Moses, *A Guide to American State and Local Laws on South Africa,* Investor Responsibility Research Center, 1992.
25. Ibid. According to the IRRC, other kinds of South Africa–related laws passed by U.S. jurisdictions are: no new investment statutes, which prohibit future investments in U.S. companies; banking restrictions, which prohibit the municipality from making deposits or investments in or using the services of South Africa–related banks; selective contracting ordinances, which prohibit local governments from purchasing services from companies doing business in South Africa; "Shell-free zone" laws, which prohibit localities from buying products or services from Royal Dutch Shell or its units; and bans on purchases of South African–made goods by local governments.
26. Ibid. According to the IRRC, the success of the divestment movement reached its peak in the mid-1980s. From 1985 through 1987, 149 U.S. companies pulled out of the country, an average of 50 divestments per year. See also: "Non-U.S. Firms Set Up Direct Ties to South Africa," *Responsive Investing News,* Dec. 7, 1992, p. 1.
27. Walter Sisulu, transcript of speech before the quarterly meeting of the Social Investment Forum, Boston, Mass., June 14, 1992.
28. Margaret Price, "Investors Await ANC Call," *Pensions & Investments,* Aug. 9, 1993, p. 20.
29. The Rustenburg Declaration is a statement by South African religious leaders drawn up at a conference in Rustenburg, Transvaal, in November 1990.
30. "Non-U.S. Firms Set Up Direct Ties to South Africa," *Responsive Investing News,* Dec. 7, 1992, p. 1.
31. Ibid.
32. *Church Proxy Resolutions,* pp. 63–64.
33. Heidi J. Welsh, "A Guide to U.S. Legislation in Support of the MacBride Principles 1993," Investor Responsibility Research Center, 1993.
34. "Sears Agrees to Adopt Measures on Prison-Made Chinese Imports," *Responsive Investing News,* March 30, 1992, p. 1.
35. "Petro-Canada to Review Myanmar, Social Responsibility Policies," *Responsive Investing News,* May 11, 1992, p. 1.
36. *Church Proxy Resolutions,* pp. 56–57.
37. George E. Mowry. *The Era of Theodore Roosevelt* (New York: Harper & Row Publishers, 1958), pp. 26, 29. Social Gospel adherents splintered along ideologi-

cal lines, with more moderate groups seeking to work within the economic system as Christian capitalists, while more radical elements sought wholesale change. Each was opposed by fundamentalists Protestants. The only area of agreement was on the need for Prohibition. The imposition of the Eighteenth Amendment in 1919, and the subsequent disdain for it by the nation as a whole, diminished the Protestant churches' political influence—and killed any momentum that existed for socially screened investing. For an excellent examination of the Social Gospel's role in shaping political debate, see E.J. Dionne Jr.'s *Why Americans Hate Politics* (New York: Simon & Schuster, Touchstone Edition, 1992). It is discussed in the chapter "Hell Hath No Fury," pp. 209–241.

38. *The Better World Investment Guide* (New York: Prentice Hall Press, 1991), pp. 2–3; and Peter Kinder, Steven D. Lydenberg, and Amy L. Domini, *Investing for Good* (New York: Harper Business, 1993), p. 13.
39. Michael Crosby, "Tobacco Shareholder Actions," in Peter Kinder, Steven D. Lydenberg, and Amy L. Domini, *The Social Investment Almanac* (New York: Henry Holt and Company, 1992), pp. 185–186. It should be noted that "it was the same James who first derived serious revenue from an import duty on the weed"; see "The Weed of Liberation," *The Economist,* December 21, 1991, p. 116. The article points out that governments have a long history of ambivalence toward smoking—denouncing it as evil, taxing it heavily to discourage use, living off its revenues, and subsidizing its cultivation to ensure the tobacco industry's viability.
40. Alix M. Freedman and Laurie P. Cohen, "Smoke and Mirrors: How Cigarette Makers Keep Health Question Open Year After Year," *Wall Street Journal,* Feb. 11, 1993, pp. A-1, A-6; and "Production and Marketing of Tobacco and Related Products," Investor Responsibility Resource Center Social Issues Service, Jan. 25, 1993, p. E2.
41. Trex Proffitt, "Tobacco Divestment Debate Revives Philosophical Questions," *IRRC News for Investors,* Oct. 1991, p. 6.
42. The Big Six: American Brands, B.A.T. Industries PLC (British parent corporation of Brown & Williamson), Brooke Group (parent of Liggett Group), Loews Group (parent of Lorillard), Philip Morris Companies, and RJR Nabisco Holdings Corporation.
43. *Social Investment Almanac,* p. 189.
44. Ibid., pp. 189–190.
45. Gregory N. Connolly, "Crimes and Misdemeanors: Institutional Investors and the U.S. Tobacco Industry," 1990, a valuable if now dated article; and *Social Investment Almanac,* pp. 190–191.
46. "Production and Marketing of Tobacco and Related Products," pp. E1–E2.
47. Ibid., pp. E2–E3.
48. *Wall Street Journal,* Feb. 11, 1993, pp. A-1, A-6.
49. In 1983, Rose Cipollone filed suit against the company, whose brands she smoked for four decades. After her death in 1984, the suit was continued by her husband and son. In 1988, the case produced a $400,000 award from a federal jury—the first monetary award in a tobacco liability case. The award was later overturned. The suit was dropped in 1992 because the plaintiffs' lead attorneys said it had

become a financial drag on their firm. (John H. Kennedy, "Suit Against Tobacco Firm Ends," *Boston Globe*, Nov. 6, 1992.)

50. *IRRC News for Investors,* Oct. 1991, p. 7.
51. Ibid, pp. 7–12.
52. Christine Philip, "A 'Raging Debate' Hits Minnesota Fund," *Pensions & Investments,* March 8, 1993, p. 4; "Investment Restrictions Hits Minnesota Active International Search," *Investment Management Weekly,* Jan. 25, 1993, pp. 1, 7; and "Minnesota Makes Dramatic Changes in Portfolio, Policies," *Investment Management Weekly,* March 22, 1993, pp. 1, 7–8.
53. " 'Sin-free' Investing Has Been Costly, Consultant Finds," *Responsive Investing News,* July 6, 1992, p. 2.
54. Louis Rukeyser, "Put This Thought in Your Pipe and Smoke It," syndicated column, Nov. 11, 1992.
55. "Sin-Free Investing," *Responsive Investing News,* July 6, 1992, p. 2.
56. David Kreiger, "NBA Commissioner Discusses Gambling," *Rocky Mountain News,* June 11, 1993.
57. *Investing for Good,* p. 74; and "High Stakes for Indians," *Boston Globe,* May 11, 1993, p. 18.
58. Polly Baroe Elliott, "Nevada Casino Operator Emerges as High-Stakes Player in Game of Political Influence," States News Service, June 10, 1993; and Jeffrey L. Hiday, "Coast Lobbyist Accused of Bribing Legislator While on GTECH Retainer," and "Despite Warnings, Gambling Stocks Take Off: Some Say Competition Will Force Them Out," *Providence Journal-Bulletin,* March 2, 1993, pp, C-1, C-2.
59. *Church Proxy Resolutions,* Interfaith Center on Corporate Responsibility, Jan. 1993.
60. Timothy Smith, "Shareholder Activism," *The Social Investment Almanac* (New York: Henry Holt & Co., 1992), p. 108.
61. Ritchie P. Lowry, *Good Money: A Guide to Profitable Social Investing in the 90s* (New York: W.W. Norton, 1991), p. 28.
62. Smith, "Shareholder Activism," p. 114.
63. "Sears Agrees to Adopt Measures on Prison-Made Chinese Imports," *Responsive Investing News,* March 30, 1992, p. 1.
64. ICCR press release dated March 18, 1993.
65. William Moses, *A Guide to State and Local Laws on South Africa, 1991,* Investor Responsibility Research Center.
66. "South Africa Shareholder Proposals Show Change in Emphasis," *Responsive Investing News,* Nov. 23, 1992, p. 1.
67. "All Pay Resolutions Defeated, but Get Sizable Support; P&G Faces Compensation Vote," *Responsive Investing News,* June 8, 1992, p. 1.
68. Marlene Givant Star. "Governance Issues Fill '93 Proxies," *Pensions & Investments,* April 5, 1993, p. 16.
69. Vineeta Anand, "'93 Proxy Season Quiet but Effective," *Pensions & Investments,* May 31, 1993, p. 3.
70. Christine Philip, "Social Activists Focus on the Environment," *Pensions & Investments,* April 8, 1993, p. 16.

71. "Investors File Fewer Social Proxy Resolutions This Year," *Responsive Investing News,* March 16, 1992, p. 4.
72. "Wal-Mart Proxy Materials Must Include Resolution on EEO Data, Court Decides," *Securities Regulation and Law Report,* Bureau of National Affairs, April 23, 1993, p. 614.
73. *Responsive Investing News,* June 29, p.1; see also "Employer's Appeal of Injunction on Health Care Proposal Dismissed," *Pension Reporter,* June 8, 1992.
74. *1993 Summary Plan Description, ECLA Regular Pension Plan,* Evangelical Lutheran Church in America Board of Pensions.
75. Steve Hemmerick, "Targeted Pool Falls Short," *Pensions and Investments,* May 17, 1993, p. 6.
76. Joel Chernoff, "Defined Contribution Soaring," *Pensions and Investments,* March 22, 1993, p. 1.
77. *Big Job Gets Bigger: Investment Management 1993,* Greenwich Associates, p. 37.

2

Public Sector Pension Funds

ECONOMICALLY TARGETED INVESTING IN PRACTICE

Regardless of where one stands on the debate about economically targeted investing, there is no denying that the trend toward utilizing pension fund investments to fulfill public policy objectives is here to stay. As pension funds get larger, and as financial constraints on states and cities become more serious, the political pressure on pension funds to invest in ways that aid the economy will increase. And, if early indications mean anything, there is every reason to believe that Bill Clinton's Washington will do everything it can to encourage that trend.

Even before the Clinton Administration came to Washington, however, the issue of targeted investing was a hot topic in the state treasurer's offices, city councils, mayor's offices, and governor's mansions of the United States. The political pressure on pension funds to make investments that provide spinoff benefits to the local community is intense because state and local governments increasingly need to make their dollars work harder. To many officials, ETIs offer the chance to save for future pension liabilities while at the same time promoting economic development—and with the same funds, no less.

While ETIs are popular among politicians, they are more than just a political gimmick. Despite some frightening failures, many pension funds have found that good, responsible ETIs can and do work. Some of the programs of several larger pension funds will be outlined later in this chapter.

Washington Shows Interest

President Bill Clinton is a long-time supporter of ETI. As governor of Arkansas, Clinton pushed for legislation that encouraged the Arkansas Teacher Retirement System and the Arkansas Public Employees' Retirement System to invest at least 5 percent, but not more than 10 percent, of their assets in Arkansas-related investments. Together, the two funds, with combined assets of nearly $5 billion, had committed $245 million to targeted investments as of February 1993.[1]

During his presidential campaign, Clinton proposed the creation of a "Rebuild America Fund" to be used for infrastructure and other public investments. While the plan was short on details, campaign literature said the proposed fund would be financed in part with four $20 billion contributions from the federal government and would leverage that by selling bonds to public and private pension funds. Road tolls, waste disposal charges, and other fees generated by the projects would be used to repay the bonds.[2]

The good news is that while the administration appears serious about tapping pension dollars to meet its public policy goals, its emphasis has been on incentives and encouragement rather than mandates.

In the January 25, 1993 issue of *Pensions & Investments,* Secretary of Housing and Urban Development Henry Cisneros was quoted as saying:

> There are ways to get returns for [pension] funds and do social investment in the communities. But pension managers and retirees are very nervous about this. This is not an area where the government can mandate percentages . . . but to the degree that it can be done through incentives, it's a laudable objective and worth exploring.
>
> If we could fashion a way to protect them, yes, there's trillions of dollars that could be spent.[3]

Even before the Clinton administration came to power, such ideas had support on Capitol Hill. House majority Leader Richard A. Gephardt and Rev. Jesse Jackson, who serves as Washington, D.C.'s "shadow senator," have suggested a national investment fund similar to the one proposed by Clinton. And in testimony before the Senate Committee on Labor and Human Resources, Felix G. Rohatyn, senior partner with Lazard Freres & Co. and chairman of New York City's Municipal Assistance Corp., called for a "new domestic order" to include the creation of a public investment fund that would sell "investment rated bonds, which could be acquired by private and public pension funds and other institutions."[4]

Late in 1992, the Senate's Infrastructure Investment Commission, which was established to find alternative ways to finance infrastructure, gave further support to the idea of utilizing pension dollars for such projects. Again, the emphasis was on the carrot, not the stick. In a working paper released in November 1992, the commission wrote:

> Pension funds are a ready and willing source of new capital for infrastructure investments, but only where investments allow them to meet their fiduciary duties without mandates.
>
> Pension funds represent a $3 trillion potential source of capital for infrastructure finance. Fund representatives have impressed upon the Commission the importance of their fiduciary responsibilities in ensuring market rates of return, asset liquidity and investment credit worthiness. Experts have indicated that properly structured infrastructure financial opportunities can compete successfully for fund assets.[5]

The commission's working paper made numerous suggestions about how the government could encourage pension funds to invest in infrastructure. Among the ideas was a new "quasi-governmental entity for national infrastructure policy implementation," the establishment of an infrastructure bond insurance company, and the creation of a "taxable infrastructure security backed by a pool of projects with revenue streams and a guarantee from the federal government."

Also in 1992, a working group of the Department of Labor's Employee Retirement Income Security Act (ERISA) Advisory Committee, which advises the secretary of labor on pension-related issues, suggested that the department could do more to encourage ETIs. Among the panel's suggestions was that the DOL compile a database of ETI performance and establish so-called "safe harbor" guidelines for determining what is and is not an appropriate ETI. Such safe harbors could include a requirement that pension funds find other "non-ETI-motivated investors" before a deal can go forward, or the development of benchmarks for evaluating the performance of ETIs, according to Ronald D. Watson, chair of the working group. (Such a new policy would represent a stark departure from the Department of Labor's previous policies on ETIs, Watson told *Responsive Investing News*. Based on hearings held by the working group, the department, though officially neutral on targeted investing, has historically been perceived by many pension fund officials as "skeptical at best, and probably hostile" to such investments by pension funds, he said.)[6]

After Clinton was sworn in, his appointees made it clear that the Department of Labor would work to encourage, but not force, pension funds to make targeted investments. In July 1993, new Assistant Secretary of Labor Olena Berg, head of the Pension and Welfare Benefits Administration, said that she would work to promote the growth of ETIs, but added that persuasion, rather than mandates, is the best way to get the message out. Berg said the Department of Labor will take on a "bully pulpit role because funds are so individually different in terms of size. Every individual fund starts off from its liability strand and what's the appropriate asset mix . . . so I don't think there's a formula and a regulatory approach that works everywhere."[7]

State and Local Pressure

At the state and local level, the trend toward ETIs is being moved forward by a combination of overt political pressure and gentle prodding, with mixed success.

One success has been New York State's Excelsior Capital Corp., a quasi-public targeted investment program created at the urging of Gov. Mario Cuomo. Excelsior has been able to attract sizable investments, not only from public pensions, but from union and corporate pension funds as well. Excelsior so far has launched two investment programs, a $100 million pool to provide affordable mortgages in the state and a $150–250 million pool for loans to middle-market firms in New York.[8]

In other cases, jurisdictions are rethinking old investment restrictions, seeking to replace old "legal lists" of permissible investments with the "prudent person" rule, which would give fund officials the same discretion in selecting investments that is now enjoyed by corporate pension plans. Most often, the primary motivation for loosening investment restrictions is to increase the overall diversification of fund investments—by allowing funds to invest assets internationally, or increase their exposure to the stock market for example—but, clearly, this trend also paves the way for funds to make targeted investments.

Where states and localities cannot bring themselves to give up their restrictions entirely, the legal lists are being amended to include more investment categories or "basket clauses" that allow fund officials to invest a small portion of the plan's assets without restrictions except those imposed by prudent person standards. Such strategies allow the pension funds to engage in a number of innovative investment strategies—including ETIs—while allowing the state or locality to maintain restrictions on the bulk of the portfolio.

The Center for Policy Alternatives (CPA), which has become a leading cheerleader for targeted investing, concluded in a recent report that "one way for lawmakers to facilitate ETIs is to enact statutes that give pension managers more discretion over the selection of investments."

Thus, among its suggestions for encouraging targeted investing, the liberal think-tank recommends that states eliminate their legal lists or adopt basket clauses.[9]

In 1991, New York State substantially modified its legal list, in part because officials wanted to give pension funds the ability to use their 7.5 percent basket clause for additional ETIs—including investments in Excelsior Capital Corp. The changes raised the ceiling for equities to 60 percent of total assets, up from 50 percent, and added foreign securities and commingled investments to the list of permissible securities.[10]

Legislative pressure on pension funds to make targeted investments is also on the rise. By early 1993, legislators in at least three states—Maryland, Illinois, and Maine—had introduced bills that would encourage, though not require, their public sector pension funds to make targeted investments, following the suggested state ETI policy developed by the Center for Policy Alternatives. CPA predicted that similar bills would eventually be introduced in as many as 12 states.[11] Because pension funds generally resist any attempt to legislate investment guidelines, such legislation can be expected to face vocal opposition from fund officials.

Pension Fund Interest is Growing

While there is little doubt that the political pressure on pension funds to make ETIs is growing, it would be incorrect to attribute the growth of targeted investing entirely to politics. Most public pension funds, in fact, make some investments aimed at helping the community, such as municipal bonds and securities backed by agencies that provide a secondary market for mortgages.

Pension funds, traditionally the most conservative of investors, have resisted the cutting edge, preferring to stick to tried and true asset classes with known track records and predictable returns. In the past, public pension officials centered on avoiding being forced into making "social investments," many funds are now actively seeking ways to make safe, often guaranteed investments that may or may not fit neatly into conventional investment categories—and they are doing so regardless of legislative mandates or other kinds of political interference.

In some cases, pension funds have hired staff specifically to seek out and manage their ETI portfolios, just as they might hire in-house managers to oversee bonds, equities, or any other asset class. In most cases, however, funds are able to incorporate a limited amount of targeted investments into their portfolios without adding additional personnel.

The California Public Employees' Retirement System, the nation's largest public sector pension system (which, like most public pension funds, is not required to allocate assets in the state), announced in early 1992 that it would invest $225 million in three limited partnerships to invest in California housing. The fund made the investment because its trustees felt the plan was a good way to take advantage of a promising financial opportunity while assisting the sluggish economy. Investment officials at the fund said the move provided a way to take advantage of a good investment opportunity, while also helping the state's economy.[12]

Later that year, the California fund announced plans to invest up to $25 million in venture capital funds that finance minority- and women-owned businesses in the state.

In the summer of 1992, the Seattle City Employees' Retirement System (which, like the California pension fund, is in no way required to invest locally), began studying whether it could find a place for targeted investments in its portfolio. A study written for the pension fund by the Seattle law firm of Preston, Thorgrimson, Shidler, Gates & Ellis, concluded that "a legal foundation exists supporting the assumption that 'financially comparable' ETIs may generally be considered to meet the prudent person standard under common-law."

While warning that the fund must first meet "traditional goals" before considering "non-traditional objectives" such as targeted investing, the report suggested that the pension system "develop policy criteria to solicit and analyze specific ETIs." The report said the fund could then consider such initiatives as a loan program in conjunction with the Seattle Housing Authority, a certificate of deposit program with women- and minority-owned financial institutions, and a Small Business Administration variable rate loan portfolio.[13]

Roger Howeiler, executive director for the pension fund, told *Responsive Investing News* that the Preston Thorgrimson report contained some "very worthy ideas" and that the fund's board of trustees would consider it seriously. "I have no problem with investing in ways that help the community, if it meets fiduciary standards," he said.[14]

That qualifier, "if it meets fiduciary standards," is among the most repeated phrases one hears when discussing ETIs with pension fund officials—and justifiably so. Clearly, the first duty of any pension fund is to meet its financial obligation to plan participants. Every percentage point in lost investment returns by a large public fund can, over time, translate into millions of dollars in increased contributions of tax dollars and/or a significant decrease in the benefits to the teachers, fire fighters, police officers, or other public employees served by it. It is no surprise, then, that pension fund officials and trustees often use words like "sacred" and "public trust" when describing their fiduciary duty.

So the challenge of targeted investing, as some observers have put it, is to serve two masters: to find ways to help the local community while earning the same risk-adjusted rate of return that could be earned in more traditional investments. The huge losses of the Kansas pension fund and the souring of Connecticut's stake in CF Holdings prove that the task can be tricky, but there are numerous success stories as well.

Following are a few examples of how public funds are trying to meet that challenge.

New York City Pension Funds[15]

As with social issues proxy voting, the city of New York pension system, particularly the public employees' fund (NYCERS), has been on the forefront of funds allocating assets to economically targeted investing. And the growth of the city's targeted investing portfolio, like its increased proxy activism, has much to do with former City Comptroller Elizabeth Holtzman (who, during her tenure from 1990 to 1994, was a vocal advocate of ETI) and City Finance Commissioner Carol O'Cleireacain (see Table 2-1).

The city's commitment to targeted investing has been controversial among public pension systems nationally. (Some observers, for example, suggested that Holtzman pursued ETIs, in part, to gain popular support for her failed senatorial campaign in 1992). However, both Holtzman and O'Cleireacain argue that, with sufficient guarantees and safeguards, public pension funds can earn a market-rate investment return while making investments in affordable housing, small business lending, local commercial development, and other socially motivated ventures.

As O'Cleireacain points out, funds often have to take a creative pro-active role if they want to make such investments. In 1992, she wrote:

> There are those who argue that markets are perfect and that "capital gaps" do not exist. By definition, then, if, through ETI, a pension fund invests in a venture, or a neighborhood or an industry that has not been receiving investment, it must be because the fund is getting a riskier investment for the same rate of return or a below market rate of return for average risk. That appears to be an ideological rather than an experience-based position.[16]

TABLE 2-1 New York City Targeted Investing Programs

Project Name	Project HOME	CPC Program*	Apartment Rehab	Red-lined Neighborhoods Aid	Main Street Fund	Small Business Loans	Exporters Loan Program
Money Allocated (millions)	$100	$350	$100	$226	$30	$50	$30
Pension Funds Involved	NYCERS	NYCERS Police Teachers	NYCERS	NYCERS Fire Police Teachers Bd. of Ed.	Teachers	Police	Police
Purpose	New home mortgages at low interest & low down payments	Rehabs apartments & builds stores in minority areas	Spurs lending for apartment rehab	Invests in red-lined neighborhoods; single family home mortgages	Rehabs mixed-use buildings with stores & 4–5 apartments	Start-up & working capital for small businesses	Loans to exporting companies in the city
Guarantee to Fund(s)	Fannie Mae–backed securities	SONYMA	SONYMA	Ginnie Mae	SONYMA/ NYC REMIC	Federal SBA	Export-Import Bank of the United States
Participating Groups	New York City Partnership	CPC, HPD & others	Three NYC lenders	Fleet/Norstar	Lenders to be identified	Seven lenders	New York State Job Development Authority

* Housing and Commercial Programs.

O'Cleireacain pointed to the example of the city police fund, which found a safe way to finance $50 million in small business loans in cooperation with the Small Business Administration.

According to figures provided by the Comptroller's office, the New York City pension funds had committed almost $900 million to various ETI programs up to that point, of which $339 million has been invested. More than half of that commitment has been made since Holtzman took office in 1990. Overseen by a full-time staff of four, the ETI programs finance home mortgages, the rehabilitation of affordable apartment housing and stores, and provides loans for small businesses in the city.

While aggressive when it comes to allocating assets to such programs, the city has been rather conservative in its selection of individual investments. To date, every ETI made by the pension funds has been either in government-backed securities or in other kinds of deals that include some sort of state or federal guarantee. Such securities and guarantees have been provided by agencies such as the Federal National Mortgage Association, the Government National Mortgage Association, the Small Business Administration, and the State of New York Mortgage Authority.

And, as with most ETI programs, the city has emphasized investments in affordable housing, considered to be the safest and most well-developed area for targeted investing. Of the nearly $900 million committed, over $800 million has been devoted to this area.

In order to track the performance of its ETI portfolio, the city Comptroller's office, which oversees the roughly $50 billion pension system, measures its annualized rate of return against that of the pension funds' general bond market investments and, by that benchmark, the targeted investments perform well. During the five years ended June 30, 1992, the annualized rate of return for the ETI portfolio was 13 percent, compared to 9.92 percent for the bond portfolio, according to the Comptroller's office.

Project HOME

Under the city's $100 million Project HOME (Home Ownership Made Easy) program, established in 1990, NYCERS purchases securities from Fannie Mae backed by loans to low- and moderate-income families for the purchase of one- to three-family homes in the city.

City-owned vacant lots are selected for development by the New York City Housing Partnership and the New York City Housing Preservation Department (HPD) and then made available at low cost to qualifying developers. In addition to receiving a favorable price on the land for development, the homes can be subsidized up to $40,000 by the city and the state. Qualifying purchasers—those with incomes no more than 165 percent of the city's median income—can then purchase the homes with a down payment of as little as 5 percent of the purchase price.

According to the city, the $100 million allocated to the project has the potential to house 1,600 families—800 as owners and another 800 as renters. As of May 1992, 217 homes, with a total of 434 family units, had been purchased under the program and commitments were in place for another 85 homes with 120 units.

Community Preservation Corporation Program

Since the program was created in 1984, NYCERS, the Police Fund, and the Teachers' Fund have committed $342.7 million to provide financing to the Community Preservation Corp. CPC, an intermediary dedicated to the rehabilitation of existing rental housing, with an emphasis on low-income communities, and the HPD.

The pension funds provide a pool of money at market rates to finance mortgages for the rehabilitation of apartments, which are guaranteed by the State of New York Mortgage Authority (SONYMA). The HPD provides subsidized financing at rates of one to three percent. CPC coordinates the financing and building rehabilitation.

Through this program, the city pension funds have so far financed the rehabilitation of 15,000 apartments in 250 buildings in Manhattan, Brooklyn, the Bronx, and Queens, according to the Comptroller's office.

The CPC initiative also includes a program to provide commercial loans, called CPC Commercial. Under this program, the City Employees' fund has committed $7.5 million for the construction of new stores in areas served by the CPC. The investment is guaranteed by SONYMA.

Public/Private Apartment Rehabilitation

Initiated in 1990, the Public/Private Apartment Rehabilitation Program seeks to encourage private banks to lend money for the rehabilitation of apartments in the city for low- and moderate-income families.

NYCERS has committed $100 million to the program, in which the fund provides financing for loans made by three participating lenders—Chase Manhattan Bank, Chemical Bank, and Dime Savings. The pension fund receives a market rate of return and all of the loans are guaranteed by SONYMA. Like the CPC program, this program offers developers additional, subsidized financing from the city's Housing Preservation Department.

The Comptroller's office reports that in 1991, the program resulted in commitments of $2.1 million to renovate 128 apartments. The program has the potential to assist in the renovation of 5,000 units, the Comptroller's office estimates.

Red-Lined Neighborhood Aid

All five of New York's pension funds have so far invested a total of $226 million in the Red-Lined Neighborhood Aid Program, begun in 1981. Under this program the pension funds purchase mortgages in minority and low-income areas of the city where home buyers have often had trouble obtaining more traditional mortgages.

Federal Housing Administration mortgages, which are guaranteed by the federal Department of Housing and Urban Development, are originated by Norstar Mortgage Co., which then converts the loans into Government National Mortgage Association securities (Ginnie Maes). The Ginnie Maes are then purchased by the city pension funds.

This program resulted in purchases of 4,200 homes, 55 percent of which were in minority neighborhoods. However, lending under this program was inhibited during the real estate boom of the 1980s. Because the value of New York homes generally exceeds the $125,00 ceiling FHA sets for the value of a home that can be financed through its program, no such mortgages have been purchased in recent years, the Comptroller's office reports.

Main Street Fund

The Teacher's Fund has committed $30 million to the Main Street Fund, which is designed to provide financing for the rehabilitation of mixed-use buildings in low-and moderate-income neighborhoods. This program, started in late 1991, specifically targets properties that contain a store or commercial space on the ground floor and two to 10 apartments on the upper floors.

Funds invested under this program will be guaranteed by SONYMA and the city's Rehabilitation Mortgage Insurance Corp. Requests for proposals from lenders were issued in May, 1992.

Small Business Loan Program

The Police Pension Fund's small business loan program, which was started in 1990, is designed to provide start-up capital to new enterprises in the city utilizing $50 million committed by the pension fund. The program makes medium- to long-term loans of $25,000 to $1 million through seven participating banks: Abacus Federal Savings Bank, Banco de la Provincia de Buenos Aires, Business Loan Center, Chase Manhattan Bank, Chemical Bank, Banco Popular, and Norstar.

The federal Small Business Administration guarantees 90 percent of all loans below $155,000 and 85 percent of the loans above that amount. The pension fund buys only the SBA-guaranteed portion of those loans through Meridian Capital Markets.

Since its inception, the small business loan program has provided $6 million in loans to 27 businesses, saving or providing about 150 jobs, the Comptroller's office estimates. About 40 percent of the loans have gone to women- and minority-owned businesses. Businesses assisted have ranged from a tool rental shop on Staten Island to a Caribbean restaurant in Harlem to a sportswear manufacturer in Brooklyn, according to the Comptroller's office.

According to a pamphlet distributed by the Comptroller's office, the Small Business Loan program offers financing at 2.25 percent above the prime rate (the rate banks offer to their best customers) for terms under seven years and at 2.75 percent over prime for terms of seven or more.

Excelsior Capital Fund

In late 1992, NYCERS committed to invest $50 million in the Excelsior Fund, an investment pool to provide financing for middle-market firms organized by the quasi-public Excelsior Capital Corp., which was set to close in March 1993. According to press reports, the pension fund is the single largest investor in the fund, which is expected to start with $150 million.

Organized at the suggestion of Governor Mario Cuomo's 1989 Task Force on Pension Investment, Excelsior Capital was set up to provide pension funds with market-rate investments geared toward aiding New York state's economy. The Comptroller's office and the City Employees' Pension Fund have been actively involved with Excelsior Capital since its inception.

Export-Import Bank Program

In October 1993, the New York's Police Pension Fund committed $30 million to a program designed to provide loans of $25,000 to $2.5 million to exporters in the city and those in the metropolitan area that ship their products through New York's port or airports.

Under the terms of the program, the New York State Job Development Authority will make the loans, which will be guaranteed by the Export-Import Bank of the United States. According to a statement released by the Comptroller's office, all of the loans will be AAA-rated and will pay rates of interest comparable or higher than that of other AAA-rated securities in the pension fund's portfolio.

Initially, the loans will be made for terms of up to one year, but eventually the program will provide financing for up to five years, the statement said.

State of Wisconsin Investment Board

The State of Wisconsin Investment Board controls over $30 billion in state pension, insurance, and other assets, and actively seeks out investments in Wisconsin-based companies through special programs utilizing every asset category the board invests in. As of June 1991 (the most recent data available at press time), the board had just over $5.4 billion in Wisconsin-related investments, and had plans to invest as much as another $2.4 billion in the state by the end of five years.[17]

The board's Wisconsin-related investment portfolio included $1.9 billion in the securities of Wisconsin-based corporations and another $3.5 billion in the securities of companies with more than 20 employees in the state. Of that, about $2.9 billion is in stocks, $326.6 million in bonds. Another $1 billion was in liquid assets, $1.1 billion was in private placements, and just under $100 million was in mortgages and real estate, the report said.

While it is not required to set aside any specific amount for Wisconsin-related investments, the board is required to report every two years on its five-year goals for the in-state portfolio. That report is coupled with a report by the state's Department of Development, evaluating the investment board's Wisconsin investment program and including non-binding suggestions for new in-state programs.

In its latest report, the Department of Development offers high praise for the board's efforts to steer investment dollars into the state: "Over the past several years, [the investment board] has achieved an exemplary record in Wisconsin, and has set objectives for future investment that will help sustain its Wisconsin focus."

Among its more innovative investments, the board agreed in 1992 to put up $50 million for a new commingled targeted investment trust, if the organizers of the investment pool can find other institutions to invest an additional $250 million.

Designed to give investors the benefit of diversification while meeting its targeted investing goals, the Commonwealth Diversified Trust, organized by Commonwealth Capital Strategies, offers institutions with $50 million or more the chance to direct an amount equal to its contribution to its owns geographic region. But, instead of owning the local investments outright, each institution owns a piece of the trust's entire portfolio, allowing the investors a chance to spread risk over a broader asset base. As of the fall of 1993, no other pension funds had committed to the trust, but several major pension systems were evaluating the plan, according to David Sand, president of Commonwealth Capital Strategies.

Massachusetts State Teachers and Employees Retirement System

In 1991, Massachusetts State Treasurer Joseph Malone wanted to find ways to utilize the investment prowess of the state's pension funds to help the state's economy. At the time, Massachusetts, like the rest of New England, was suffering from a severe recession that was made worse by the failure of numerous local banks and savings and loan associations. Because traditional lenders had become so constrained in their ability to make new loans, it seemed crucial that the state explore alternative ways to get capital in the hands of businesses in order to get the economy moving again.

In the fall of that year, Malone put together a "blue ribbon" panel to explore whether economically targeted investments could be incorporated into the portfolio of the Massachusetts State Teachers' and Employees' Retirement System (MASTERS). The panel was simultaneously assigned to decide what kinds of policies should be adopted to ensure that the investments were made prudently, and with proper oversight.

In its report, issued in December, the panel recommended that the pension fund set up a formalized targeted investing program, staffed with full-time personnel, to oversee an allocation of up to 5 percent of its portfolio—then about $300 million—to targeted investments over time.

Such investments, the panel said, should provide a return equal to or better than that of other investments with similar risks while filling "capital gaps" by providing financing that otherwise was not available because of "habit, bureaucracy, lack of attention, lack of information, or lack of liquidity." Furthermore, the report said, the targeted investments made by the pension funds should conform to all applicable state laws and, to the greatest degree possible, "transfer credit risk away from the local economy."

To meet this last requirement, the panel suggested utilizing federal insurance and "quasi-government guarantees"—such as that offered by the Federal Housing Administration and Small Business Administration and the Federal National Mortgage Association—whenever possible. "Corporate guarantees may also be useful, particularly if the corporation is geographically diversified," the report said. However, the panel stated that, while such guarantees are recommended, "The MASTERS ETI program will not be able to meet this criterion for all targeted investments. . . . Minimal local credit risk is recommended as a goal, not an absolute standard."

Largely as a result of the panel's work, the MASTERS pension trust has invested in three targeted investing programs described below, but as of early 1993, the system had not yet moved to hire a full-time ETI staff.

Middle Class American Dream Program

Under the MASTERS pension trust's Middle Class American Dream program, the fund has purchased $250 million in Federal Home Loan Mortgage Corp. (Freddie Mac) securities backed by loans to middle-class families in the state. In early 1992, $125 million was purchased, and a second equal-sized purchase was announced later in the year.

In exchange for MASTERS' commitment to buy the securities, Freddie Mac agrees to relax underwriting requirements, allowing home buyers to obtain mortgages at favorable interest rates with a down payment of as little as 5 percent. In addition, mortgage payments can equal 33 percent of the borrower's household income, instead of the usual 28 percent.

The state treasurer's office estimates that each $125 million investment provides about 1,000 mortgages in the state.

LIMAC/*Freddie Mac Program*

In 1992, MASTERS committed $50 million to a program developed by Freddie Mac and the New York–based Local Initiatives Managed Assets Corp. (LIMAC) that is designed to provide a secondary market for multi-family loans.

In this trial program, Freddie Mac agreed in 1991 to swap AAA-rated securities for mortgages on multi-family buildings, which typically are not packaged into securities and sold to institutions the way single-family mortgages are. So that the loans can meet Freddie Mac's fiduciary standards, LIMAC and the lenders retain part of the risk. The Freddie Mac securities are then sold to institutional investors.

ARK *Program*

The MASTERS fund also has invested in a program set up to help small businesses hurt when their bank or savings and loan fails and its loan portfolio is liquidated. The Small Business Administration buys performing loans and re-sells the guaranteed portions of these loans as AAA-rated securities.

Under the ARK program, MASTERS has committed to purchase $50 million of such securities, representing the guaranteed portion of loans to Massachusetts businesses.[18]

Pennsylvania

Another outspoken advocate of ETI, Pennsylvania State Treasurer Catherine Baker Knoll has initiated six separate targeted investment programs, totaling about $845 million, since taking office in 1989.

Like New York City's Elizabeth Holtzman and Carol O'Cleireacain, Knoll is a proponent of considering the social implications of their investment policies since they have become so large. In late 1992, Knoll, who often speaks in favor of targeted investing at meetings of pension fund officials, told a conference sponsored by the Center for Policy Alternatives: "Our pension funds can no longer view themselves as islands unto themselves. The future of our pension funds and their beneficiaries is inextricably tied to the economic success of our country."[19]

However, like the New York officials, Knoll is quick to add that pension funds cannot be asked to subsidize public policy projects and so, should never accept less than a market-competitive rate of return. And like the New York City funds, Pennsylvania's targeted investments utilize a variety of government and quasi-government guarantees.

HomeStart

In 1991 and 1992, the state treasury purchased a total of $200 million in Federal National Mortgage Association securities backed by home mortgages of

Pennsylvania residents. Under the HomeStart program—which is similar to the state of Massachusetts' Middle Class American Dream program—Fannie Mae agrees to certain underwriting concessions in exchange for the state's commitment to purchase the mortgage-backed securities.

As in the Massachusetts program the first- and second-time home buyers obtained mortgages at favorable interest rates with a down payment of as little as 5 percent of the home's purchase price.

According to the state treasury, the first $100 million in Fannie Mae securities provided the state with an 8.6 percent return at a time when 30-year federal Treasury notes were yielding 7.54 percent. The second $100 million in Fannie Maes yielded 7.49 percent, compared with 7.02 percent for Treasury notes.

Pennsylvania Lease Purchase Home Program

Begun in 1991 with a commitment of $10 million, the state's Lease Purchase Home Program provides assistance to people who want to enter into lease-to-own home purchase arrangements.

The state treasury purchases bonds from the Pennsylvania Housing Finance Agency which uses the proceeds to make low-interest loans to non-profit and for-profit developers of new homes. The developers lease the homes for up to three years to Pennsylvania families, setting aside a portion of the rent payments for closing costs and a down payment at the end of the lease. Pennsylvania Housing Finance Authority (PHFA) then provides permanent financing to the families.

The state treasury said this investment was yielding 4.53 percent annually as of early 1993.[20]

Save Our Cities

In the wake of the Los Angeles riots in the spring of 1992, the Pennsylvania treasury committed $50 million to its Save Our Cities program, which is designed to create housing and jobs simultaneously in inner-city areas. The treasury agreed to buy $10 million in bonds every year for five years from the Pennsylvania Housing Finance Authority to be used for the creation of affordable housing.

The money, which will be loaned at 15 basis points above the rate available on two-year federal Treasury notes, will allow the state agency to finance 1,200 units of housing per year, a treasury spokesman said at the time. Much of the construction under this program will be done by unemployed workers in the Pennsylvania Job Training Centers program, according to the Treasurer's office.[21]

Infrastructure Programs

The treasury has developed two programs designed to pump a total of $90 million into infrastructure projects in the state. Under its $15 million Acquisition Development and Construction loan program, the treasury provides financing to help developers build infrastructure such as roads and water and sewage lines that are necessary for the construction of single-family homes. Such loans earn 25 basis points above five-year federal Treasury notes.

In early 1993, the Pennsylvania Treasury finalized terms for a program called Treasury Initiative for Education, which will provide $75 million in loans to state school districts for infrastructure and equipment. Under this program, 75 percent of the money will be for infrastructure utilizing domestic steel, while 25 percent will be earmarked for the purchase of U.S.-built equipment. These loans are expected to yield at least 45 basis points more than two-year Treasury notes.

PHEAA Investment

In the years 1990, 1991, and 1992, the Pennsylvania treasury purchased a total of $500 million in securities from the Pennsylvania Higher Education Assistance Agency (PHEAA), which provides student loans to Pennsylvania residents. The treasury's investment is collateralized with student loans guaranteed by the federal government and earns a rate equal to 50 basis points above three-month Treasury bills with a floor of 4.05 percent.

This program had provided loans to 87,000 students by 1992, the state treasury reports.

Depository Programs

In addition to the ETI programs, the Pennsylvania treasury has organized programs that utilize the state's hundreds of millions of dollars in bank deposits to finance loans that are seen as beneficial to the state's economy. In January, 1991, the treasury, in conjunction with the Pennsylvania Public School Retirement System and the Pennsylvania State Employees' Retirement System, initiated a program to deposit $100 million in certificates of deposit with 206 depository institutions in the state. The lending institutions then use the money to make loans in their local communities. The participating depositories are located in 64 of Pennsylvania's 67 counties.

In addition, the state has made about $96 million in so-called "linked deposits." Under this program, the state treasury makes deposits at Pennsylvania banks and savings and loans that agree to make specific loans to businesses at one percent less interest than the institutions would normally charge. Such loans have created or retained 8,500 jobs in the state, the treasury claims.

State of Connecticut Trust Funds

In February 1993, Francisco L. Borges, the outgoing treasurer of Connecticut, announced a significant expansion of a largely dormant targeted investment program, the Connecticut Programs Fund. Originally launched in 1988, the Programs Fund was created to invest up to three percent of the pension fund's total assets in investments designed to help the state's economy—provided that the investments also can provide a market rate of return.

Until 1993, the state's only Programs Fund investment had been a $25 million stake in CF Holdings (formerly the firearms division of Colt Industries), which went into bankruptcy in 1992.

While the many details about the new Programs Fund investments were not available as of March 1993, a statement issued by the Connecticut treasurer's office said the new initiative would concentrate on "venture capital including minority focused venture capital . . . mezzanine financing for companies seeking expansion capital," and "financing for sound middle sized companies that do not have access to capital markets due to changes in banking and insurance lending regulations and policies."

In this last category, the statement said, "equity financing needs for balance sheet restructuring or for expansion will be the primary focus."

The investments, Borges announced, would be made through four limited partnerships that would split up an initial commitment of $155 million. He said the new expansion of the Programs Fund would supplement, but not replace, a separate in-state venture capital fund through which the pension funds have invested $14 million in 27 companies since 1987.

Connecticut also operates a $160 million affordable home mortgage program in conjunction with Fannie Mae. Called the STAR Mortgage program, it is similar to the affordable home mortgage financing offered to Massachusetts residents by the Massachusetts State Teachers and Employees Retirement System.

PENSION FUNDS AND PROXY VOTING

As was discussed earlier, a shareholder who objects to a company's conduct has two choices: he or she can sell the stock, or can become an active shareholder. The active shareholder strategy is particularly well-suited to pension funds because, as large investors, they often do not have the privilege of simply selling the stock of companies that do not behave responsibly. The portfolios of institutional investors have grown so much in recent years, that, due to the demands of diversification, such investors must hold a wide variety of stocks and bonds.

In many cases, portfolios are passively invested in an index, such as the Standard and Poor's 500, effectively eliminating the ability of fund officials to pick and choose particular companies. This means that officials must find a comparable replacement for any stock eliminated from the portfolio for social or political reasons—a daunting, and often impractical task, particularly when ethical restrictions are placed on a portfolio of millions or billions of dollars. The "Wall Street walk," therefore is often not an option.

Putting aside ethical arguments, poor social and environmental performance can have a large, negative impact on a corporation's bottom line and, thus, its return to shareholders. This is true if the company's behavior results in boycotts, adverse publicity, labor disputes, or large financial liabilities resulting from environmental misconduct or other violations of the law.

Therefore, while ethical, moral, and political considerations are very often at the heart of social proxy resolutions, long-term investors often throw themselves behind these initiatives to protect the bottom line.

The argument that good corporate behavior is good business has long been a part of the social proxy activism of the New York City Comptroller's Office, which overseas the city's pension system.

For the 1992–1993 proxy season, New York City's five pension funds, which sponsor more social issues shareholder resolutions than any other public sector pension system, sponsored at least 37 such resolutions. One of the city's most successful social issue shareholder campaigns has been its program to persuade companies to abide by the MacBride Principles, a code of conduct for doing business in Northern Ireland. As of August, 1993, the city had reached such agreements with 23 U.S. corporations.

The Department of Labor's Position

Another reason pension funds have shown an increased interest in proxy activism is that the Department of Labor has made clear, in recent years that it considers proxies to be an important asset and that voting proxies is an important part of the fiduciary duty of pension fund officials under the rules of the Employee Retirement Income Security Act (ERISA). (While ERISA rules do not apply to public sector pension funds, the Labor Department's rulings have, nonetheless had an important impact on those funds because many of them either work within rules patterned after ERISA or have adopted investment policies that incorporate important aspects of the statute.)

Two well-known opinion letters, one addressed to Helmuth Fandl, chairman of the retirement board of Avon Products, and another written to shareholder activist Robert A.G. Monks, referred to as the Monks Letter, clearly outline the Labor Department's position.

In the Avon letter written in 1988, Deputy Assistant Secretary of Labor Alan D. Lebowitz wrote: "In general, the fiduciary act of managing [pension] plan assets which are shares of corporate stock would include the voting of proxies appurtenant to those shares of stock." Furthermore, the letter states, the trustees of the pension fund "have the exclusive authority and responsibility for voting these proxies" unless the plan makes the trustees subject to the direction of some other fiduciary, or if the trustees delegate management of plan assets to investment managers.

If the management of the assets is delegated to investment managers, the letter states, those managers then take on the responsibility for voting those proxies, unless the trustees of the fund retain the voting responsibility for themselves in delegating fiduciary duty to the manager:

> [ERISA does not grant] an investment manager the powers of a named
> fiduciary to allocate or designate the investment management function
> for [pension] plan assets to other persons. . . . Therefore, to the extent
> that anyone purports to direct an investment manager as to the voting
> of proxies, or to the extent that an investment manager purports to
> delegate to another the responsibility for such voting decisions, the man-
> ager would not be relieved of its own responsibilities and related
> liabilities. . . . The manager would continue to have full responsibility
> (and liability) for the exercise of the proxy voting decision.[22]

And, the letter states, it is the duty of pension fund trustees to be aware of
how the fund's shares are being voted even when proxy voting authority is
delegated to managers:

> Finally, the Department notes that [ERISA] requires the named fiduciary
> appointing the investment manager to periodically monitor the activities
> of the investment manager with respect to the management of plan
> assets. In general, this duty would encompass the monitoring of deci-
> sions made and actions taken by investment managers with regard to
> proxy voting.[23]

In the Monks letter, the department states explicitly that trustees, or any
other named fiduciary of a pension plan, must not only be familiar with its
money manager's proxy voting policy, but must also be able to review every
individual proxy vote. Lebowitz wrote:

> It is the Department's view that in order for the named fiduciary to carry
> out his fiduciary duties under ERISA . . . he must be able to review peri-
> odically not only the voting procedure pursuant to which the investment
> manager votes the proxies appurtenant to plan-owed stock, but also the
> actions taken in individual situations so that a determination can be
> made whether the investment manager is fulfilling his fiduciary obliga-
> tions in a manner which justifies the continuation of the manager
> appointment.[24]

For the most part, pension funds have concentrated on resolutions dealing with the governance of corporations in which they hold stock, since those
resolutions often appear to be most closely tied to the economic bottom line.
Members of the corporate governance reform movement have sponsored resolutions asking for compensation policies that tie the pay of top executives to
performance, the adoption of confidential voting or proxies, the annual election of directors, and the appointment of more directors from outside the
company, among others.

Pension funds have also voted for resolutions aimed at eliminating so-
called "poison pill" defenses designed to make unfriendly takeovers costly by
giving existing shareholders the chance to buy stock at a discount, in the event

of a takeover attempt. In the view of many investors, such defenses serve to entrench management and discourage economically beneficial mergers.

However, the line between social and corporate governance activism can get a bit fuzzy at times. Even some investors who are reluctant to take political stands have found reasons to support "social" proxy proposals. For example, the California Public Employees' Retirement System, which has been much better known for its corporate governance activity than for social activism, often votes in favor of resolutions dealing with environmental performance. The reasoning is simple: environmental clean-up liabilities cost money and erode shareholder value.

Conversely, many corporate governance resolutions that have been sponsored or supported by social investors who feel that companies that are more responsive to shareholders (in a sense, more democratic), are more likely to be good corporate citizens. In 1993, members of the Interfaith Center on Corporate Responsibility coalition—which sponsors the bulk of social issue proposals—also introduced numerous corporate governance resolutions asking companies to tie executive compensation to performance (environmental and financial) and called for the adoption of confidential proxy voting.

Whether proxy resolutions are designed to make a company more profitable or more moral, the Labor Department made clear that it is the obligation of every pension fund to carefully evaluate these proposals and vote its proxies in accordance with the best interest of the fund and its participants and beneficiaries. Funds that fail to take this obligation seriously risk not only the possibility of violating their fiduciary duty, but also forgo an important opportunity to influence and improve the performance of companies they invest in. In the 1990s and beyond, the Wall Street walk is a luxury few pension funds can afford.

Two Leaders: CalPERS and the New York City Pension Systems

CalPERS

Where does an 800-pound gorilla sleep?

Most everyone knows the answer to that question. Here's another: When can an investor with over $80 billion in assets, stock holdings in virtually every major U.S. company, extensive foreign holdings of foreign securities, and a lot of clout in the institutional investor community, get the attention of management at the nation's leading corporations. Exactly as you might have guessed—just about any time it wants to.

The giant California State Employees' Retirement System (CalPERS), based in Sacramento, is the pension fund equivalent of the proverbial 800-pound gorilla. Partly because of its vast size and partly due to the political skills and sophistication of its investment staff, the fund has had a profound impact on the way corporations are governed in the Unites States. Thanks in large part to the activities of CalPERS, corporations as well-known and powerful as General Motors Corp.; International Business Machines; Sears, Roebuck & Co.; Boise Cascade; Champion International; and Westinghouse Electric Corp. will never look at shareholder relations in the same way ever again.

Every year, the giant pension fund selects about a dozen U.S. companies, picked from among the poorest performing companies in its portfolio, for special attention by the staff. Depending on the situation, the pension fund then asks companies to adopt any of a number of corporate governance reforms, such as appointing an independent director to the position of chairman of the board, appointing a monitoring committees of shareholders, repealing anti-takeover defenses, or simply maintaining more direct contact with major shareholders.

According to a CalPERS memo, the pension fund's strategy is first to contact a company's chairperson to make him or her aware of CalPERS concerns and to ask for a meeting with the company's outside directors and the chief executive. Then, only if the company rebuffs CalPERS request for dialogue or if no agreement is reached to address CalPERS concerns, the pension fund files a shareholder proposal to be considered on the next proxy statement. For the 1993 proxy season, the memo states:

> Potential corporate governance issues approved by the Board were numerous and varied, but center around two central themes: the need for effective director oversight of management, and the need for effective participation by shareholders in the director election process.[25]

In 1993, the fund kept the names of its so-called "Focus 12" companies secret "until a shareholder resolution is filed or negotiations are completed."[26]

In addition to its Focus 12 program, CalPERS, which maintains a huge portfolio of non-U.S. securities, initiated a limited international corporate governance campaign during 1992 and 1993.

For that period, the fund, concentrated its efforts on Japan and the United Kingdom, in which CalPERS has the greatest holdings outside the United States. In Japan, the fund concentrated on analyzing the impact of the country's *keiretsu* system of interlocking corporate ownership and directorships. In the U.K., the emphasis has been "aimed primarily at strengthening CalPERS' relationships with organizations within that country that already have active corporate governance programs."[27]

CalPERS' 1992–1993 corporate governance campaign was enormously successful. On the home front, the fund reached agreements with 11 of the Focus 12 companies without the need to file a shareholder resolution.[28]

Among its successes, in 1992, the fund reached an accord with Westinghouse under which the company: created a nominating and corporate governance committee made up of outside directors; rescinded its poison pill anti-takeover defense; eliminated staggered terms of service for board members; adopted secret proxy voting; agreed to appoint a majority of outside directors; and increased the number of annual board meetings to 12 from eight.

In another case, CalPERS was involved in Time Warner's efforts to reform its corporate governance structure in late 1992. Time Warner agreed to reduce the size of its board from 22 (including eight insiders) to 12 (with two insiders) and to adopt confidential proxy voting. The company also eliminated all "golden parachute" separation provisions from executive pay agreements and agreed to appoint a majority of outside directors to its board.[29]

In the international arena, CalPERS made headlines in September, 1992 when it sent a representative to the annual meeting of France's BSN to publicly denounce a management-sponsored proposal that limited shareholder voting rights to 6 percent.

In a statement read at the meeting, the CalPERS representative said: "this attempt to limit shareholder rights is transparently no more than a defensive maneuver by management anxious to defend itself from a possible [takeover attempt]." He said that, in CalPERS' view, such voting restrictions "devalue the most basic rights of shareholders who own this company." At the time, CalPERS owned about 12,000 shares of BSN stock worth $2.5 million.

Despite the efforts of CalPERS' and other U.S. shareholders which also voted against the proposal, the measure was easily passed by shareholders. However, a CalPERS official said at the time that the fund had no intention of selling its shares in the wake of the vote.[30]

CalPERS conducts its international corporate governance campaign with the help of its outside international proxy voting service, Global Proxy Services.

At least one study suggests that the corporate governance activity undertaken by CalPERS has provided, in addition to numerous moral victories for the fund and its staff, increased profits on a massive scale.

In a paper published in early 1992, Stephen L. Nesbitt, a senior vice president with Santa Monica-based Wilshire Associates, a consultant to the pension fund, argued that the shareholder activism of CalPERS (which he called "a recognized leader in corporate governance") provided tangible benefits in terms of helping to produce higher stock prices than might otherwise have been achieved.[31] Based on its analysis of the results of 42 corporate governance shareholder proposals at 27 companies, the Wilshire study concluded:

> Shareholder proposals initiated by large pension funds produce excess
> returns [defined as the difference between a company's total return and
> that of the S&P 500 stock index] to stocks of targeted companies. This

> supports the notion that actions taken to enhance management account-
> ability to directors of shareholders increase shareholder value.[32]

Wilshire found that the companies targeted for action by the California pension fund underperformed the Standard & Poor's 500 stock index by 9.3 percent during the six months before the shareholder action was announced. But, from the time the action was announced until the time the issues were resolved (through shareholder votes or negotiated settlements), the stocks outperformed the index by 5.7 percent.

Based on those results of its research, Wilshire estimates, CalPERS earned an additional $137 million as a result of stock price appreciation resulting from its corporate governance campaign. That's a hefty payoff from a corporate governance program that costs the pension fund about $500,000 per year to operate.

While the study is less than conclusive—Wilshire can say with only 85 percent certainty that the higher stock prices were not the result of chance—the results are compelling. Furthermore, CalPERS activity is intriguing because, unlike some of the activities undertaken by large shareholders in recent years, the benefits of corporate governance activity, when it results in higher share prices, helps to enrich numerous small shareholders along with the pension fund.

"What is good for CalPERS is good for the little guy," Wilshire's Nesbitt asserts, "It is not true that what was good for [famous corporate "raider"] Boone Pickens was good for the little guy."[33]

New York City

Unlike CalPERS, the shareholder activities of the City of New York's pension system reach far beyond strict corporate governance activity to include a myriad of social issues which, directly or indirectly, could have an impact on a corporation's bottom line over the long term.

While very active on corporate governance issues like the repeal of poison pills and the appointment of more outside directors, the city's resolutions have also dealt with such issues as job discrimination in Northern Ireland, national health care, South Africa, equal employment rights for homosexuals, and environmental conduct. Much of this emphasis on social issues can be credited to the leadership of former City Comptroller Elizabeth Holtzman.

In addition, the Office of the Comptroller, which oversees the pension system, has been at the forefront of challenging recent Securities and Exchange Commission decisions that have allowed corporations to exclude more and more social resolutions from their proxies. In some cases, the Comptroller's office has been successful in getting the courts to force companies to include resolutions that the SEC had ruled to be excludable for various reasons.

It would be naive to suggest that political considerations do not account for at least part of the motivation behind the city's active involvement in social issue shareholder proposals. However, officials there insist that all of the city's resolutions have been aimed at ending practices that, the pension fund trustees feel, could expose companies to serious liabilities, stifle accountability or lead to a consumer backlash and, in the end, reduce the value of the shareholders' investment.

In response to charges that the city's pension funds have been too involved in so-called "social investing," Holtzman asserted in 1991 that: "In fact, we've eliminated the 'S' word [social] from out vocabulary. We've replaced it with a better word. It's an 'R' word—'responsibility.' "[34]

According to information provided by the ICCR, the New York funds filed more than 30 shareholder resolutions in 1993, dealing with issues of corporate governance, national healthcare policy, equal employment in Northern Ireland, involvement in South Africa, and tobacco advertising practices.

Among its more notable social issue campaigns, NYCERS has been the only public pension fund to sponsor shareholder resolutions related to the Coalition for Environmentally Responsible Economies' (CERES) Principles (such proposals were filed with Exxon, Occidental Petroleum, USX, and Louisiana Pacific in 1993). The fund has also led the effort to gain corporate acceptance of the MacBride Principles, a code of conduct for companies doing business in Northern Ireland. As of August 1993, 25 U.S. companies had reached agreements pledging to abide by the MacBride Principles to the extent legally possible, in exchange for the withdrawal of shareholder resolutions.

In 1992, the employees' pension system was the first shareholder ever to file a shareholder resolution dealing with the rights of homosexuals. That resolution, filed with Lebanon, Tennessee–based Cracker Barrel Old Country Store, was excluded from the company's proxy after a ruling by the Securities and Exchange Commission. But, as it has done in the past, NYCERS decided to challenge that decision in court. At press time, the SEC was preparing to appeal a federal court decision in favor of NYCERS' position.

On the corporate governance front, NYCERS has used shareholder resolutions to persuade companies to adopt a variety of reforms. Among its successes in 1992, NYCERS persuaded Digital Equipment Corp. to appoint a committee of outside directors to nominate new board members; reached an agreement whereby Masco Corp. will appoint a majority of outside directors, and helped convince Boise Cascade and Coca-Cola to adopt confidential proxy voting. In all cases, the pension fund withdrew its proxy resolution as a result of the change in policy.

Holtzman's successor, Alan Havesi, has stated that he will maintain the city funds' tradition of active shareholder involvement.

PUBLIC PENSION FUNDS AND EMERGING MONEY MANAGERS

In recent years, state and local governments have shown a great deal of interest in utilizing small, young money management firms—especially the numerous women- and minority-owned firms that have sprung up—to invest a portion of their pension fund assets. Recent activity involving these so-called "emerging managers" includes the following:

+ The Oregon Treasury Department, which oversees $22 billion in pension and other state investment assets, announced in June 1993 that it will invest $400 million in a trust portfolio. The trust, in turn, would invest money with a number of small women- and minority-owned money management firms. Like numerous other pension funds, Oregon chose to invest via an emerging manager trust because the cost of administering several small portfolios with such firms can be seen as burdensome.[35]

+ The $18 billion Minnesota State Board of Investment announced plans to hire a roster of at least five money managers with $50 million to $250 million of assets under management to invest a total of $300 million. The bidding was opened to all small firms, not just those owned by women and minorities.

+ The $700 million Government Employees' Retirement System of the Virgin Islands hired two emerging firms, Chicago's Holland Capital Management and Woodford Capital Management, New York, to manage a total of $17 million.[36]

An "emerging" money manager is a small firm, often less than five years old, that has fewer assets under management than is generally required to compete for business from large pension funds—$100 million and up, and often $250 million or more. Because many of these firms are owned by women and minorities, pension funds often seek to do business with them as a way to achieve affirmative action goals. (For a list of emerging managers, see Appendix 3.)

In the past, the growth of emerging money managers has been hindered by a sort of chicken-and-egg dilemma. Most public pension funds required that all money managers be in business a certain number of years (often five years or more) and have a sizable amount of money under management to be considered for contracts. But gaining assets to manage and surviving long enough to qualify for pension fund business is difficult for firms that cannot even get through the door to tell their story.

In order to open the door to new firms, and in the process, increase opportunities for women and minorities, pension funds have increasingly been breaking down barriers—some of which resulted merely from habit and inertia—that had kept emerging managers on the sidelines.

To accomplish this, the pension funds will sometimes specify that a certain amount or money (or percentage of total assets) will be allocated to emerging firms. Other times, funds will seek to increase opportunities for such firms in a more informal way, without setting specific goals, thus avoiding the appearance of creating a quota of "set-aside" allocations. In cases where it is not practical or cost-effective for pension funds to employ a number of small firms, funds have invested in emerging manager trusts. In these situations, a third-party acts as a "manager of managers," distributing a portion of the trust's assets to a variety of smaller firms.

Very often (as in the case of Minnesota), programs to employ emerging managers, sometimes referred to as "farm teams," are set up to include all new, small firms, whether or not they are owned and operated by women and minorities. Such rules avoid giving farm teams the taint of favoritism and can open up opportunities for a variety of good, up-start money managers. In most cases, pension funds set up such programs with the primary aim of increasing the amount of assets managed by women, minorities and, in some cases, the physically handicapped.

One example of an aggressive program to hire emerging money managers is the effort of the New York City pension funds begun in 1990. In an effort to facilitate the hiring of more woman and minority firms, the city changed its rules to allow firms with at least $20 million under management and five years in business to compete for business. Formerly, managers were required to have $300 million under management. As a result of the new rules, the five city pension funds had, by late 1992, hired 16 small firms to manage $800 million (out of just under $50 billion in total assets). Of those 16 firms, 14 were owned by woman and minorities.

Much of the enthusiasm for emerging money managers comes from pension trustees and staff members who are motivated both by a desire to encourage minority participation and by the chance to add a "farm team" of young, eager firms to their money manager rosters. At the time its emerging managers program was announced, Minnesota State Treasurer Michael McGrath told a trade publication that the state decided to make the allocation in order to encourage the growth of new money management firms and to foster new ideas.

"The old line firms are more susceptible to developing patterns of behavior where performance can suffer," McGrath told a trade publication. "But the new firms often have a new perspective that we are committed to. We think there can be a lot of value to a new perspective."[37]

Enthusiasm aside, it is also true that numerous governors, legislators, and state treasurers, eager to see their state's public pension funds embrace the affirmative action goals of other state agencies, have waged a concerted political effort to encourage the use of such firms.

At a conference held in September 1992, the National Association of State Treasurers issued a resolution that called on its members to:

✦   . . . [U]se their voice and the powers of their respective offices to increase the extent of participation by qualified minority and female-owned firms as fund managers and broker dealers for public pension funds.

✦   [In addition,] state treasurers who sit as trustees of public pension funds or are custodians of public pension funds [should] call on their fellow board members and fund administrators to vigorously encourage the participation of qualified minority- and female-owned firms as fund managers and broker dealers for public pension funds.

✦   [And] call upon their fellow elected officials . . . to join with them in this historic effort to ensure that all Americans, regardless of race and gender, have truly equal opportunity to participate in the management, acquisition, and sale of assets of America's public pension funds.

In addition, some states have passed, or are considering, legislation that would require or encourage state pension systems to utilize women- and minority-owned money managers.

For example, a bill recently passed by the Illinois state legislature encourages the state's 13 public employees pension funds—which control about $35 billion in assets—to utilize women- and minority-owned money managers to the "greatest extent feasible within the bounds of financial and fiduciary prudence." In addition, the new law requires the pension funds to report annually on their use of such firms, the percentage of total assets managed by them, actions taken to increase the use of minority- and women-owned firms, and actions taken to encourage the funds' other money managers to use such firms as subcontractors.[38]

It would, however, be unfair to suggest that legislative action was needed to force the funds to adopt affirmative action. Even before the bill was passed, several of the largest state funds in Illinois had, for some time, employed women- and minority-owned firms to manage a portion of their assets.

In Louisiana, State Senator Marc Morial said in March 1993 that he was considering legislation that would require the state's public pension funds, which control $10 billion in assets, to hire women- and minority-owned money management firms. Morial said the idea was part of his plan to "put laws on the books that insure and require the participation of minority-

and women-owned firms in all categories of the state's financial services contracts."[39]

As in the case of Illinois, such action is being considered despite the fact that the major state pension funds already employ emerging firms as asset managers.

PUBLIC FUNDS AND SIN STOCKS: THE CASE OF MINNESOTA

Among public pension funds, those that screen out sin stocks are rarer than smokers in the workplace. And their ranks are thinning. In March 1993, the Minnesota State Board of Investments ended its 20-year prohibition on the ownership of stocks in tobacco and alcohol companies.

The reasons were simple: the board found the ban had cost the state pension system millions of dollars in opportunity losses and was having no discernible effect as a social policy.

The board used looser stated criteria than those of many socially conscious investment managers, excluding companies that derive 50 percent of gross revenues from the manufacture or sale of tobacco or alcohol. (The Domini 400 Social Index has a stated cutoff of 4 percent.) But the effect was the same. Some of the biggest and best corporate performers of the 1980s, such as Philip Morris, were kept off Minnesota's books.

In late 1992, the board carried out a study comparing its actual five-year performance with a model portfolio that included the forbidden equities. The study found that the $16 billion state pension funds, for which the board invests, lost up to $7 million a month in opportunity costs, for a total of $150 million.

The study coincided with the board's hiring of its first international stock specialists and its exposure of up to $800 million in assets to foreign equities. The board thought the ban would drag down international return because, in even greater proportion than in the United States, top performing companies overseas are in the sin industries. Looking ahead over the next five years, several board members projected that continuing the sin prohibitions would result in opportunity losses of $185 million.[40]

For the board, the choice came down to a "fundamental belief in the role of a pension trustee," state Treasurer Michael McGrath told *Pensions & Investments*. "Are we truly to look for investment opportunity wherever we find it? Or are there secondary considerations which should be taken into consideration?"[41]

The decision may have been made easier by the conclusion, stated by Laurie Fiori Hacking, executive director of the Minnesota Public Employees Retirement Association, that there was no clear evidence linking the restrictive policy to a decrease in the consumption of tobacco and alcohol.[42]

Minnesota's decision to end the ban leaves only one fund, the Cambridge, Massachusetts, Retirement System, with a similar sin stock policy. The Cambridge fund's guidelines state it is the board's "intent to encourage the manager to restrict investment" in companies engaged in the manufacture and sale of tobacco products, said executive director Anne Leduc. No study of the policy has been made, nor has the fund noticed any costs of the variety stated in the Minnesota study.

NOTES

1. Christine Philip, "Gov. Clinton Sought In-state Investments," *Pensions & Investments,* Feb. 22, 1993, p. 32.
2. Bill Clinton, *Putting People First: A National Economic Strategy for America,* 1992.
3. "Cisneros Thinks Pension Assets Could Be Put to Work," *Pensions & Investments,* Jan. 2, 1993, p. 8.
4. Testimony at hearing, Sept. 29, 1992.
5. Working paper released Nov. 19, 1992.
6. "Dept. of Labor Group Encourages Federal Support for ETI Programs," *Responsive Investing News,* Nov. 23, 1992, p. 1.
7. Patricia B. Limbacher, "Berg to Use 'Bully Pulpit' for ETIs," *Pensions & Investments,* July 12, 1993, p. 1.
8. "Excelsior Pool Nabs Corporate Funds," *Pensions & Investments,* Feb. 22, 1993, p. 32.
9. Richard Ferlauto, Robert Stumberg, and Robin Sampson, *State Policy Support for Targeted Pension Fund Investment,* Center for Policy Alternatives, May 1992.
10. "New York Frees Up More Pension Capital for ETI," *Responsive Investing News,* Aug. 5, 1992, p. 1.
11. "State Pension Funds Tugged Toward ETIs," *Pensions & Investments,* Feb. 22, 1993, p. 4.
12. *Responsive Investing News,* Feb. 3, 1992, p. 5.
13. *A Policy Framework for Economically Targeted Investing,* prepared by Alan Asaki, an attorney with Preston, Thorgrimson, Shidler, Gates & Ellis; and Peter Moy & Associates.
14. "Seattle Completes ETI Study, Explores Options," *Responsive Investing News,* Aug. 31, 1992, p. 1.
15. Much of the detail on specific programs was taken from *Bulls-Eye: How Targeted Investments Can Enrich Pension Funds and Help New York City's Economy Grow,* a report released by the New York City Office of the Comptroller in July 1992, and from press releases issued by the city.

16. Carol O'Cleireacain, "Pension Funds and Social Investment," *Social Investment Almanac* (New York, Henry Holt, 1992), p. 509.
17. *Wisconsin Investment Program, Management Objectives, Five Year Investment Goals,* State of Wisconsin Investment Board, June 30, 1991.
18. Richard Ferlauto and Jeffrey Clabourn, *Economically Targeted Investments by State-Wide Pendion Funds,* Center for Policy Alternatives, 1993, p. 25.
19. "Pension Funds Can Do Good, Do Well, Conference Told," *Washington Post,* Dec. 12, 1992, p. f1.
20. "PA Develops Rent-to-Own Home Purchase Program," *Responsive Investing News,* Nov. 11, 1991, p. 2.
21. "PA Treasury Allocates $50M for Urban Housing, Jobs," *Responsive Investing News,* June 22, 1992, p. 1.
22. Letter from Alan D. Lebowitz, Deputy Assistant Secretary of Labor, to Helmuth Fandl, chairman of the retirement board, Avon Products, Feb. 22, 1988.
23. Ibid.
24. Letter from Alan D. Lebowitz to Robert A.G. Monks of Institutional Shareholder Services, Jan. 23, 1990.
25. CalPERS memo dated Jan. 12, 1993.
26. Ibid.
27. Ibid.
28. Vineeta Anand, " '93 Proxy Season Quiet But Effective," *Pensions & Investments,* May 31, 1993, p. 3.
29. CalPERS memo.
30. *Responsive Investing News,* Oct. 12, 1992.
31. *Rewards from Corporate Governance,* Feb. 1992, Wilshire Associates.
32. Ibid.
33. Ibid. See also: Allen R. Myerson, "Pension Populism Gets a Critical Lift," *New York Times,* July 20, 1992, p. D4.
34. William Murphy, "Boardrooms Feel Pension Fund Clout," *Newsday,* March 4, 1991, news section, p. 21.
35. "Oregon to Invest $400M in Emerging Manager Trust," *Money Management Letter,* June 7, 1993, p. 1.
36. "Virgin Islands System Hires Two Emerging Firms," *Money Management Letter,* Aug. 16, 1993, p. 9.
37. "Minnesota to Recruit Emerging Managers for $300 Million," *Money Management Letter,* Aug. 16, 1993, p. 1.
38. Mark Fortune, "Illinois Bill Gives Emerging Managers a Come Hither Smile," *Money Management Letter,* March 15, 1993, p. 1.
39. "Louisiana Lawmakers to Address Women and Minority Issues," *Money Management Letter,* March 29, 1993, p. 11.
40. "Investment Restrictions Stall Minnesota's Active International Search," *Investment Management Weekly,* Jan. 25, 1993, p. 1.
41. Christine Philip, "A 'Raging Debate' Hits Minnesota Fund," *Pensions & Investments,* March 8, 1993, p. 4.
42. Ibid.

3

Foundations and Social Investing

FOUNDATIONS SLOWLY BUILD THEIR SOCIAL INVESTING

Boston's Dudley Street is about as far removed from cutting-edge investment as one can imagine in an American city.

Just two miles from the high-rises of the city's Financial District, the neighborhood residents are among the poorest in the city and the least likely to be employed.

And yet the Dudley Triangle is the site of an important experiment in community development. In March 1993, with the aid of the Ford Foundation, the Dudley Street Neighborhood Initiative (DSNI), a storefront nonprofit agency, broke ground for six apartment units. Eventually, DSNI hopes to build 296 housing units for low- and moderate-income residents and two community centers where young people and elderly residents can congregate.

Ford's investment in the project—a $2 million, 1 percent loan—was critical to its becoming a reality. According to Clayton Turnbull, a member of DSNI's board, "It's not just the $2 million. Its a strong statement from one of the biggest foundations in the country." The confidence Ford showed solidified the venture, in which the city and federal government also contributed financing, and technical and legal support. Said Turnbull of Ford's presence: "The real significance of this is that we're going to prove this kind of process works."[1]

The nation's 32,000 foundations, with $142.5 billion in assets, have an enormous social and economic influence. In 1992, they made grants of $8.3 billion to support the arts, education, health care, the environment, economic justice, and other causes.[2] They can also further their goals through their investments. Like other institutions, they can apply ethical screens to their portfolios or they may choose to invest directly in for-profit enterprises that produce good returns and illustrate their social mission. Or they can make concessionary, program-related investments in projects like Dudley Street's.

They have been reluctant to use those social investment tools, however. "Foundations have been notorious latecomers in not having their money match their charitable mission," said Marcy M. Murninghan, a writer, teacher, and consultant in Cambridge, Massachusetts. But, increasingly, she said, there are signs that foundations are, "like Sleeping Beauty," awakening to their potential to foster social change through their investment strategy.

SCREENS

Foundations that adopt ethical investing guidelines say they are necessary to avoid potential conflicts between investments and programs. These principles are far from universally shared. According to Christie Baxter, director of the Project on Social Investing at the Massachusetts Institute of Technology, "there is very little screening."

Statistics are rare, but according to the Social Investment Forum, foundations invested about $500 million in socially screened funds in 1991. *The Chronicle of Philanthropy* reported in 1992 that, of the nation's 10 largest foundations, with $36.5 billion in assets, seven reported no screens on investments. The Ford Foundation, the nation's largest fund, with $6.5 billion in assets, has barred investments in corporations operating in South Africa that have not signed the Statement of Principles. The fourth-largest foundation, the Robert Wood Johnson Foundation, shuns tobacco, as do the Rockefeller Family Fund and the Henry J. Kaiser Family Foundations.[3]

But it is the smaller, politically progressive foundations that do the most social screening. The Unity Foundation in St. Paul, Minnesota, avoids a roster of corporations, including polluters, weapons manufacturers, and those that perform non-medical tests on animals or have violent advertising. The Haymarket People's Fund of Boston, a $4 million fund, has an especially tight set of investment guidelines.

Named for the 1886 Haymarket Affair in Chicago, a watershed event in the labor movement's drive for an eight-hour workday, Haymarket makes grants to grass-roots New England groups working for gay and lesbian rights, the environment, and the homeless, among other issues. It prohibits investments in corporations with poor environmental and labor records or those involved in alcohol, tobacco, gambling, or pornography. The restrictions even extend to U.S. Treasuries, since they go to finance a federal deficit due, in large part, to "wasteful defense spending," according to the fund's guidelines.[4]

"They are completely, consciously connected," said executive director Pat Maher of the fund's financial and social guidelines. "To invest without a consciousness of the political or social impact of the investment would go completely against the grain of what Haymarket is all about."

Likewise, the Samuel Rubin Foundation in New York screens out the 200 largest Defense Department contractors and businesses with ties to South Africa. And it has no plans to change. "Why should we?" said Cora Weiss, president of the $12 million fund, which supports groups working for peace and justice. "If you're giving money to socially responsible entities, you should invest in socially responsible entities."

Those cases aside, most foundation are loathe to invoke ethical investing guidelines. There are a number of reasons for their reluctance. Foundation trustees historically viewed their roles as ensuring that investments produce enough of a return to meet federal payout requirements—the Internal Revenue Service mandates that foundations make grants equal to 5 percent of assets—and protecting the foundation's asset base. And since these boards are largely insulated from the types of interest groups—students, faculty, church congregations, and the news media—that can raise a fuss, they are free to follow a strict fiduciary course. Furthermore, foundation executives register the same complaints about screened investing as do officials with other institutions: that it inhibits decision-making, is time-consuming, does not achieve its aims and, most important, sacrifices return on investment.[5]

John W. English, vice president and chief investment officer of the Ford Foundation, expressed his doubts to *The Chronicle of Philanthropy:* "Since all the foundation's investment gains are used to do good works, I think our objective is to maximize the investment return in order to do good works throughout the world."[6]

Others agree. The Jessie Ball duPont Religious, Charitable and Educational Fund, a $165 million foundation in Jacksonville, Florida, has no restrictions. "The trustees decided in an affirmative way that they didn't want to inhibit . . . the return from the funds," said Willard Wheeler, chief investment officer for the Northern Trust Bank of Florida, which oversees the foundation's portfolio. At the Rhode Island Foundation, a $275 million community foundation, trustees have never discussed setting up screens. And the $60 million Olin Foundation, one of the few funds with a sunset provision, invests "simply with the idea of maximizing return and securing the body of the endowment," said program officer William Voegeli.

DIRECT INVESTMENTS

When they have found negative screens inadequate to deal with complex, rapidly changing social issues, a few foundations have turned to direct investments that build on cutting-edge technology, innovative financing, or emerging companies. If successful, they have the advantage of carrying forth the foundation's mission without sacrificing return. Some philanthropies choose to invest through special mutual or loan funds that target their areas of interest. A handful have undertaken studies and pilot projects that bring their investments in line with their missions.

None is doing it in a bigger way than the John D. and Catherine T. MacArthur Foundation. The $3.3 billion fund is putting a significant portion of its assets into a three-part program that will promote energy conservation, environmentally sensitive development, and private capital investment. MacArthur had considered setting up a model portfolio, with 1 to 3 percent of assets put through screens and invested in experimental programs. But the foundation decided it could make a more compelling argument if it put more of its assets on the line. Said William F. McAlpin, MacArthur's director of investments related to program: "This makes it more real."

The foundation's decision was forced, in part, by the unusual makeup of its portfolio. About a third of its holdings are in real estate, including about $370 million in downtown Chicago. To make the buildings better investments and to show that conservation pays off, MacArthur decided to invest in energy efficiency. The project includes installation of tighter windows and doors; better lighting and heating, ventilation and air conditioning systems; insulation; and software systems used to create "smart buildings."

Retrofitting has begun in the Marquette Building, the turn-of-the-century Chicago landmark where the foundation is headquartered, and will soon expand into other properties. If successful, the program could persuade utilities to invest more heavily in energy conservation; expecting a 20 to 25 percent return "is not wild-eyed," McAlpin said.

The second part of MacArthur's investment strategy is to develop some of 40,000 acres (worth approximately $730 million) it owns in the Loxahatchee Slough, a wetlands region feeding Florida's Everglades. A master plan for a high-density yet environmentally sensitive development was due to be completed this year by the Conservation Fund, headed by a former president of the Nature Conservatory. Based on "sound science," the plan will set aside a large portion of the property for conservation, MacAlpin said. And it will limit the amount of roads and build in environmental protections.[7]

"We don't think it's inconsistent with asset value" to develop the property, McAlpin said. He pointed to Miami planner Andres Duany's award-winning village designs, such as Seacoast on Florida's panhandle, as a model MacArthur might follow.

Third, MacArthur hopes to act as lead investor in a $30 million to $50 million private capital pool. The fund, for which MacArthur is seeking limited partners, would enable the foundation to make more adventurous investments in emerging companies, McAlpin said. The foundation could also place more of its short-term cash in community development in Chicago.

McAlpin, a former program officer and treasurer for the Rockefeller Brothers Fund in New York, has been directing MacArthur's investments related to the program since 1991. It is the first time since the Ford Foundation did a study in the 1970s, that a foundation has undertaken such a large-scale examination of its investments. McAlpin said MacArthur hopes to break a logjam in the philanthropic community.

"I think that there's a stigma attached to this, and that has to be overcome," he said. "We are trying to show some leadership, sort of demystifying it and say that you don't necessarily have to take a hit on the return side" when investing in a socially responsible manner.

Stephen Viederman, president of the Jesse Smith Noyes Foundation in New York, said MacArthur's work is "great and tremendously important." Viederman's foundation, which advocates ecologically sound, sustainable agriculture and the long-term survival of farming communities, is developing its own set of guidelines.

"There are some who argue that the problem with tainted money is that there 'tain't enough of it," Viederman said. "They say you should take as much of that money as you can and launder it. We decided that's not something we wanted to do. We wanted to remove, if you will, the cognitive dissonance."

The $60 million fund, based in New York, wrote social investing rules in 1990. (Those guidelines led to its dumping of one of its best performing stocks, Philip Morris, because of concerns that tobacco farming is environmentally detrimental.) Still, the foundation discovered that "things kept popping up that just don't fit," Viederman said. Rather than use the standard ethical investing approach of negative screens, the foundation, with its managers and consultants, is developing a system of positive screens that identify whether there are "companies out there that fit [our mission] and can make a profit," Viederman said.

As part of that effort, the foundation plans to make early-stage venture capital investments in companies that make environmentally safe products. In 1993, it made its first such investment in Natural Chemistry, a Connecticut company that makes a household cleaning product that uses enzymes rather than chemicals.

Other foundations are devoting limited portions of their holdings to mutual funds and progressive lenders. The Northwest Area Foundation, a

$270 million fund based in St. Paul, Minnesota, allocates 5 percent of assets in the Regional Fund of First Asset Management of Minneapolis, which supports emerging small businesses from Minnesota to Washington.

In 1991, the foundation redefined its mission to focus on alleviating rural and urban poverty and promoting sustainable development in the region. The fund fits those goals, the foundation said, because studies suggest most job creation will take place in the small-business sector and because the fund promotes much-needed economic diversity.

PROGRAM-RELATED INVESTMENTS

Another significant way in which foundations are involved in social investing is through program-related investments. PRIs are high-risk, low-interest loans, loan guarantees, or equity arrangements—made with community development, environmental, or other non-profit groups, like Boston's Dudley Street Neighborhood Initiative—that are consistent with a foundation's program mission. Some are also made to for-profit enterprises unable to get conventional financing.

PRIs count toward a foundation's 5 percent distribution requirement as though they were grants. And as they are repaid, PRIs enable philanthropies to recycle their money—to use it for other projects—instead of making grants in which the money is disbursed one time. "Thus, the foundation is able to continue its growth at a greater pace than would be possible if the entire payout were made in the form of grants," according to a report for the Social Venture Network.[8]

Along those lines, Paul E. Lingenfelter, director of program evaluation for the MacArthur Foundation, wrote that "because PRIs are not included in [the] asset base, they have a 5 percent head start on regular investments. In terms of the effect on total assets, a PRI earning 3 percent may be compared favorably with a regular investment earning 8 percent." Further, the practice of designating 10 percent of a foundation's annual distribution to PRIs, he wrote, "will pay for itself and increase the funds available for grants."[9]

PRIs are among the more promising tools in social investing. Few conventional investors would, on their own, seek to invest in low-income, inner-city housing, or sustainable development in the Third World. But the presence of loans or equity capital from a major foundation often represents a vote of confidence in projects—and draws banks and insurance companies into what would otherwise be untouchable investments. Lingenfelter wrote:

> In essence, a program-related investment should fill an economic gap,
> the gap between what is possible in the normal economy without philan-
> thropic intervention and what can be achieved only through a direct

grant. Philanthropic involvement in this segment of economic life is highly leveraged almost by definition; PRIs support philanthropic activities that are almost, but not quite, self-supporting, and they usually help bring non-philanthropic capital to the task.[10]

Figures on the amount and growth of program-related investing nationwide are elusive, although clearly, in the field of social investing overall, the amount is small. The Foundation Center, which compiles information from federal tax documents, found the amount of loans from foundations to other organizations in 1991 totaled $134.9 million, or about the amount the city of Providence, Rhode Island, spends on schools. Those documents do not have a separate category for PRIs, however. The Ford Foundation places the figure near $75 million a year. Most experts accept the Ford figure as the more precise.

Ford is clearly the leader in PRIs. Since the mid-1980s, it has made $13 million to $15 million in PRIs a year; at the end of 1992, it had $113.1 million in PRIs outstanding. MacArthur made $10.6 million in PRIs in 1992, and has $53.1 million outstanding. Among the other top PRI investors are the Metropolitan Life Foundation (with about $30 million outstanding), Pew Charitable Trusts ($23 million), Robert Wood Johnson Foundation ($20.3 million), and Charles Stewart Mott Foundation ($11 million).[11]

As for PRI growth, Ford and MIT's Project on Social Investing, which conducts seminars teaching foundations about PRIs, say there is anecdotal evidence suggesting they have been used more often and by more foundations. Edward Skloot, president of the Surdna Foundation and author of a 1984 study on PRIs, said, "I think there's some increase, but I don't think we're seeing a wave. People are more interested. Social investing is getting more cachet. But I don't think there's much more."

Program-related investments can be traced to the Ford Foundation's Gray Areas Project in the early 1960s. Gray Areas provided education, health, legal and employment services in a half dozen cities, and introduced precursors to many federal programs, including Head Start, championed by Lyndon Johnson in his War on Poverty.

Mitchell Sviridoff, the director of the most successful Gray Areas program, in New Haven, Connecticut, became vice president for national affairs for the Ford Foundation in 1966. During his tenure, assistant director Louis Winnick developed an idea that he had formulated earlier in the decade for an alternative to grants. Encouraged by the foundation's trustees, who wanted a new way to attack persistent urban social problems more effectively, Winnick teamed with John Simon, law professor at Yale University. Simon, later the co-author of *The Ethical Investor,* called for setting aside the requirement that foundations get maximum return and permitting funds to make investments in important social projects. Largely through their efforts, the Tax Reform Act of 1969 contained the first legal definition of program-related investments.[12]

For almost a decade after that Ford had the PRI field virtually to itself. The program had a rocky start. Mixed with the successes—a $600,000 loan to the Harvard Community Health Plan in Cambridge, Massachusetts, launched what is now one of the nation's largest health-maintenance organizations—were a number of missteps. Ford loaned money to publishers, bakers, fast-food franchisees, and a "dairy goat farm in Arkansas, that nobody wanted to read 200-page reports about," Winnick said. "We learned a lot of things not to do." The program had a high default rate in the first few years. Later, a Ford staffer said: "We were making substantial loans to small enterprises run by inexperienced entrepreneurs in the poorest neighborhoods. It's surprising that we lost only 35 percent."[13]

Two things happened to change the nature of PRIs. First, Ford moved the program out of its administrative area and integrated it with its grant program. That was a signal that PRIs should not be considered investments themselves but supplements to grantmaking, a bridge between finance and social programs. Second, Ford shifted its focus away from PRIs for individual business and toward the foundation's central mission: alleviating poverty in urban and rural areas and encouraging development in the Third World. That moved the benefit of PRIs from small groups of entrepreneurs to the community at large.[14]

Ford also nurtured the concept of community development corporations (CDCs), small, community-based non-profits that develop housing in distressed neighborhoods. And in 1979, Ford founded the Local Initiatives Support Corporation (LISC), an intermediary organization (headed for the first seven years by Sviridoff) that links national donations and investments with CDCs. LISC, now headed by Paul Grogan, also gives technical advice to CDCs, and helps them raise matching funds from local sources. In its history, LISC has raised more than $880 million from corporations, foundations, and other investors, opened more than 44,000 housing units and 7 million square feet of commercial and industrial space.[15]

The matching dollars help spread the financial burden and risk for investors. Today, Ford makes the most of its PRIs to intermediary organizations.

Other foundations made their first PRIs in the 1970s and early 1980s, and then established formal programs. They were spurred in part by a greater recognition that programs and investments can be integrated; by the emergence of a new generation of leaders, many of them Ford alumni, who were interested in innovative investing; and by a recognition that, in an era of scarce resources, grants can only go so far.

The Tax Reform Act of 1986, which included the Low-Income Housing Tax Credit, put PRIs on a new stage. The credit attracted other investors, especially insurance companies and some banks, to community development projects that had been getting PRIs but little other investment. Foundations now boast that each PRI dollar leverages another five dollars, on average, from other investors, bringing their impact far beyond the initial investment.

"They've gotten a lot better at it," said Winnick, now a senior consultant with the Fund for the City of New York. The fund is a major PRI investor, primarily through bridge loans to non-profit agencies and businesses that need short-term cash while awaiting payment for government contracts.

The Ford Foundation's special interest in alleviating urban poverty led it to Dudley Street. The project is an example of how a foundation can nurse a project along in a way a conventional lender would not.

DSNI was formed in 1986, when it wrote a master plan for the neighborhood. The city of Boston worked closely with DSNI and made the plan its official neighborhood zoning map. What attracted Ford was the fact that the city gave DSNI power of eminent domain in the area. It was the first time an independent non-profit group in Massachusetts, and perhaps the nation, had been given such authority.

"That makes it some kind of national model" for community development, said Kerwin Tesdell, a program investment officer for Ford. DSNI and Ford began talks in 1988; it was not until 1992 that the foundation made the loan. Payable over eight years, the loan will go to the purchase of condemned land and help pay for operating expenses.

"Without their funds and support, this project would not have happened," said Paul Yelder, director of DSNI's non-profit land trust subsidiary. "There were a lot of legal issues. It wasn't easy, either. But clearly they helped us move forward with the loan, unsecured as they are. It's really been a plus." By mid-1994, the group hopes to have 38 housing units built.

The MacArthur Foundation, established in the late 1970s, is relatively newer to program-related investing and pursues a slightly different course than Ford. MacArthur makes a number of PRIs from its corpus, rather than from a discrete budget, as Ford and most other PRI investors do.

In 1993, MacArthur devoted $4 million in assets to PRIs. Those investments were in the middle range of risk, between low-return PRIs and the foundation's regular investments, for which maximum return is paramount. This practice, MacArthur says, uses PRIs more directly as a means of pursuing the goals of its grant programs.

MacArthur has wide philanthropic interests. And its PRIs reflect interest close to, and far from, home. MacArthur's first PRI, in 1983, gained it

$620,000 in preferred stock in the Illinois Neighborhood Development Corporation, later called Shorebank, the parent of South Shore Bank of Chicago. It has since made a number of PRIs with Shorebank, the nation's top social investment bank; a number of loans in the mid-1980s to Shorebank subsidiaries were used to open a shopping center in the Austin section of Chicago and hire neighborhood residents for jobs in a Shorebank-financed supermarket. MacArthur helped a Shorebank affiliate, Southern Development Bancorporation, in its drive to open a development bank in Arkansas in the late 1980s and made an investment in a rural development bank on Michigan's Upper Peninsula managed by Shorebank.

Farther away, in 1990 MacArthur made a $500,000 low-interest loan to Costa Rica's National Institute for Biodiversity to conduct an inventory of all plants and animals in the country's rain forest region. The survey prompted the pharmaceutical company Merck—intrigued by the possibility of finding treatments for AIDS, high blood pressure, and other illnesses in the rain forest—to sign a $1 million contract with the institute. In 1991, the foundation committed a loan of $1 million to Cultural Survival Enterprises, the Massachusetts-based importer that creates markets for goods produced by indigenous people living in environmentally threatened areas, including rain forests. (One of Cultural Survival's best-known products are the brazil nuts used in Ben & Jerry's Rainforest Crunch ice cream.) The loan was intended to help Cultural Survival raise funds needed to match a $3 million grant from the U.S. Agency for International Development, financing that would help it vastly expand its importing capabilities.[16]

Another leading PRI investor, the Robert Wood Johnson Foundation, made its first PRI in 1983 and developed a more complete program six years later.

In 1990, the foundation made $9 million in program-related loans to develop housing for the chronically mentally ill. One of the nine recipients, a non-profit organization in Columbus, Ohio, used the foundation's 10-year loan to buy and build housing. It then received favorable, longer-term financing (up to 3 percent for 30 to 40 years) from the Ohio Housing and Finance Authority. The financing deal enabled the group to use the PRI as "sort of a revolving loan fund" to acquire and construct more housing than it could have with the original $1 million loan, said Peter Goodwin, the foundation's vice president for financial monitoring. By early 1993, the group had housed 254 chronically mentally ill people.

In 1991, the Robert Wood Johnson Foundation made a $500,000 PRI to convert a 25-bed community hospital in Scotland Neck, North Carolina, to a primary care facility that also provides long-term care and housing for elderly patients. The loan, combined with state and federal financing, will bring better care to an area that, like much of rural America, has unmet health care needs.

"The money was leveraged with other money to get something bigger," Goodwin said. "So we got more than a $500,000 [investment] out of it."

Foundations have invested in small-loan funds since Ford made a $770,000 PRI to the Grameen Bank in Bangladesh, the pioneer in peer lending, in 1981. Microlending is now an important way of bringing credit to impoverished areas in the United States. In 1987, Ford and the Northwest Area Foundation made PRIs of $500,000 and $100,000, respectively, to the Lakota Fund, which administers two small-loan programs on the Pine Ridge Indian Reservation in South Dakota. The PRIs were used to capitalize the fund and pay operating expenses.

Financially, the program has worked, said executive director Elsie Meeks. In the five years the Lakota Fund held the PRIs, it made more than 200 loans averaging $1,800. Most went to provide supplemental income to reservation residents; 65 percent were for arts-and-crafts-related work, the remainder for service and retail businesses. Meeks said the fund has a relatively high rate of delinquency, but it has a smaller default rating, 7 percent, than the 30 percent it projected.

As for its effectiveness in the lives of individuals, Meeks said there is some anecdotal evidence. "We're seeing changes in people. They are not showing up late. They're more strategic" about their businesses, she said. The fund is working on its methods of evaluating the success of the program. Both PRIs were paid off in 1992. Ford has since made a $100,000 grant to the program; Northwest renewed its PRI.

Service agencies, perhaps because they offer little or no collateral, receive fewer PRIs than those tied to tangible assets. One of the exceptions is the Council on Adult and Experiential Learning (CAEL)—a Chicago-based non-profit that helps businesses, labor unions, and government agencies set up programs to train and educate workers—that received $1.4 million in PRIs from the Joyce Foundation and the MacArthur Foundation in 1993.

Joyce made a $200,000 PRI, after having given $500,000 in grants, because of its interest in making training accessible to lower-income, less-educated workers. The 4 percent, seven-year loan is earmarked to expand the CAEL's upper management and to develop public policy, such as CAEL's role in helping a state task force in Indiana design a plan to bring training to small and mid-sized companies.

MacArthur's 12-year, $1.2 million loan is designed to help CAEL establish a citywide workforce training system in Chicago. Previously, CAEL concentrated on its contracts with one or two major corporations in the cities in which it has operations—Chicago, Denver, and Philadelphia. The MacArthur PRI would enable CAEL to pursue agreements with small and mid-sized firms; those contracts would provide "a scale, when enough companies come together," to create an integrated adult education program, said

CAEL president Pamela Tate. The agency's goal is to create a national training model for cities within five years.

The potential value of the PRIs is immense. If each program is successful, CAEL will generate an average annual revenue increase of 22 percent in Chicago. For an agency with a $4.5 million budget that would mean significant growth in size—and, more important, influence. "We feel this is a tremendously exciting time to get this PRI," Tate said. "I hope I'm right, but it feels like . . . the PRI is a gift to gear up and rapidly capitalize on what's going on."

Joel Getzendanner, Joyce's vice president of programs, said that, from the foundation's perspective, the public impact of the project, not the investment, is what's important. "We apply the same rigorous standards [to PRIs as to] any grant. If it fails, its not fine with us. But we don't expect every project to succeed," he said. And if it works? "We get our money back and the kind of benefit we think a program like this would have on the community, broadly defined, will be of significant value."

Of course, not all PRIs work. The Mott Foundation and the Hitachi Foundation each lost $100,000 when an employee-owned bakery in Pittsburgh, for which they provided a loan and a loan guarantee, respectively, suffered heavy losses.

In 1990, the foundations joined a Who's Who of religious and social investors, the AFL-CIO, the state of Pennsylvania, and a quasi-governmental industrial development group, the Steel Valley Authority, in a complex deal to finance the City Pride Bakery. The authority used the power of eminent domain to block the demolition of a century-old bakery shut down during a corporate restructuring by Continental-Ralston-Purina, which owned the plant. After the plant turned out to be worthless, the investors built a new 102,000-square-foot facility that employed 100 of the 250 workers who lost their jobs when the old bakery closed. Management had hopes of creating 200 more jobs. City Pride also secured $26 million in sales orders from local supermarkets. Liberal social activists hailed City Pride as an example of the new thinking needed to restructure the American economy.[17]

But things quickly went sour. After delays in opening and production problems, the consortium sold the bakery to a deep-pocketed local businessman.

According to Mott program officer Jack Litzenberg, due diligence indicated City Pride had what it took to succeed. Had it worked, it would have been a textbook example of what PRIs can be. But its struggle points out the risks associated with making such investments. "That's why we're in it, that's why we make PRIs," Litzenberg said. "City Pride—I think I'd do that again. I thought it would work."

There are a number of directions in which PRIs may turn during the rest of the decade. Marcy Murninghan, author of *Undimmed by Human*

Tears: American Cities, Philanthropy and the Civic Ideal, a study of major charitable institutions in the wake of the Los Angeles riots, expects growth in grass-roots community development that not only builds housing but also addresses the overall welfare of the residents: "I think that this is really where the big money is going to go in social investing, or ethical investing, or what I like to call civic investing, in organized philanthropy."

She pointed to a three-year effort, the National Community Development Initiative, as a PRI program that—with its combination of big dollars and community-level rehabilitation and service delivery—could be a model. Eight investors, led by the Rockefeller Foundation, Lilly Endowment, and Prudential Insurance Company of America, put up $62.5 million to build 2,000 housing units in 20 cities from Boston to Los Angeles. Prudential loaned $15 million at 7.5 percent; the foundations $27.5 million at 3 to 5 percent. The rest of the money, $20 million, was made in the form of grants.[18]

NCDI secretary James Pickman said that, by pooling their resources, the funders have more of an impact and can demand more accountability. "It ties things together which might not have been tied together as much if the funders gave individually," Pickman said.

The program is operated for the funders by LISC and a second national intermediary, the Enterprise Foundation. And, as with other projects involving intermediaries, the original funding is matched by grants and loans at the local level. The NCDI claims the program could attract up to $500 million in total funding and lead to the construction or rehabilitation of 7,000 housing units. Another part of the program, intended to create a secondary market for low-income, multi-family housing loans, has NCDI working with the Federal Home Loan Mortgage Company (Freddie Mac) and LISC's Local Initiatives Managed Asset Corporation (LIMAC).

Development is being carried out by CDCs, so the program is tailored to individual cities. In Philadelphia, for example, the emphasis is on multi-family rental housing; in St. Paul, Minnesota, on single family homes. In recognition that community development goes beyond bricks and mortar, the program includes financing for some support services. In New York, it will provide child care facilities for 900 children and employment services for another 250 children and their families.

In July, Housing and Urban Development Secretary Henry Cisneros proposed a $25 million grant to NCDI to build the capacity of CDCs. The program is part of the National Partnership for Community Investment, a $1.2 billion partnership between HUD and the AFL-CIO's Housing and Building Investment Trusts. The arrangement represents a new direction for HUD, which has traditionally not taken a passive role in grantmaking. But Cisneros told the *Washington Post* that the expertise of non-profit community organizations grew dramatically in the 1980s, as HUD became less effective, and ought to be tapped. "There is a lot of talent out there," Cisneros said. "It is clear that a lot less of what we do will be 'top down.' "[19]

Foundations will continue to be important partners on smaller projects as well. Their experience in correcting the capital markets through PRIs will be critical to banks feeling pressure to live up to the Community Reinvestment Act; many experts believe that philanthropies will be much sought after, both as information sources and as partners in PRIs, in poor and minority areas that lenders have traditionally passed over.

Another area of significance in the 1990s will be the growth and maturation of non-profit agencies. Many no-longer-young non-profits, such as the established CDCs now entering their third decade, can't continue to operate on an ad hoc basis.

Indeed, Judy Samuelson, Ford's PRI director, said PRI investors will have to address the issue of building capacity and stability in non-profit agencies: "As the non-profit world continues to expand and mature and looks for a way of becoming more permanent, non-profit agencies need [offices], they need buildings, they need some way of anchoring where they reside, and that calls for capital."

Such steps have already begun. In 1990, the Ford Foundation loaned $1.5 million to the Nonprofit Facilities Fund, which provides financing, technical aid, and building services to New York City non-profits. The fund was begun in 1980 as a Ford subsidiary to help agencies buy cost-cutting energy conservation measures. But the organization, which went independent in 1984, found that the energy issues stemmed from poor building management and hampered the organization's work.

Ford's 10-year, 2 percent loan, along with a $750,000 loan by Morgan Guaranty Bank, greatly enhanced the Nonprofit Facilities Fund's capital base. And in 1992, it made 22 loans—three times the average lending—to organizations ranging from the Nuyorican Poets Cafe to the Cathedral of St. John the Divine.[20]

In the late 1980s, California non-profit organizations, especially those providing child and elder care, had difficulty obtaining affordable and reliable liability insurance. The Packard Foundation made a $250,000 loan to the group, the Nonprofit Insurance Alliance of California (NIAC), to form a risk pool, in which they are covered by a common reserve fund. The 2 percent loan, part of a $1.5 million capital reserve, is designed to allow NIAC to use the excess interest to pay operating expenses and build reserves that could replace the PRI within seven years. The plan is made to accommodate 300 small non-profits.[21]

Many PRI investors said foundations have to provide more equity capital than they have in the past. PRIs have tended to be in the form of short- or mid-term loans; even when partnered with other financing, they haven't made borrowing organizations more stable. Instead, they worry as much about paying off the loans as delivering services.

"There's a lot of talk about making PRIs and using them to leverage other pots of money from banks or other financial institutions, and that's not the way it works in the financial world," said Trinita Logue, executive director of the Illinois Facilities Fund, which finances group residential care programs for people with disabilities, children, and the homeless. "I think PRIs are not the way, with what we do, because without equity we can't grow."

Finally, it is important to note the synergistic relationship between philanthropy and government. In the past, foundation programs have influenced federal policy, as the Gray Areas Project did during the Johnson administration, and government affected foundation investment, as the tax acts of 1969 and 1986 did with PRIs.

Pamela Tate of CAEL said of program-related investing: "I honestly think that this is an important statement for foundations, and perhaps could be an example for federal and local governments" to act on important social issues.

The significance of PRIs lies not so much in their size. A PRI can have ramifications beyond the neighborhood or the issue it was directed toward. Perhaps Dudley Street, CAEL, or NCDI will become the next Gray Areas Project: the program that sets the agenda for the nation.

NOTES

1. "Program-Related Investing; Mixing Investing with Philanthropy," *Responsive Investing News,* July 6, 1992, pp. 1, 7–8.
2. Ann E. Kaplan, ed., *Giving USA: The Annual Report on Philanthropy for the Year 1992* (New York: AAFRC Trust for Philanthropy, 1993), pp. 74, 76.
3. Stephen G. Greene, "Using Assets for Social Good," *The Chronicle of Philanthropy,* Feb. 25, 1992, pp., 1, 36–37; and Stephen G. Greene, "Economic Woes Curb Growth of Foundation Assets," *The Chronicle of Philanthropy,* Feb. 23, 1993, p. 52.
4. Haymarket People's Fund mission statement and investment criteria, 1993.
5. "Using Assets for Social Good," *The Chronicle of Philanthropy,* Feb. 25, 1992, p. 36.
6. Ibid.
7. Anne Lowrey Bailey, " Devalued Fla. Land Slows MacArthur's Asset Growth," *The Chronicle of Philanthropy,* Oct. 6, 1992, p. 14.
8. Frances Brody, John Weiser, and Matthew McCreight, "Alternatives for Socially Responsible Investing," 1992, p. 6.
9. Paul E. Lingenfelter, "Program Related Investments: Do They Cost, or Do They Pay?" John D. and Catherine T. MacArthur Foundation, 1988, pp. 3–5.
10. Ibid., p. 7.

11. "How the 10 Largest Foundations Invest Their Assets," *The Chronicle of Philanthropy,* Feb. 23, 1993, p. 52; and Brody & Weiser, *Program Related Investment Primer* (Washington, D.C.: Council on Foundations, 1993), p. 47.

12. *Investing for Social Gain: Reflecting on Two Decades of Program-Related Investments* (New York: The Ford Foundation, 1991), p. 5.

13. Ibid., p. 8. In the early years of PRIs, Ford and other foundations—including John Simon's Taconic Fund—also tested the concept through the Cooperative Assistance Fund, a pooled capital fund designed to stimulate business development where it is most needed. Today, with many of the same funders, CAF is targeting businesses owned by minority and low-income residents of Washington.

14. Ibid., pp. 7–9.

15. "From Within Our Cities: 1992 LISC Annual Report," p. 1.

16. "The MacArthur Foundation's Programs," *The Chronicle of Philanthropy,* Oct. 6, 1992, p. 14; and *Program Related Investment Primer,* p. 68.

17. Ann Crittenden, *Killing the Sacred Cows: Bold Ideas for a New Economy* (New York: Penguin Books, 1993), p. 161; and *Program Related Investment Primer,* p. 62.

18. Marcy Murninghan, *Undimmed by Human Tears: American Cities, Philanthropy and the Civic Ideal* (report to the Council on Foundations), 1992, pp. 69–70. Besides Prudential, the Lilly Endowment and Rockefeller Foundation, each of which committed $15 million, the participants were the William and Flora Hewlett Foundation ($6 million), Knight Foundation ($5 million), Pew Charitable Trusts ($5 million), MacArthur Foundation ($1 million), and Surdna Foundation ($500,000).

19. Henry Cisneros, "Cisneros' Legislative Program," *National Mortgage News,* Sept. 27, 1993, p. 4; and Guy Gugliotta, "Shallow Pockets and Big Needs Prod 'Small' Thinking at HUD," *Washington Post,* July 13, 1993, p. A-6.

20. *Program Related Investment Primer,* p. 68.

21. Ibid., pp. 68–69.

4

Unions: New Frontiers for Labor?

When Senator Robert Taft was crafting the Labor Management Relations Act of 1947, he built in measures to suppress union influence over pension assets. His interest, Taft said, was to protect beneficiaries and prevent the funds from turning into "union war chests."[1]

He need not have worried. Over the last five decades, union pension funds have been anything but tools of labor. The Taft-Hartley Act created the collective bargaining plan, under which union workers and several employers make pension contributions determined in labor talks. Labor and management share equally in the control of pension assets. And despite (or perhaps because of) the presence of elected union representatives, these jointly trusteed funds, which today have more than $250 billion in assets, have been largely closed to types of investing that may have helped the labor movement.[2]

Not that Taft is solely responsible. The strictures of the Employee Retirement Income Security Act of 1974 (ERISA) and the hostility toward targeted investing by the U.S. Labor Department during the Reagan and Bush administrations were also significant obstacles. But none of these factors entirely explain union funds' caution.

The truth is that Taft-Hartley funds have often lagged behind other institutional investors operating under the same or similar restrictions. In the name of fiduciary conservatism, they have been reluctant to employ innovative strategies. Their comparatively late entry into equities, their slowness in achieving diversification, and their prohibitions against international investing have helped do something Taft could not have foreseen.[3] The funds treat-ed union interests as separate from beneficiaries'. In the process, both may have been hurt.

The most influential name in labor, the AFL-CIO, hopes to end the division. In 1993, the federation's executive council adopted guidelines on domestic and international pension investing that mix social concerns with purely financial aims. The council views the guidelines as a way to safely use union pension funds to further its number one goal: protecting U.S. jobs.

"The growing importance of pension funds in both the domestic and international capital markets has broadened the labor movement's responsibilities and created new opportunities for asserting the voice of working people in matters directly affecting their lives," John T. Joyce, president of the International Union of Bricklayers and Allied Craftsmen, told the board.[4]

While taking pains to point out that all investments must meet common rules of prudence, the guidelines call for a strategy in which funds place a premium on the continuous employment of participants; long-term economic health of employers; promotion of local economic development and job creation; and corporate responsibility to shareholders, workers, and communities (see Tables 4-1 and 4-2).

The AFL-CIO was motivated by what it sees as the failure of government and private-sector investors to boost American infrastructure and employment, as well as by the flight of capital, jobs, and technology overseas. The executive council's recommendations also point out that labor realizes that political and demographic trends are forcing it to rely more on its economic power. After all, the United States' economic base has shifted from the manufacturing to the service sector, where unions have held less sway; the percentage of unionized workers is declining; jobs in heavily unionized industries, such as automobiles, steel, and electronics, have moved to other shores; and the political influence that has been so much a part of labor's power since the New Deal era is ebbing, despite the outcome of the 1992 presidential election. The one area in which labor, indirectly, is gaining strength is in the growing value of the pension funds of union workers.

TABLE 4-1 Number of Shareholder Proposals Sponsored by Labor Unions

Type	1991	1992	1993*
Corporate governance	13	17	18
Social issues	13	15	12
Total	26	32	30

* Preliminary

Source: D.F. King & Co., Inc. (New York).

TABLE 4-2   Types of Resolutions Proposed by Labor Unions, 1993

Type	Number	Sponsor
Corporate governance		
Poison pills	5	UBCJA (4)
		IUOE (1)
Classified board	3	UBCJA
Confidential voting	2	UBCJA
Accumulative voting	2	UBCJA
Independent nominating committee	2	UBCJA
Majority independent directors	2	UBCJA
Golden parachutes	1	OCAW
Employee on subsidiary's board	1	OCAW
Social issues		
Health care policy	3	UBCJA (2)
		ACTWU
Health and safety policy	3	UBCJA
Endorse CERES Principles	1	OCAW
Low-income minority lending	1	UBCJA/Pension
PAC contributions	1	UBCJA
Plant closings	1	CWA
Report on equal employment	1	ACTWU
Safety performance	1	UBCJA

Key
ACTWU — Amalgamated Clothing and Textile Workers Union
CWA — Communications Workers of America
IUOE — International Union of Operating Engineers
OCAW — Oil, Chemical and Atomic Workers
UBCJA — United Brotherhood of Carpenters and Joiners of America
Source: D.F. King & Co., Inc. (New York).

Any changes in the investment of those assets to a pro-jobs, pro-union strategy will not happen overnight, if at all. A few funds have some of the recommended elements in place—the Bricklayers, for instance, have a strong targeted investing program. No fund has all of them. And the process of persuading the hundreds of local unions and their funds to follow along will be cumbersome, said Meredith Miller, formerly the AFL-CIO's assistant director of employee benefits and now an official in the Labor Department.

The federation plans to work in stages, Miller said, to encourage the many types of funds representing union workers—Taft-Hartley, public and single-employer pension plans—to adopt the guidelines. It also hopes to cultivate a roster of investment managers who will offer vehicles that adhere to a pro-labor philosophy. But it has no timetable in which to achieve its goals.

To some observers, the guidelines are the triumph of hope over experience. Taft-Hartley funds have been extremely conservative, and, even if some in the union movement are now bent on change, they will have to overcome the institutional inertia and complacence present since Taft's time. Initiatives emanating from the AFL-CIO's Washington headquarters have tended to peter out by the time they reach the thousands of unions, pension trustees, and administrators. Said one consultant, "We've heard this before."

ECONOMICALLY TARGETED INVESTING

A key recommendation of the AFL-CIO report is that more union-affiliated funds make economically targeted investments (ETIs). The federation defines these as investments that, besides meeting the standards of prudent investing, provide "a corollary benefit to the fund's plan participants and beneficiaries, geographic area, demographic group or industry." Those benefits might include more jobs, better schools and health care facilities or environment, more affordable housing, or promotion of economic growth.[5]

ETIs help fill inefficiencies in the capital market, bringing financing to regions or projects ignored by conventional lenders, the labor federation says. Depending on who's counting, estimates of targeted investing run as high as $10 billion nationally.[6]

Taft-Hartley funds devote a higher percentage of assets to ETIs than any other fund type. According to a 1992 General Accounting Office study of 15 ETI housing programs, more than $1.3 billion in private-sector assets, mostly from Taft-Hartley funds, were committed to the projects. (Public-sector funds, which represent a much larger portion of the pension fund pool, placed $3.4 billion in the same ETIs.) Still, those projects are a small portion, less than 1 percent, of all Taft-Hartley assets.[7]

Among the greatest success stories in targeted investing are four funds operating under the aegis of the AFL-CIO. The pooled-asset real estate funds invest solely in construction project built by union labor. The funds have more than $2 billion under management for hundreds of pension funds.

The oldest of the funds, the AFL-CIO Housing Investment Trust (HIT), a mortgage fund, was established in 1964, well before targeted investing was an investment catch-phrase. Along with the five-year-old Building Investment Trust (BIT), it has supported 220,000 building trades jobs, created 31,000 housing units and 2.8 million square feet of commercial property, the AFL-CIO claims. In 1992, HIT was investing $646 million for 312 pension funds, most of them union-affiliated, and BIT $200 million. Officials project the two funds will have more than $1 billion in total assets by the end of 1993.

The AFL-CIO's Union Labor Life Insurance Company (ULLICO) has managed the third mortgage fund, J for Jobs, since 1977. Today, it invests more than $472 million for 175 funds. The fourth fund, the Multi-Employer Property Trust, an open-end real estate fund, began in 1982 with $16 million and five clients; today, it manages $720 million for 99 retirement plans. It has never had a losing quarter.[8]

According to a 1992 study by the Marco Consulting Group of Chicago, a leading consultant to jointly trusteed funds, these real estate investment funds, and others with pro-labor standards, perform better than competitors without social agendas.

Among six mortgage funds, HIT had a 13 percent return over a 10-year period ending in 1991, tops in the category, and J for Jobs 11 percent. Over a three-year period, HIT had an average return of nearly 14 percent and J for Jobs and BIT just under 8 percent. Another labor-oriented mortgage fund, Prudential Insurance's Union Mortgage Account, averaged a 13 percent return. In both the short- and long-term periods, the funds outdistanced Aetna's Participating Mortgage Separate Account, a non-union fund. As for the open-end Multi-Employer Property Trust, it had an annualized 10-year return of more than 9.5 percent and three-year average just under 7 percent, both ahead of the Evaluation Associates Inc.'s Open End Equity Funds Median, the industry benchmark for such funds. A study of its five-year performance through 1992 showed an average annualized return of 5.6 percent.[9]

Jack Marco, president of Marco Consulting, attributed the performance of the funds to their conservative nature as well as the quality of the work in the projects. Though new construction projects are typically risky, the four funds are quite selective. The Multi-Employer Property Trust, for example, invests only in substantially leased properties. And because the work must be done by unions, construction is handled by established contractors, Marco said. A joint study by the National Science Foundation and North Carolina State University supports his contentions. It showed that productivity on union contractors in commercial office construction was at least 30 percent higher than for non-union contractors.[10]

The Bricklayers have been heavily involved in the funds since 1981, when, in the teeth of the recession, their trustees set aside 10 percent of pension assets for HIT and J for Jobs. The investment proved so successful that the Bricklayers today earmark 15 percent of assets, about $80 million, for the four funds. And they may push the limit even higher.

Explained L. Gerard Carlisle, the Bricklayers secretary-treasurer and trustee for the $530 million jointly trusteed fund: "It creates jobs, we get a good investment return, it's good for the community and it builds projects that might not get built otherwise."

Other unions have gotten with the program, many for differing reasons. The $4.6 billion National Electrical Benefit Fund, the retirement trust for the International Brotherhood of Electrical Workers, has invested $300 million (much of it though the AFL-CIO funds, some through its own successful programs) in union-built construction, because of the solid return. In three years, the investments have averaged a 10 percent yield.

The $2.5 billion 1199 Health Care Employees Pension Fund, the fund for the Health and Hospital Workers Local 1199, placed $5 million in the Housing Investment Trust in 1991. Although the fund has undertaken a study of affordable housing investments in New York City, its trustees deadlocked over whether they should actually make the plunge; the HIT investment has served as an introduction to targeted, affordable housing investments.

The Pacific Coast Roofers Pension Plan, which represents 4,500 workers and retirees, chose ULLICO's J for Jobs as an investment vehicle in 1988, placing $3 million in the account. That investment has grown to $5.4 million. John Banister, a management trustee, said the fund chose the investment to diversity the funds assets and to create jobs. It also helps the small businesses in the building trades secure contracts and provide jobs, he said.[11]

Other, independent ETIs have also shown good results. The Massachusetts State and Local Laborers' Pension Fund and Bricklayers and Masons Pension Fund have had a happy experience with a program they developed in 1988. The Taft-Hartley funds operate a non-profit development company that builds affordable housing with union labor, a program that the company's president, Thomas J. McIntyre, called "simple but not easy"—"simple" because its goals are clearly defined, "not easy" because of the economic obstacles it faces.

The linked-deposit program ties the union funds' deposits in local banks to the amount of loans made to the unions' jointly held company, the Non-Profit Housing Corporation. The loans finance the construction of low- and moderate-income housing. The arrangement allows development loans to be made at up to 4 percent below prevailing rates and enables the banks, led by U.S. Trust Company, to satisfy their Community Reinvestment Act requirements. The retirement trusts benefit from having Federal Deposit Insurance Corporation protection of up to $100,000 per plan participant.

In five years, the corporation has built 230 housing units, mostly one- to three-bedroom condominiums, in such struggling neighborhoods as Charlestown, Mission Hill, Roxbury, and South Boston, McIntyre said. The condos sell for as low as $87,500 for a three-bedroom unit, a bargain in the high-priced Greater Boston real estate market. The total value of the projects exceeds $35 million.

The Non-Profit Housing Corporation builds on land donated by the city of Boston and receives grants from a city-managed "linkage trust," a fund developers pay into when they build downtown office space. The money is then used to help the city's neighborhoods. The city subsidies and the low cost of borrowing have kept development costs at least 40 percent lower than normal, even with the price of union help.

"This provides the union openings, besides the issue of jobs, to do something at the grass-roots, of accomplishment of good in the community," McIntyre said. "Not to get too philosophical, but people have given up on cities and they shouldn't. Cities are a great jewel."

Elsewhere, failures of construction-related ETIs, coupled with intense federal scrutiny, have had a chilling effect on many union funds. Operating Engineers Local 675 in Pompano Beach, Florida, invested 60 to 70 percent of assets in real estate construction in its home base of Broward County. The types of projects were diverse; the financial quality was not, and the fund suffered huge losses. In Denver, the Labor Department hauled the Centennial State Carpenters Pension Trust Fund into court for allegedly placing an inappropriate amount, nearly one-quarter of assets, in construction mortgages on union-built projects.[12]

Many fund administrators and trustees said that the two cases, and the specter of costly lawsuits during the Reagan and Bush presidencies, prevented them from joining even proven ETI projects. Indeed, the Labor Department's ERISA Advisory Council noted in 1992 that, though officially neutral on ETIs, the department was perceived as "skeptical at best, and probably hostile" on the subject.[13]

Not only has that outlook changed in the Clinton administration, but labor has been given something more: a piece of the action. President Clinton—who as Arkansas' governor steered public pension fund money to housing and job-creating projects—has given labor access to big-time investments it had been locked out of. Within three months of his inauguration, his Housing and Urban Development secretary, Henry Cisneros, announced the National Partnership for Community Investment, a joint venture with the AFL-CIO's Housing and Building Investment Trusts.

Under the plan, the trusts will invest $660 million in affordable housing. Federal, state, and local governments and private investors will kick in another $550 million. The financing will be used to build 12,000 units of affordable housing and 1 million square feet in commercial office space in 30 cities. Up to 20,000 construction jobs will be created.[14]

Besides giving unions a foot in the door on federal projects, the partnership takes care of a key labor concern, investment safety. HUD will provide $100 million in seed money and Section 8 rental assistance, to ensure a revenue stream. And pension money will be protected through the Federal National Mortgage Association (Fannie Mae) and other government and private programs. "We will not sacrifice our returns just to make a social investment," Muriel Cohen, the AFL-CIO's director of affordable housing, told the *Christian Science Monitor*. "Our goal is to demonstrate that pension funds can invest in rebuilding our cities, producing affordable housing and creating new jobs without damaging funds' safety and security."[15]

The housing partnership is part of a favorable shift in federal policy toward ETIs over the last year, one that labor has ardently sought. The Labor Department's ERISA council in 1992 asked regulators to give ETIs favorable treatment if the investments offered a market rate of return. The Senate Infrastructure Committee, which studied ways of using pension money to rebuild the nation's public properties, concluded that pension funds are "ready and willing" to put up capital for infrastructure, if proper incentives and guarantees are provided.[16] The administration convened an interagency task force to follow up on the issue.

CORPORATE GOVERNANCE, PROXY ISSUES, AND DIALOGUE

Union-affiliated funds have come to fulfill what, in 1976, management icon Peter Drucker called "pension fund socialism": workers, through their retirement trusts, control the means of production. As investment banker David F. Sand wrote, "[W]hile their political power had diminished, their economic importance was ascending. In an ironic twist—as unimaginable to theorists from Adam Smith to Karl Marx as to labor leaders like John Lewis and George Meany—workers had come to *own* much of the outstanding stock of American corporations."[17]

Today, corporate, public, and Taft-Hartley funds are the real capitalists in the United States. These assets give labor "a lot of direct and indirect influence" on corporate America, Sand said in an interview. And, in the mid-1980s, unions began to use those assets, albeit in a limited way, to wield their influence.

In the mid-1980s, union funds found themselves, like other large investors, unable to maneuver in the marketplace. The growth of pension funds was so great that it reduced their ability to move their money—another irony, given that unions worked so hard to ensure their members had adequate retirement plans and that the very growth of those plans appeared to be undermining them. So union funds took one step that Lewis and Meany surely would have understood: they formed coalitions.

Since 1986, a handful of jointly trusteed funds have been members of the Council of Institutional Investors. The Washington-based association was formed in response to takeover activities that it thought threatened benefits. Today, it monitors federal laws and regulations and studies corporate governance issues on behalf of members. The council includes 80 plans, such as the American Express Retirement Plan, California Public Employees Retirement System and 1199 Health Care Employees Pension Fund, with assets exceeding $500 billion. The 24 Taft-Hartley funds that are members have about $11.5 billion in assets.

The council's efforts, and those of its members, have opened up corporate governance, increased shareholder democracy, and toppled unresponsive CEOs, like those at American Express, General Motors, International Business Machines and Westinghouse. And major institutions have won a number of changes in Securities and Exchange Commission rules, such as those in 1992 making it easier for them to meet, correspond, and exchange information without the prior approval of the commission. Anne Hansen, the council's vice president, said, "This has made the owners [pension funds] more powerful."[18]

Formal networks like the Council of Institutional Investors, and other informal links, have helped multi-employer plans further union goals. In 1990, the United Mine Workers of America (UMWA) workers with the Pittston Company signed a contract, ending a tumultuous 46-week strike in which more than 3,000 people were arrested. The dispute stemmed from Pittston's refusal to abide by an agreement reached with other corporations in the Bituminous Coal Operators Association (BCOA) and its move to cut health benefits for retired and disabled workers. UMWA officials used their ties with other institutional and social investors to attempt to oust Paul Douglas, Pittston's chairman, from the board of Philip Morris; they also sought out companies whose officials were Pittston directors, seeking their resignations. The efforts helped turn public opinion against the company.[19]

The UMWA tried similar tactics in 1993. During prolonged negotiations with the BCOA, union officials met with members of the Council of Institutional Investors, telling them it was in their best interests as investors that a fair, timely settlement be reached. It asked them to convey to company officials that the talks be settled quickly. Without the focus on a single corporate villain like Pittston, the going appeared more difficult, and negotiations with the BCOA dragged on through much of the year.

According to Kenneth Zinn, the UMWA's director of special projects, miners have a long tradition of taking their case to the ultimate decision makers—the owners. In 1914, he said, labor agitator Mother Jones shepherded a contingent of Colorado miners to the door of John D. Rockefeller, whose anti-labor policies led to the Ludlow Massacre in which 33 people were killed.

Seventy-nine years later, the nature of corporate America is entirely different. So, Zinn explained, the union makes a subtler case to major investors; namely, that miners and shareholders have more common interests than differences. The workers, many of whom have "invested decades of sweat equity in the industry," have nowhere else to go, he said; investors, too, cannot simply walk away from the market since, in many respects, they are the market. They have billions of dollars to invest and reinvest each year. Their best bet, Zinn said, is to work for responsible management of the corporations they invest in.

"This really isn't new to us. Historically, the union has understood you always have to go to the decision makers. Only today, instead of Rockefeller, it's CalPERS," Zinn said.

Another way in which unions began acting as a member of the marketplace was to introduce proxy issues and to engage in dialogue with companies.

The roots of shareholder activism extend to the 1970s corporate campaign led by the Amalgamated Clothing and Textile Workers Union (ACTWU), which represents workers in the apparel and textiles industry, against sheet manufacturer J.P. Stevens. It was the first labor-run campaign to inject Wall Street into a labor-management battle. The fight was fierce, the outcome muddy. Stevens, the subject of two leveraged buyouts in the 1980s, closed a number of factories. And the domestic textile industry has looked on wanly over the last two decades as thousands of jobs have left for cheaper Third World factories.[20] But the campaign was labor's Bunker Hill, an early and inconclusive battle that it declared a victory.

It was only in the mid-1980s, however, that unions (rarely their pension funds) became more deeply involved in proxy campaigns. And even that role is limited. Among groups that bring social-issue shareholder issues, unions are among the least prominent. Of the 263 socially oriented proxies introduced in 1993, 11 were sponsored by unions, led by the United Brotherhood of Carpenters and Joiners of America, the most active union on shareholder topics, which introduced seven; one was sponsored by a Taft-Hartley pension fund, the Carpenters' fund. Forty-one were sponsored by public pension funds representing unions; none were sponsored by corporate pension funds.[21]

Joseph Uehlein, an AFL-CIO official who helps unions run corporate campaigns and wage proxy fights, said labor's role is limited "because so many local unions . . . just haven't gotten on the bandwagon yet."

Labor's only outright proxy win in a vote of shareholders occurred in 1989 on a corporate governance issue pitting the UMWA against Pittston. The union led a three-issue proxy campaign to increase shareholder democracy, a cause dear to institutional investors. One of the resolutions, requiring the company to make voting confidential, won a majority of votes at the annual meeting. Not coincidentally, the victory carried a reported price tag of several hundred thousand dollars.

In recent years, several unions have focused shareholder resolutions on the retail industry, which has a mainly non-union workforce. Their prime target has been the discount retail giant Wal-Mart, a favorite among social investors for its growth—it has gone from $16 billion in annual sales in 1988 to $44 billion in 1992—and outstanding profit record. But to unions, Wal-Mart is disastrous. Sixty-two percent of its payroll goes to minimum-wage jobs, according to the AFL-CIO. It is closely held, with the family of the late CEO, Sam Walton, controlling about 38 percent of shares. It seldom discloses anything but minimally required information and limits shareholder democracy, routinely challenging social-issue proxies in court. And, most galling to labor, Wal-Mart has trumpeted its "Buy American" campaign while using overseas manufacturers and suppliers.[22]

The antagonism has resulted in two court decisions that some proxy issues experts believe could boost labor's ability to challenge corporations.

In 1992, the AFL-CIO's Food & Allied Service Trades Department (FAST) sponsored a resolution asking Wal-Mart to set up a committee to investigate whether any of its imports from China were made with prison labor. FAST, which is composed of 16 unions, bypassed the usual shareholder-resolution process of seeking access to the company's proxy statement. Instead, it sponsored a separate resolution and asked for access to Wal-Mart's shareholder list so it could contact investors directly. The company complained in Delaware Chancery Court that FAST wanted the list to organize its employees. The motion to block the resolution was denied, and FAST gained access to the list. The decision was seen by some proxy watchers as having the potential to open shareholders' meetings to a wide range of labor-related issues.[23]

At the shareholders meeting, Wal-Mart CEO David Glass "stuffed" Hongda "Harry" Wu, a fellow at the Hoover Institute at Stanford University and a political prisoner in China for 19 years, who presented the resolution, said Jeffrey Fiedler, FAST's secretary-treasurer. The resolution received just 4.9 percent of the vote, nearly 25 million shares. Supporters included the New York State Teachers Retirement System, the five New York City funds, a Pennsylvania state fund, and 2,000 individuals.

Wu and Fiedler later upped the ante. In December 1992, Wal-Mart was the subject of a Polk Award-winning report on NBC-TV's *Dateline* program, which showed Bangladeshi children as young as 11 years old sewing Wal-Mart labels into garments. Wal-Mart called that accusation, previously leveled in a resolution introduced by the United Food and Commercial Workers, untrue. But the company acknowledged the truth of another charge, that at least one store (*Dateline* said 12) had placed "Made in America" signs above foreign-made merchandise. The *Dateline* report also accused Wal-Mart of importing garments with labels claiming they were made in Malaysia or other countries and not in their true originating country, China, in order to circumvent a quota on Chinese-made products. Wal-Mart company denied that, but immediately ended its association with the Hong Kong supplier it bought the merchandise from. The main sources for the story were Wu and Fiedler.[24]

FAST did not have to file another resolution. Immediately after the NBC report, Franklin Research & Development Corporation, the Boston investment advisory firm, filed a resolution asking the company to comply with legal and ethical standards on labor. After three months of dialogue between Wal-Mart officials and the Interfaith Center on Corporate Responsibility (ICCR), Wal-Mart agreed to an expanded set of standards for its suppliers; Franklin withdrew the resolution.[25] It can be debated whether FAST, as the confrontational "bad cop," or Franklin and ICCR, as conciliatory "good cops," was more effective. But Franklin would not have intervened— nor Wal-Mart conceded—as quickly if FAST had not used its pre-Miranda approach. Fiedler said FAST is continuing to monitor and research Wal-Mart and may take some unspecified further action against it.

In the second key case, ACTWU joined a coalition of religious investors in filing a lawsuit against Wal-Mart and the SEC in 1992. The suit challenged the SEC's decision to uphold Wal-Mart's exclusion from the proxy statement a resolution asking the company to disclose its equal opportunity practices.

The resolution asked Wal-Mart to disclose the percentage of women and minorities by job category; summarize its affirmative action efforts; attempt to increase the number of female and minority managers; and describe any outreach programs it has to women- and minority-owned suppliers. Other retailers, including J.C. Penney, have included similar information in their proxy statements.

With the approval of the SEC, Wal-Mart kept the resolution off the ballot in 1992. The company intended to strike the measure from the proxy statement again in 1993, but in April federal District Judge Kimba Wood, responding to the original suit, issued an injunction preventing Wal-Mart from doing so.[26] Wal-Mart chairman Rob Walton relented and the company agreed to include the information in its 1994 annual report. The case is considered important, especially in combination with Wood's later decision in the Cracker Barrel case, because it may hinder the SEC's ability to keep social issues from coming before shareholders.

Another ACTWU resolution brought Sears, Roebuck & Co., the nation's third-largest retailer, to change its review policy. In 1991, after reports by the human rights group Asia Watch that Chinese prison factories produced goods for exports and then sold them through third-party trading companies to hide their origin, the union introduced a shareholder resolution, similar to that FAST brought against Wal-Mart, to require Sears to investigate its suppliers in China. In early 1992, less then four months after the resolution was filed,

ACTWU and Sears reached an agreement. Sears pledged to inform its Chinese suppliers of its anti-slave-labor policy and incorporated such language into its contracts. And it agreed to certify the source of the goods by maintaining a list of the manufacturing plants and periodically visiting those sites.[27]

Uehlein, executive assistant to the president in the AFL-CIO's industrial union department, said that what unions ultimately want, as in the Sears case, is to discuss major issues with management. But they can generally get to the boardroom only by sponsoring resolutions. He pointed to a confidential-voting question sponsored by an Akron Beacon-Journal reporter, a union member, at Knight-Ridder. The measure won more than 30 percent of shareholders' votes in 1991. When it was reintroduced in 1992, company management offered to permit confidential voting if the resolution was withdrawn. It was.

"What that says from our point of view is that a company responds and a relationship can develop that goes beyond the immediate issue," Uehlein said. "If we can get to the dialogue, we consider that a victory."

While unions themselves have played the activist's role in proxy campaigns, their pension funds have been barely visible. Again, that is due, in part, to the distance put between workers and their pension money by Taft and later laws. Still, the funds could help advance labor's cause by its voting on proxies. Which is why the AFL-CIO issued advice to Taft-Hartley funds on proxy voting in 1991 and sent out an updated version two years later. The federation's advice stems from the Labor Department's "Avon letter," which, in 1988, stated that "to act prudently in the voting of proxies (as well as in all other fiduciary matters), a plan fiduciary must consider those factors which would affect the value of the plan's investment."[28]

While not mandatory, the advisories are intended to provide union funds with a framework for establishing their own written policies in accordance with what the AFL-CIO sees as the best interest of union members.

The guidelines require fiduciaries to closely review each proxy resolution dealing with issues that have a material effect on the operation of a company—including those involving corporate governance, changes in control, and a variety of social issues—and to vote against management's position on these matters when appropriate.

In the case of corporate control and governance issues, the fiduciary is required to conduct "an independent and thorough cost benefit analysis" before voting to evaluate "the long-term business plans of the competing parties" and to vote in a manner consistent with the "long-term economic best interests of plan participants and beneficiaries," even if that means forgoing some short-term gain in the process.

The guidelines give numerous specific examples of cases in which fiduciaries would vote in favor of or against these kinds of resolutions. For example, the guidelines say, the voting fiduciary may support reincorporation

where "there is no significant negative impact on matters of corporate governance, management accountability, and the interests of employees."

In another example, the guidelines say, the fiduciary may support a
management-sponsored proposal to change the number of directors "provided
a satisfactory explanation justifying the change is given in the proxy statement." However, if the change means that the number of "outside," or independent directors is decreased in the process (this is often the case), the voting fiduciary should attempt to maintain a reasonable balance between the
two. Because, while more independent directors may increase a company's
responsiveness to shareholders, the guidelines point out, insiders often are
more sensitive to the concerns of employees and the community.

Likewise, the guidelines say that the fiduciary should weigh the same
factors when dealing with shareholder resolutions asking companies to create
boards made up of a majority of outside directors.

With certain other kinds of proposals, including those dealing with
social issues, the guidelines require that the fiduciary vote in favor of the proposals where it finds that a resolution "enhances the long-term economic best
interests of [pension] plan participants and beneficiaries" or will have no
impact on those interests.

Examples include resolutions that call for: the creation of special policy
review and shareholder advisory committees; studies of the impact of national health care reform on a company's operations; withdrawal from South
Africa; adherence to the MacBride Principles; and the adoption of the CERES
Principles. Fiduciaries are also instructed to vote in favor of resolutions that
call for "affirmative action compliance with" regulations on nondiscrimination or public reporting on policies regarding "basic labor protections," so
long as the votes are not harmful to the long-term interests of the pension
plan.

In addition, the AFL-CIO guidelines instruct fiduciaries to initiate
"alternative action," to address "issues which may have a significant economic impact . . . [but] are not addressed in the company's proxy. Such action can
include sponsorship of shareholder resolutions, meeting with a company's
management, or requesting special reports.

AFL-CIO's guidelines leave fiduciaries free to vote with management
on routine matters, such as those dealing with executive stock option plans
and director liability and indemnification, but adds that fiduciary duty
requires that "each shall be reviewed individually to ensure that no factors
detrimental to the long-term economic best interests of participants and beneficiaries are present."

For example, the fiduciary should consider whether stock option plans
are "overly generous and not closely tied to performance" and whether direc-

tor indemnification does not "limit directors' or officers' liability where a court finds illegal insider dealing, gross negligence or a breach of the duty of loyalty."

INTERNATIONAL INVESTING

Pension funds [should] actively pursue an investment and administrative policy which is directed at increasing domestic economic and employment growth. This would include the establishment of guidelines which embody a heavy bias in favor of companies and industries that have stable or expanding employment prospects for American workers. . . . In short, they must do everything prudent and feasible at home before going abroad and, if they do go abroad, investments should be undertaken according to standards and principles designed to protect the long-term economic interests of plan participants and beneficiaries.
—*Pensions in Changing Capital Markets*[29]

In their effort to protect American jobs, unions have called on their funds to limit international investing. But, like it or not, union-affiliated funds are foreign investors. Whether through direct investments in foreign firms, generally made by corporate or public pension plans, or stock ownership in U.S.-based multinationals, unions are party to foreign investing. And, as the world economy becomes more interdependent, distinguishing domestic investing from foreign investing will be increasingly difficult.

Recognizing that trend, the AFL-CIO has asked union funds to scrutinize their investments more closely. And it has identified foreign investment vehicles that satisfy its concern with protecting workers and the funds' fiduciary responsibilities to participants and beneficiaries. These vehicles, which apply the principles of targeted investing to the international arena, are still theoretical. They are either unfunded or are looking for investors. And they may take years to get off the ground. But they represent a first stab at applying the integrated approach to investing abroad as well as domestically.

In its guidelines, the AFL-CIO states: "In examining the issues surrounding international investing by pension funds, it is not a theoretical question of whether funds should be investing internationally. The fact is, the majority of pension funds are *already* involved in international investing and the extent to which they are is significant."

In a 1992 *Pensions & Investments* survey, 127 international and global managers handled $133.7 billion for U.S. tax-exempt institutions. And in 1991, the top 200 institutional investors invested $75.5 million in foreign securities. Of those investors, 89 percent were corporate and public sector plans which represent 13.5 million workers and 60 AFL-CIO affiliates. Among the plans with major international holdings: American Telephone &

Telegraph, with $2.5 billion; United Technologies, $1.1 billion; and the California Public Employees Retirement System, $9.5 billion.[30] The figures for jointly trusteed multi-employer plans are less clear. Remi Browne, managing director for international investments for Ark Management, said less than 1 percent of Taft-Hartley assets are in direct international investments.

Most plan sponsors and money managers believe that figure will rise to 2 to 5 percent, a potential market of $12.5 billion. A 1991 survey by the International Foundation of Employee Benefit Plans found 72 percent of plan administrators projected that foreign investments by Taft-Hartley funds would increase by the mid-1990s. At the time of the survey, just 17 percent of respondents said their plans invested internationally. Indeed, a number of jointly trusteed funds, even the smallest, are putting their toes in international waters for the first time. For example, the trustees of the Plumbers & Pipefitters Local 77 fund in New Bedford, Massachusetts, a 200-member, $22 million fund, voted in 1993 to explore allocating up to 5 percent of assets to international equities as a way of diversifying its portfolio.[31]

In addition, union funds invest in "American" companies that have significant assets and operations abroad. In a 1992 report, Lazard Freres & Company said that Exxon had $51 billion in assets, or 58 percent of its total, overseas; Federal Express $1.5 billion, or 28 percent; H.J. Heinz Company $2.6 billion, or 43 percent; and Texas Instruments $2.2 billion, or 43 percent. In the case of Exxon, the AFL-CIO report says, "[Fifty-eight] cents of every dollar of retained earnings of new investment . . . will, in effect, go to support those operations."[32]

The labor federation worries that union-affiliated funds have been—and will increasingly be—putting substantial amounts of their assets abroad. Thus, money that could be invested domestically is supporting competitors of U.S. workers or has financed U.S. companies engaged in "runaway" tactics— that is, shutting down plants here and opening operations on other shores.

The AFL-CIO argues that there are a number of reasons to avoid foreign investing, saying that foreign investing fails to achieve the diversification of risk and asset type that is often claimed; that the higher price of asset management abroad may negate any increase in return; that U.S. shareholders have less of a voice in corporate affairs, through shareholder votes, than at home; that government regulations in other countries are less generous to shareholders than in the United States; and that, because union-affiliated funds are so slow to act, the best investment opportunities in new markets like Eastern Europe will be swallowed up by more aggressive Western European investors. The AFL-CIO states that investment abroad "should be undertaken only in the context of a domestic policy which seeks full employment at home" and should be avoided when it has a direct negative impact on domestic employment. Therefore, it said, "[T]he funds should establish policies which filter investment options for compliance with minimum standards and their impact on domestic interests; filters which, while they may not exist in current financial community practices and standards, are feasible and will be created if pension funds, as a major market, require them."[33]

The AFL-CIO has identified a vehicle that, though unproven in the market, could help labor stay true to its principles and, yet, conquer what it called the "new frontier" of international investing. The concept is "foreign locals."

Foreign locals are companies engaged in businesses—such as utilities, construction, food retailing or service—meant for internal markets and, therefore, not directly competitive with U.S. companies. The theory was developed by Ark Management's Browne. Under Browne's hypothesis, thriving foreign locals expand overseas economies, provide larger export markets for American goods and services, and create jobs here at home. For example, a power plant built abroad could create demand for machinery produced in the United States, or tap the expertise of U.S. engineers, advisors, and consultants.[34]

Ark tested the theory by measuring the performance of a model portfolio comprised of foreign firms with no international revenue against that of Morgan Stanley Capital International's Europe, Australia, Far East index (MSCI EAFE) from 1983 to 1991. The study found the foreign locals had an annualized return of 21.78 percent, compared to the EAFE's 21.77 percent. The study also found foreign locals had a greater effect on diversification of risk.[35]

No fund has been constructed to follow the foreign locals model. Browne said Ark has wooed the AFL-CIO, trying to interest it in financing one, so far to no avail.

Other groups of investment managers are building targeted investment vehicles abroad. One such group is close to opening a fund that would provide start-up or expansion capital for promising companies in Poland, where the most dramatic—and to date successful—economic reforms of the former Eastern Bloc have taken place. The Poland Partners Limited Partnership, which has been seeking investors for two years, primarily from labor and public pension funds, anticipates returns of 20 percent.

The partnership is being developed by British and American investors, including Butler Associates, whose principal, Landon Butler, is a board member of the AFL-CIO's Multi-Employer Property Trust and former Carter White House aide. The idea was launched in 1989, when Polish labor leader (and now president) Lech Walesa toured the United States as a guest of the AFL-CIO.

Investments will be limited to companies that comply with the International Labor Organization's fair labor standards. The partnership may make direct investments or join with several international lending organizations. In addition, the principal invested in the partnership will be guaranteed by the Overseas Private Investment Corporation, a U.S. government agency that evaluates projects for their effect on domestic employment and compliance with standards on human and worker rights, health, and safety. The agency is prohibited from providing guarantees for investments detrimental to the American economy. The partnership will, like other venture capital funds, try to protect assets by seeking seats on the companies' boards of directors.[36]

The partnership, which is still trying to raise capital, arranged a tour of Poland for management trustees of Taft-Hartley funds in 1993 in hopes of drumming up interest. Labor trustees had toured the country in 1991.[37] Butler expected a $50 million fund to be up and running by the end of 1993. The Bricklayers, who were represented on each of the trips, are among the more likely investors.

THE OUTLOOK

The AFL-CIO expects turning its guidelines into reality—getting investors to make more ETIs, vote proxies wisely, tread carefully overseas, and conduct a top-to-bottom review to ensure consistent pro-labor investments—will take some time.

According to Meredith Miller, the former AFL-CIO employee benefits official, the federation will follow a staged approach in working with unions. At first, it hopes to convert the Taft-Hartley funds and at least two-thirds of public pension funds, which represent a heavily unionized workforce, to the guidelines. The federation's member unions and their funds are not obligated to follow the suggestions, but "the executive council's word carries a lot of weight," Miller said.

At single-employer corporate funds with more than $2.3 trillion in assets, no cooperation is expected. The AFL-CIO aims to push its goals through shareholder resolutions and by seeking federal legislation giving unions representation on investment committees, Miller said. Several bills, including one sponsored in 1990 by Representative Peter Visclosky, D-Indiana, to give labor equal representation on corporate pension boards have fared poorly. Currently, few funds have labor representatives on benefit panels.

Given the lack of central control of labor unions by the AFL-CIO's Washington headquarters, and separation of unions from the management of their funds, can the federation's guidelines make a real difference?

Some funds—like the Bricklayers, who already have what Miller called some of the most "current, cutting-edge investment strategies" around—have begun reviews. The International Brotherhood of Teamsters, whose two headquarters and affiliates funds have assets of more than $575 million, has discussed the funds' ban on investments outside the United States and Canada. The $2.8 billion Bakery, Confectionery and Tobacco Workers Union fund, an avid investor in the Housing and Building Investment Trusts, has taken a fresh look at foreign investing.

If union-affiliated funds fall into line—a big if—money managers could be affected as well. The AFL-CIO began working on the guidelines after a fruitless meeting with investment professionals in New York in 1992. Nobody there knew how to develop a pro-union investment strategy with concern for the environment, human rights, and the domestic economy, Miller said. The federation hopes to recruit managers who can service such an integrated strategy and will conduct seminars on the subject for them.

ETI proponent Jack Marco said that following the guidelines would mean "Wall Street is going to have to respond. Instead of offering stock and bonds, they're going to have to say, 'How about this product that might help your client?' "

Michael Steed, senior vice president for investments for Union Life Insurance Company, said money managers will have to design ETIs for pension funds—or face legislation requiring them to do so: "Without that, Washington in some way, shape or form, through a punitive tax or some other measure, will mandate some type of investment."[38]

In each case, that may be wishful thinking. The financial industry took a while, for example, to react to the desire of some labor funds for targeted funds like the Multi-Employer Property Trust. And pension legislation favorable to unions has gotten an unsympathetic hearing, even in the heavily Democratic Congress. Still, Marco sees the AFL-CIO guidelines and union funds' increased use of ETIs and other strategies as signs of emerging "common sense investing." No longer should trustees follow investment advice when it winds up costing union jobs, he said. The days of anyone—whether it is Taft or overly cautious union trustees or Wall Street—separating beneficiaries' interests from unions' are over: "That's ancient history. Nobody thinks like that anymore."

NOTES

Portions of this chapter appeared in an article in the April 1993 issue of *Plan Sponsor* magazine.

1. Richard Blodgett, *Conflicts of Interest: Union Pension Fund Asset Management* (New York: The Twentieth Century Fund Inc., 1977), p. 5.
2. Stephen Clark, "Who's Afraid of the Lunchpail Trustee?" *Institutional Investor,* March 1990, p. 73.
3. Ibid. A Labor Department study, used by opponents of a 1990 proposal to put union trustees on corporate pension boards, showed the poor performance of multi-employer pension plans relative to their corporate counterparts. From 1977 to 1986, the study noted, the annual average return of Taft-Hartley funds was a full percentage point below that of non-union corporate plans, 10.8 percent versus 11.8 percent.

4. "Report to the AFL-CIO Executive Council by John T. Joyce, AFL-CIO Pension Investment Committee," Feb. 17, 1993.

5. *Pensions in Changing Capital Markets* (Washington, D.C.: American Federation of Labor and Congress of Industrial Organizations, 1993), p. 53.

6. Joel Chernoff and Christine Philip, *Pensions & Investments*, Feb. 22, 1993, p. 33.

7. *Pensions in Changing Capital Markets*, p. 57. Landon Butler, a trustee with the Multi-Employer Property Trust, said most Taft-Hartley assets in real estate are in ETIs.

8. *Pensions in Changing Capital Markets*, pp. 58–60, and Steve Hemmerick, "Fund Capitalizes on Union Label," *Pensions & Investments*, April 3, 1989, pp. 21–22.

9. "Union Targeted Real Estate Funds Were Top Performers Last Year," *Responsive Investing News*, April 27, 1992, pp. 1–2.

10. *Responsive Investing News*, April 27, 1992, pp. 1–2; *Pensions & Investments*, Feb. 22, 1993, p. 1; and *Pensions & Investments*, April 3, 1989, pp. 21–22.

11. "Management Trustee John Banister Speaks Out on J for Jobs," *ULLICO Bulletin*, Aug. 1993, p. 14.

12. *Pensions & Investments*, Feb. 22, 1993, p. 35.

13. "Dept. of Labor Encourages Federal Support for ETI Programs," *Responsive Investing News*, Nov. 23, 1992, p. 1.

14. David C. Waters, "Pension Funds May Join Push to Rebuild Cities" and "AFL-CIO Pension Investment Plan Builds on 30 Years of Experience," *Christian Science Monitor*, April 9, 1993, p. 8; and James B. Parks, "HIT, HUD Launch Funding Partnership," *AFL-CIO News*, June 28, 1993, p. 15. In the year before the partnership was announced HIT invested $68 million in affordable housing.

15. "Pension Funds May Join Push to Rebuild Cities," *Christian Science Monitor*, April 9, 1993. p. 8.

16. "Dept. of Labor Encourages Support for ETI Programs," *Responsive Investing News*, Nov. 23, 1992, p. 6; and "Second Semi-Annual Review: 1992," *Responsive Investing News*, Dec. 22, 1992, p. 1. Labor has actively voiced its concern. In 1992, AFL-CIO Secretary-Treasurer Thomas R. Donahue told the Infrastructure Committee that the government should "assist in the development of spending priorities, financing mechanisms and the appropriate role of the federal and local governments in financing such projects." The federation was interested in infrastructure projects if appropriate vehicles were found and participation were voluntary, he said. The implication was that the federal government should not only create and encourage opportunities for ETIs, but also guarantee some of the investments. Also, labor consultant Randy Barber wrote a report, circulated widely after Clinton's election, recommending government encouragement of pension funds that "provide clear, long-term benefits to the economy."

17. Peter D. Kinder, Steven D. Lydenberg, and Amy L. Domini, *The Social Investment Almanac* (New York: Henry Holt & Company, 1992), p. 678. Chapter on labor issues by David F. Sand.

18. Patricia Lamiell, "Shareholders, Angry over Poor Corporate Performance, Give CEOs the Boot," *Associated Press*, Dec. 31, 1992; and "SEC Rules Changes Please Large Investors," *Responsive Investing News*, Oct. 26, 1992, p. 3.

19. Peter D. Kinder, Steven D. Lydenberg, and Amy L. Domini, *Investing for Good* (New York: HarperBusiness, 1993), pp. 157–158; and "Who's Afraid of Lunch-pail Trustees," *Institutional Investor*, March 1990, p. 73.

20. *The Social Investment Almanac*, p. 677–678. Chapter on labor issues by David F. Sand.

21. *The Corporate Examiner*, Volume 21, Number 9, 1992; and "Review of Share-holder Proposals Presented by Labor Unions in 1993 (Preliminary)," D.F. King & Company, Inc.

22. Wendy Zellner, "OK, So He's Not Sam Walton," *Business Week*, March 16, 1992, p. 56.

23. Jason Zweig, "Proxy for Action," *Forbes*, June 27, 1992, p. 45; and "Wal-Mart Shareholders Confront Chinese Imports Resolution," *Responsive Investing News*, June 8, 1992, p. 1.

24. Thomas C. Hayes, "Wal-Mart Disputes Report on Labor," *The New York Times*, Dec. 24, 1992, pp. D-1, D-4.

25. Simon Billenness, "Franklin Research Dialogues with Wal-Mart," *Investing for a Better World*, April 15, 1993, p. 3.

26. "Shareholders Sue over SEC Decision at Wal-Mart," *Responsive Investing News*, July 6, 1992, p. 5; "Wal-Mart's Proxy is Held by Court For Race-Policy Data," *Wall Street Journal*, April 20, 1993, p. B6; and "Wal-Mart Ordered to Include Minority Hiring Resolution in Proxy," *Bloomberg Business News*, April 26, 1993.

27. "Sears Agrees to Adopt Measures on Prison-Made Chinese Imports," *Responsive Investing News*, March 30, 1992, p. 1.

28. "Labor Department letter on proxy voting by plan fiduciaries," from Alan D. Lebowitz, Deputy Assistant Secretary of Labor, to Helmuth Fandl, retirement board chairman, Avon Products, *BNA Pension Reporter*, Feb. 29, 1988, p. 392.

29. *Pensions in Changing Capital Markets*, p. 88.

30. Ibid., p. 77–78 and Appendix A. The study did not include figures on Taft-Hartley funds' ownership of foreign securities.

31. "Plumbers Seek to Tap into International Market," *Investment Management Weekly*, April 12, 1993, p. 4, and *Pensions in Changing Capital Markets*, p. 79.

32. *Pensions in Changing Capital Markets*, p. 78 and Appendix A.

33. Ibid., p. 87–88.

34. Remi Browne, "Investing Internationally for Taft-Hartley Funds," *The Journal of Investing*, Summer 1992, p. 47.

35. Ibid.

36. *Pensions in Changing Capital Markets*, pp. 92–93.

37. "AFL-CIO Debates Policy on Eastern Europe Investments," *Responsive Investing News*, May 27, 1991, p. 3.

38. *Pensions & Investments*, Feb. 22, 1993, p. 33.

5

Two Cheers for the Insurance Industry

In 1971, Donald S. MacNaughton, then president of Prudential Life Insurance Company of America, made a statement that at once stated the lofty ideals of his industry and threw down a challenge to it: "We have a responsibility to place our investment funds, and they are considerable, where they will inure to society's benefit. This is not inconsistent with maximum yield because, in determining yield, we must take into consideration the effect of our investments on society as a whole and over the long, not the short, haul."[1]

MacNaughton's statement came in the midst of a massive effort, involving 160 life insurance companies, to rebuild urban America. In 1967, after riots erupted from Watts to Detroit to Newark, the industry launched the five-year, $2 billion Urban Investment Program. According to an industry evaluation, the program created 116,000 housing units, 40,000 to 50,000 permanent jobs, 60 day care centers, 40 nursing homes, and two industrial parks, and made additional investments in hospitals and minority colleges and banks.[2]

In the two decades following the Urban Investment Program, members of the American Council of Life Insurance and Health Insurance Association of America poured more than $1 billion a year into social investments, according to industry estimates. In 1991, the last year for which complete figures are available, the industry invested $1.94 billion for social purposes (see Tables 5-1 and 5-2).[3]

Stanley G. Karson, director of the industry's Center for Corporate Public Involvement, said the record shows companies have done a "pretty

135

TABLE 5-1   Industry-Wide Investments for Socially Desirable Purposes (1991)*

Type	Amount
Housing, 1–4 family	$490
Housing, multi-family	96
Hospitals	3
Nursing homes	17
Clinics	15
Other health facilities	55
Commercial	91
Economic development	15
Arts/cultural	**
Social service	1
Environment	15
Minority financial institution deposits	985
Education	15
Other	146
TOTAL	$1,944

* Total reported by 197 life and health insurance companies that made social investments in 1991.

** Less than $500,000.

Source: 1992 Social Report, Center for Corporate Public Involvement.

amazing" job of fulfilling MacNaughton's credo: "[His] view is still the right view, one that we're striving for and one that we're trying to get more companies involved in."

For all the idealism of MacNaughton's statement, there is a strong element of self-interest in the industry's program. Executives are not shy in pointing out that by improving the lot of inner-city homeowners or upgrading medical treatment facilities, the industry is investing in *its* future. After all, better neighborhoods make better markets for insurance products.[4] In addition, as a state-regulated industry, the insurance community can keep the wolf of Community Reinvestment Act–style federal supervision from its door, in part, by making socially conscious investments.[5]

Whatever the motivation, the insurance industry's program—the only voluntary, industry-wide social investing plan—is intriguing. And it raises questions about what constitutes social investing and what the balance between fiduciary responsibility and public citizenship should be.

"Amazing" as the industry has been, critics raise questions about the companies' commitment and the effectiveness of their investments. Has this $1.5 trillion industry, with $140 billion in premiums a year, placed its assets

TABLE 5-2 Selected Types of Social Investments by Core Companies (in millions)*

	1991	1990	1989	1988	1987
Housing, 1–4 family	$222	$545	$444	$285	$787
Housing, multi-family	69	102	160	28	41
Hospitals	3	33	1	16	50
Nursing homes	8	12	2	10	2
Clinics	6	1	3	**	5
Other health facilities	1	3	4	21	60
Commercial	84	250	17	419	70
Economic development	9	14	17	33	55
Arts/culture	**	**	4	**	**
Social service	1	5	3	4	3
Environment	7	**	8	40	86
Minority deposits	985	673	64	555	473
Education	1	1	5	44	28
Other	136	74	97	36	30
TOTAL	$1,532	$1,717	$825	$1,491	$1,890

* Core companies are the 36 life and health insurers that made social investments in each year from 1987 to 1991.

** Less than $500,000.

Source: 1992 Social Report, Center for Corporate Public Involvement.

where they "inure to society's benefit," or is it overly concerned with the bottom line? Are companies in the game for the long haul? Is the industry, in fact, living up to MacNaughton's ideals?[6]

The complaints fall into two not unrelated categories: first, that the industry does not go far enough in making social investments and, second, that its claims about social investing go too far.

The Woodstock Institute, a Chicago advocacy and research center specializing in community investment, is in the first camp. In its balanced 1989 study *The Silent Partner: The Insurance Industry's Potential for Community Reinvestment,* the institute found that while individual companies take leading roles in advancing housing and economic development, the industry as a whole is not a major player in underserved markets. Said Woodstock vice president Kathy Tholin: "We like what they do. There's just not enough."

Indeed, the number of companies participating in social investing is low. In its 1989 study of social investing funded by the Ford Foundation, the Center for Corporate Public Involvement found that 102 of 157 companies surveyed, or 65 percent, did not make social investments. And in its 1992

Social Report, the center stated that 197 companies, of 397 that voluntarily provided data, made at least one social investment the prior year (see Table 5-1). The same report found that only 36 "core companies" made social investments each year from 1987 to 1991. There are more than 6,000 life and health insurance companies in the United States.[7]

The amount of money invested in social projects is far from consistent. The center's 1992 report found that social investing among the core companies dipped from $1.89 billion in 1987 to $825 million in 1989 before recovering to $1.53 billion in 1991 (see Table 5-2).[8]

In the second category of critics are those who believe that while insurance companies are overly cautious in making social investments, they are much too anxious to point out their merits.

The industry defines social investments as those that "would not otherwise be made under the company's customary lending standards, or in which social considerations played a substantial part in the investment decision."[9] The Center for Corporate Public Involvement, which encourages volunteerism, philanthropy, and social investing by life and health insurers, compiles the industry's list of social investments each year based on reports from contributing companies. The final tally depends largely on what the companies believe to be social investments, Karson said. "Social investing varies. It's in the eye of the beholder."

The flexible standards are necessary, he said, because of the differences in underwriting concerns and social investing history. Some companies, like Protective Life Insurance Company in Birmingham, Alabama, make social investments through their investment divisions, expecting to get conventional yields. Others, like Aetna Life & Casualty, provide subsidy or opportunity cost budgets to social investment offices to cover higher administrative costs and lower returns. A third group, including Metropolitan Life Insurance Company handles social investments through foundations; in the case of Met Life, it has made 35 percent of its assets, about $30 million, available for low-yielding program-related investments, expecting that the remainder of its portfolio will gain stronger returns. Furthermore, Karson said, a company in its first year of social investing might be held to a less strenuous standard than one in its 20th.

Using those criteria, the industry counted $985 million in deposits in minority-owned financial institutions in 1991. Those deposits, which comprised 50.7 percent of the industry's total social investment that year, are especially debatable. Mostly short-term deposits, they include some tax withholdings held in the banks for as little as one business day.

The insurance industry contends that the deposits are made for little or no yield, boost bank balances, accrue fees and interest income for the banks and may help persuade other corporations to make similar investments or deposits. As such, they are as important to the financial institutions as longer-term investments are to, say, community development corporations.

"These funds could be put into other very high-yielding investments. There are all kinds of places to put money where it's going to do very well," Karson said. "They could put it in Chase [Manhattan Bank] if they wanted to."

Critics said the deposits demonstrate the underlying passivity of the insurance industry's social investing and fail to show the longer-range vision MacNaughton spoke of. Frances Brody, a partner in the Connecticut consulting firm Brody & Weiser, said, "There is nothing wrong with that [the bank deposits], but this is not what I would call aggressive social investing."

In the area of housing, critics suggest the resolve is lacking. Investments in government-backed securities such as those issued by the Government National Mortgage Association (Ginnie Mae) have been routinely included in the industry's tally of social investing. The bonds are generally regarded as safe—indeed, conventional—investments. A. Steve Williams III, chairman of the industry's Socially Responsive Investing Technical Advisory Group (SRITAG), acknowledged that their inclusion allows "the magnitude of what has been done to be questioned by some people."

Furthermore, Edward Skloot, author of a 1989 report, *Social Investment and Corporations,* which had kind words for several insurers' programs, said that companies remove so much risk in their social investments—and still receive returns that fit the general profile of their portfolios—that often what they are doing is not making social investments at all. Rather they are making low-risk conventional investments dressed up as social investments. "The social investment business of the insurance industry is the most high touted," Skloot said, but ". . . I think there's a huge amount of public relations there."

Many insurers make housing investments through pooled investments or intermediaries, such as the Local Initiative Support Corporation (LISC), which act as go-betweens for investors and non-profit community development organizations. Twenty years ago, each concept was unproved. But over two decades, they have established themselves as generally safe investments. Besides, pools and intermediaries spread risk to such an extent, and over such a large group of investors (in the case of LISC, both national and local), that risk is relatively small. Yet insurers routinely rely on other institutions, notably religious funds and foundations, to take subordinate positions or lesser returns or to underwrite capital costs of investments, so they may realize a solid, low-risk return.

At the same time, Skloot said, insurers offer few discounts on rates, at least commensurate to their minimal risk. And many companies have benefited from such government breaks as the Low-Income Housing Tax Credit, which allowed investors to subtract from their yearly tax bills up to 9 percent of the purchase, construction, or rehab costs of low-income housing for 10 years. Combined with other provisions, returns have shot up to 20 percent.[10]

Speaking about the combination of safety and solid returns, Skloot said, "That's not real social investing as far as I'm concerned."

Williams agreed that the industry has not done enough social investing—not because it takes on too little risk on particular investments, but because insurers, uncertain what social investing is, seal themselves off from the concept completely.

The typical insurance executive believes that social investing must necessarily involve high costs, low return, and an inordinate amount of staff resources, he said. The industry's 1989 study bears him out. Among companies that made no social investments, 64 percent cited the long maturity they said is required for social investments compared with standard investments was an obstacle. Others cited the difficulty evaluating potential projects (64 percent) or borrowers (61 percent); monitoring projects once they began (61 percent); and high transaction costs associated with underwriting the projects (61 percent). Fifty-four percent said the small size of social investments compared with ordinary investments was a deterrent.[11]

For the last two years as chairman of the social investment group SRITAG, Williams has tried to break those perceptions. In a way, he said, the industry's efforts to spread social investing to smaller companies has been hampered by the success of larger firms. Companies such as Aetna and Met Life, which can make larger, higher-risk deals than their smaller counterparts, are held in the highest esteem. When others look at those examples, and see that they could not make the same deal, they shy away from social investing.

The smaller insurers must use different investment standards than the giants, Williams said. He pointed to his company, Protective Life. If it used the same criteria as the bigger firms, Williams said, it would make far less than the $7 million to $8 million a year in social investments it averages. So, instead, Protective Life concentrates on smaller-scale projects in its area of expertise (shopping center development) that offer market-rate returns. As a result, Protective Life has brought supermarkets, retailers, and restaurants, many of them minority owned, to inner-city areas that have lacked quality, competitive commercial areas; in most cases, the projects have been rejected by traditional lenders. Yes, the company's investments have made good money, Williams said, but more important, *the investments have been made*.

"We're not trying to give this money away. You want it to be used over and over again and achieve something that might not happen otherwise," Williams said.

He chided social investment advocates for being fixated, when it comes to private enterprise, with process (that is, how an investment is made, under what financial terms, and who makes a dollar from it) rather than progress (the real-life difference the investments make in people's lives). Those critics should recognize that, while companies can make investments in socially conscious endeavors, as private enterprises their overriding obligations are to their policyholders and shareholders, he said.

"There's no magical money here. You can't expose excessive amounts of capital to undue risk, because it's not *your* money. It belongs to other people, and why some people who are so carried away with social investing don't understand that I don't know."

One undeniable truth is that insurers have been unable to maintain the level of social investing during times of economic distress. During the period of high inflation in the late 1970s and recession in the early 1980s, the commitment to social investing flagged. Similarly, the late 1980s and early 1990s introduced financial uncertainty in the industry. The poor performance of commercial real estate, demise of junk bonds, and 1987 stock market collapse dimmed the investment picture. Fierce competition and corporate mismanagement led some companies to offer overly generous guaranteed insurance contracts to policyholders, leading to huge gaps between assets and commitments.

That led to a number of casualties. Mutual Benefit Life of New Jersey, a major player in the Northeast real estate market and the nation's 18th largest insurance company, was seized by state regulators in 1991, when it was crushed by bad investments. Others, including Executive Life of California, collapsed under the weight of junk bonds. And, at the surviving companies, social investment departments or budgets were axed.

"It's very much subject to the market," said Kirsten Moy, vice president of Equitable Real Estate Investment Management. Examples abound:

Moy was an executive with the social investment department of the Equitable Life Assurance Society of America, an industry leader in housing lending until the unit was scrapped in 1990. The company was the first insurer to back the Neighborhood Housing Service of America's secondary-mortgage market. And it was one of the first to invest in LISC's National Equity Fund and the Community Reinvestment Fund in Minneapolis, which issues bonds backed by loans to community development corporations. The Equitable closed the program not because its investments soured; its Community Mortgage Portfolio, which invested $90 million in 15 states, averaged nearly a 10 percent return, with a loss rate below industry norms for commercial mortgages.[12] But the company retreated into more predictable lines of business, and its only involvement in social investing today is the maintenance of $30 million to $40 million in holdover investments.

Before 1992, Aetna invested in a variety of areas, among them minority higher education and entrepreneurship, low-income housing, and inner-city commercial development. But as corporate earnings plunged from $1. billion in 1987 to $55 million in 1992, its once-generous social investment budget declined as well. From $40 million in investable assets and a $4.5 million opportunity cost budget, Aetna now has $15 million for investment and $2 million for opportunity costs.

The lower budget led to a reassessment of its social investment priorities. The company decided it would have more impact by dropping its former areas of lending. It now concentrates on issues close to the corporation's philanthropic efforts: immunizing pre-school children and involving more poor and working-class people in the health care system.

The New England, which had made social investments since the 1960s, ended the practice in 1991. Ironically, a group within the company had just revised The New England's social investment guidelines with an eye on expanding its low-income housing loans in Boston, its home base. But the recommendations were issued just as The New England's ratings were downgraded due to heavy real estate losses. The New England's financial stature has improved sufficiently to spark hopes it will resume social investments by early 1994.

Through the late 1980s, Connecticut Mutual Life made up to $2.5 million a year available for social investing. Its projects included low- and moderate-income housing development in Hartford and a hospital in Texas. Today, the company continues to carry several million dollars in social investments, but has not made a new loan in years.

"We just don't have the resources anymore," said Bertina Williams, corporate responsibility officer. Could the program be revived? "I don't know. I suppose yes, if we went back to the fat, happy days of the 1980s. But, if things keep going as they have been, the 1990s look grim and restricted."

Indeed, the industry looks leaner and meaner, as a number of developments could further diminish enthusiasm for social investing. Companies have turned toward higher-quality fixed-rate instruments, leading to lower portfolio yields. Tougher requirements from the Securities and Exchange Commission and the Financial Accounting Standards Board may require companies to increase capitalization, open up disclosure practices and revise accounting methods. The real estate debacle of the 1980s will continue to bedevil the industry because, even though the worst appears over, many companies carry a heavy load of bad debt. (Aetna's problem and restructured loans amounted to 15 percent of its portfolio in 1992, compared with 11 percent a year earlier). Besides, expiring commercial leases will keep the vacancy rates relatively high. And the resale market looks weak. And though many big companies endorse some form of managed competition, health insurers face an uncertain future as Congress considers the Clinton administration's health care reform package.[13]

The Socially Responsive Investing Technical Advisory Group is working against those trends. In 1992, it set its sights on increasing the size, number and quality of social investments. It called for studies on stimulating investments in existing intermediaries like LISC and the Neighborhood Housing Services of America; establishing a risk-sharing mechanism; creating a workable national secondary market; and starting new collaborative investment programs.

The committee's ideas were presented to a committee of life and health CEOs, which approved further study of two proposals: risk sharing and the secondary market. Many insurers like the latter concept, reflecting the view expressed in 1992 by the National Task Force on Affordable Housing, which included leaders from throughout the financial community.[14] The thinking in the insurance industry is that a current program, LISC's Local Initiatives Managed Asset Corporation, is not winning investment dollars because it is too narrowly based.

But Williams said any change in social investment trends will more likely come from individual companies with determined CEOs. "As far as an industry initiative, as an overall thing, no, it's just not going to happen now," he said. "The chances of getting big-time money is remote."

DEPOSITS IN MINORITY-OWNED FINANCIAL INSTITUTIONS

For most of the late 1980s and early 1990s, the backbone of the insurance industry's social investment program has been deposits in minority-owned financial institutions. With the exception of 1989, when only $64 million, or 7.8 percent, of the social investments reported by the 36 core companies was placed in minority banks, these deposits have accounted for from 25 percent (in 1987) to 64.3 percent (in 1991) of those companies' total.

For those who measure social investing by dollar-for-dollar results—by the number of homes built or businesses opened in poor neighborhoods, by the number of non-profit groups that receive loans or the immunization shots given to children—the insurance companies' banking program is not the place to look.

The deposits tend to be short term, most of them overnight federal tax withholdings, so banks receive only a fractional amount of the social benefit implied by industry figures. For every $10,000 made in one-day deposits, banks receive less than $1. The transfers are helpful to the banks, which receive fees and interest without doing any heavy lifting. But their value is more symbolic—as an expression of confidence in small and, in some case, struggling institutions—than of actual financial value.

Whatever their relative merits, such deposits are on the rise. In 1991, insurance companies placed $985 million with minority-owned banks, up

$312 million from the previous year.[15] Another increase is likely to be reported for 1992.

That surge is due in large measure to the banking policies of Prudential Insurance Company of America. To its credit, Prudential regards them as a minimal part of its social investment program. In fact, the deposits are supervised by Prudential's treasurer's office, not the social investment department.

"The way we view this is we, as a large company, have to do things related to banking," said James J. Straine, vice president and assistant treasurer for Prudential. "If they [the minority-owned banks] can meet our needs . . . I think it's a win-win program."

Prudential began its minority bank deposit program in the early 1970s. Its guidelines were revised in 1987 to reflect its changing needs. The company dropped its association with minority savings and loan institutions; those institutions were, like S&Ls in general, struggling financially and, as mom-and-pop operations, did not offer services suited to a large corporation. With the revisions, the company also opened a $35 million line of credit with a national network of minority banks.

The credit line, one of three parts of Prudential's current banking program, serves as a backup to the company's prime source of borrowing, the issuing of commercial paper. Straine said the credit line, which now stands just over $30 million, has not been tapped in its six years of existence. But, he said, it enables the 51 banks in the network to demonstrate to other potential commercial borrowers that they have the confidence of a major corporation. The banks also receive a commitment fee of 10 basis points, which amounted to $39,250 in 1992.

In the second part of the program, Prudential holds $100,000 certificates of deposit with each bank in the network, for a total of $5.1 million in 1992. The permanence of the deposits helps banks that need seed money, Straine said. A benefit for Prudential is that the deposits are fully protected by the Federal Deposit Insurance Corporation.

In 1992, the CDs gave Prudential a 4.8 percent return, or $239,461, according to a company memo written in January 1993. Because the yield exceeded the anticipated return of 3.8 percent, Prudential considered itself as making no "contribution equivalent," or concession, with those deposits.[16]

The final segment of the program consists of quarterly one-day deposits of federal tax withholdings. In terms of dollars deposited, it is Prudential's largest commitment—$876,753,114 in 1992.

The program works this way: At the end of each quarter, Prudential sends federal payroll tax and other withholdings to the lead bank in the network, City National Bank, which like Prudential is headquartered in Newark, New Jersey. City National distributes the money through the consortium. The banks can lend out the money overnight at the federal funds rate, which has hovered around 3 percent to 3.5 percent, before forwarding it to the U.S. Treasury Department. Using an overnight funds figure of 3.52 percent in 1992, Prudential estimated the banks' revenue through the tax withholdings at $84,553.[17]

In total, the company estimated a contribution equivalent of the entire banking program, including an $37,981 administrative fee to City National and 375 hours of staff time, at $192,244.

The Teacher Insurance and Annuity Association, the $61 billion retirement and insurance fund for employees of educational institutions, launched a minority banking program in 1992. Working with a 14-member network headed by Drexel National Bank of Chicago, TIAA places tax withholdings worth an estimated $125 million a year with the banks. The fund also purchased a $100,000 CD from each bank, for a total of $1.4 million. Ten percent of the earnings go to a scholarship fund of the National Bankers Association, a trade group of women- and minority-owned banks.

James Shirley, president and CEO of Drexel, said the formation of networks has enabled the minority banks to, in effect, act like bigger banks and compete for business they might not otherwise get. TIAA's confidence in the network, Shirley said, could help Drexel and its partners secure similar deposits of other large corporations.

Other insurers tend to have lesser relationships, if any at all, with minority banks. State Farm has a total of $300,000 in deposits in three black-owned banks in Los Angeles. Since the city erupted in violence in 1992 after the verdicts in the first Rodney King trial, the company has considered making a larger commitment.

It is ironing out details with Rebuild L.A., the private redevelopment organization formerly headed by one-time baseball commissioner Peter Ueberroth. A State Farm spokesman said any increase in deposits would be linked to economic development in underprivileged minority neighborhoods like South Central Los Angeles.

HOUSING

Housing investment is the insurance industry's No. 2 area of social investing. The numbers show, however, that investing in this area has dropped substantially since 1987. Among the 36 core companies, the amount allocated to single- and multi-family housing fell from $828 million to $291 million. The industry overall invested $556 million in housing in 1991, or 28.6 percent of the total.[18]

Allstate Insurance Company has been among the more active investors in affordable housing. Since 1977, the company has allocated $18 million to secondary market programs operated by Neighborhood Housing Services of America.

Under one program, to which Allstate's investment division has committed $8 million, local Neighborhood Housing Services affiliates in more than 140 cities provide home repair loans for low- and moderate-income borrowers, generally in areas ignored by banks and other conventional lenders. The local groups bundle the below-market loans for sale to NHSA, which in turn sells them on the secondary market. (A raft of other social investors have taken part in the NHSA's home purchase and fix-up loan programs. They include Prudential, with a $12.5 million commitment; Equitable, $10 million; Met Life, $5 million; Aetna, $4 million; and Mutual Benefit, $1 million.) At the local level, Allstate has also invested in the NHS affiliate in Chicago and other cities in which it has operations. And it has donated money and management consulting to those affiliates.[19]

Allstate has also pledged $10 million to a secondary market fund designed to help local governments accelerate the pace of affordable housing loans. Under this plan, Allstate agreed to buy notes backed by housing loans purchased by local governments. Those governments were to use Allstate's investment to meet their housing and community development needs.

But the concept jumped ahead of demand. Just one government—the city of St. Paul, Minnesota, in 1990—has participated and only $800,000 million of the allocation has been used. Explained Michael Balmuth, the NHSA's senior vice president, "Basically what happened was the level of funding and the level of capacity at the local governments wasn't there."

The program was begun, Balmuth said, because of the NHSA's perception that many local government loan funds appeared to be "revolving very slowly." The NHSA thought having a secondary market would speed the process, making more money available more quickly. But it found that, in many cases, local government housing programs were not as well-serviced and -documented as the NHSA required. And, it seemed, local and county housing agencies were unable to handle the unfamiliar lending vehicle. So, despite receiving numerous inquiries, the program made only one commitment. A secondary market program operated by the Federal National Mortgage Association (Fannie Mae) has met similar results.

Balmuth said the NHSA is working with Allstate to keep the program available, should a market develop for it or should it be redesigned to meet demand. The company may also agree to shift some of its $10 million allocation into the NHSA's other lending programs, he said.

In 1992, the Metropolitan Life Foundation made $7.5 million in program-related investments in emergency and low-income housing. That included a $1 million investment in the Delaware Valley Community Reinvestment Fund that was described as giving a "tremendous boost to an innovative organization that was benefiting its community and [helping] test and advance a model for lending programs throughout the country."[20]

One of the premier community loan funds in the country, Delaware Valley has financed about 2,000 units of housing in the Philadelphia-Camden, New Jersey, area in its first seven years of existence—all without a single default on any of its loans. Delaware Valley used the investment to capitalize its revolving loan fund for affordable housing development.

"The Met Life loan is significant because I feel they made an investment that they would regard as unsecured," said Jeremy Nowak, Delaware Valley's executive director.

The loan also may have clinched investments by other institutions in the fund—enabling it to nearly double in size, to $12 million, in one year, Nowak said. Within months of Met Life's loan, the Ford Foundation came through with a $2 million program-related investment (and a smaller equity grant). And, following the favorable coverage in the local press, some Philadelphia-area insurance companies followed with investments of their own.

Met Life's six-year loan initially requires payment of interest only, with the principal not due until four quarterly payments in the final year. It carries a slightly higher price than Delaware Valley's typical financing. The fund pays individual and institutional investors, primarily religious organizations, returns well below market rates; the Hitachi Foundation, for example, has made a 3.5 percent loan. In turn, Delaware Valley lends to homeowners rates of about 7 percent. The spread is used to finance operations. Met Life's loan carries a floating rate that follows the prime, with a floor of 5.5 percent and a ceiling of 7 percent. That makes the margin tighter, Nowak said.

But the loan also had a provision enabling Delaware Valley to draw down the loan as it needed financing for specific projects. That enabled Delaware Valley to reduce costs (since it did not have to pay interest on money not borrowed) and Met Life to keep the unused portion of the loan in higher-yielding investments.

COMMERCIAL AND ECONOMIC DEVELOPMENT

For Protective Life Insurance Company, its commercial social investments fold neatly into its overall portfolio. The $4 billion, shareholder-owned company has 33 percent of its portfolio in real estate, nearly double the industry average, with the highest concentration in discount shopping centers. The company tries to limit its risk by securing long-term leases and, until the late

1980s real estate slump, developed properties with the intention of reselling them within four years.

Protective Life, which made its first social investment in 1973, has stepped up its program since 1989. In the last four years, it has made 11 social investments in the Sunbelt totaling $29 million. Eight loans went to developments in minority neighborhoods, three others to minority-owned enterprises.

Williams, the chairman of the industry's social investing committee and Protective Life's senior vice president for investments, said the loans are examples of how social investing can be market grade, have limited risk, *and* make a difference in a community: "We think we can do more good by making less risky deals."

In 1992, one of its loans built Heritage Town Center, an 84,000-square-foot shopping center in its hometown of Birmingham. The center serves a mixed-income minority neighborhood that, like many urban areas, lacked adequate shopping. Heritage Town Center contains a supermarket, pharmacy, discount store, and furniture rental store as well as Alabama's first black-owned McDonald's franchise and a minority-owned Baskin Robbins ice cream shop. It also provides scores of full- and part-time jobs for minority neighborhood residents.

Protective Life stepped forward when the center's developer could not get financing from another source. The insurer made a $4.8 million loan, covering 100 percent of development costs, at 9.75 percent interest, market rate at the time of the loan. The company also took an equity position, receiving 50 percent of income after debt service and expenses. "It kicked our yield up a lot higher than 9.75 percent," Williams said.

Williams said the company also took other measures to safeguard its investment. It signed up a regional grocery store chain as one of the anchor tenants, with a 20-year lease. A regional pharmacy chain and the two discounters became the other anchors, with 10-year leases. Together, leases from those stores account for 124 percent of the loan. The only real concession made was in the loan-to-value ratio, which was 84 percent.

"It's not a bad situation to be in," Williams said. "We ended up with a very good investment."

Prudential helped fill a void in Newark in 1990 by lending $8.5 million for the development of a shopping center in the Central Ward, epicenter of the 1967 rioting.

An interesting wrinkle is that the shopping center is a joint venture between a non-profit organization, the New Community Corporation, and Supermarkets General Corporation, parent company of the Pathmark chain. New Community, which developed the center, has a two-thirds ownership, with Supermarkets General holding the remainder.[21]

Prudential's investment, a 20-year 10 percent loan, was part of a $13 million financing package that included a federal Urban Development Action Grant, a 4 percent loan from the state Local Development Financing Fund, and foundation grants.

Gaining the loan from Prudential was a complex process that involved its social investment, underwriting, and capital market divisions, the latter brought in after Supermarkets General was the subject of a leveraged buyout during the negotiations, said Raymond M. Codey, New Community's development director. Still, the negotiations, which were as much about each department meeting its needs as about financing the shopping center, were wrapped up in about six months.

The result is a shopping center with a 45,000-square-foot Pathways store, pharmacy, restaurants and a print shop. Codey said it has had an enormous positive impact on the neighborhood. According to a Columbia University estimate, the supermarket gives residents, who previously had to travel long distances to suburban stores or pay high prices at local bodegas, 38 percent more purchasing power. The center also created more than 200 jobs.

In the fiscal year that ended in February 1993, the supermarket had $32 million in gross revenues and realized profits of $1.2 million. New Community uses its revenue to help finance other community service ventures—including seven day care centers (one for HIV-infected infants), an alternative school, a 180-bed nursing home, and two employment centers. For Supermarkets General, which had struggled financially and watched two key rival chains take advantage of its inability to expand, the Newark store is a profitable venture in an area virtually free from competition.

The center has been visited by the mayors of Memphis and Baltimore and by executives of other supermarket chains, all hoping to see if its operations could be duplicated. It has also been used as a case study by the Food Marketing Institute and called the best urban supermarket in the country in a report by the U.S. Department of Agriculture.

"To say that it has been successful is an understatement," Codey said.

Principal Financial Group, a $38 billion company in Des Moines, Iowa, is one of the industry leaders in social investing, with a $5.5 million annual budget. Its goal, a company spokesman said, is to "do what we can to make the state commercially more attractive, more socially viable [and] more economically viable," and create a quality of life that will enable it to better attract and retain employees.

To further those interests, Principal Financial Group five years ago invested $1.5 million in the Iowa Venture Capital Fund, a $15 million pool whose limited partners include the Iowa Public Employees Retirement System and Maytag. At least two-thirds of the resources are used to develop new instate businesses. So far, those businesses have included a bagel baker and distributor, an agriculture-related trailer company, and a combination laundro-mat-and-bar franchise. Principal Financial has received only a 5 percent return on its investment—below market return but in line with its expectations for the fund.

Across the industry, commercial and economic development accounted for $106 million, or 5.5 percent, of social investing in 1991.[22]

HEALTH

The insurance industry's fourth-largest concentration of social investments is in the field of health care. In 1991, insurers devoted $90 million, or 4.6 percent of total social investments, to hospitals, nursing homes, clinics and other health facilities.[23]

One of the more innovative health-related programs was made through a partnership with the National Cooperative Bank, a Washington-based niche market financier for cooperative enterprises, such as day care centers, tenant unions and community development corporations. Four large insurers—Equitable, Met Life, Prudential, and Aetna—made $15 million available through NCB to finance the construction and expansion of community health care centers.

Marsha Krassner, vice president-manager for NCB, said the three-year-old program has three primary financial benefits. First, NCB is able to increase its liquidity and sell off some of the risk in the loans. It also receives 10 percent of the loan amount to administer the loan and provide technical assistance to the community health providers. Second, the insurance companies gained access to a market in which they would have been unlikely to make direct deals and add to their social investment portfolios without having to do a lot of legwork. ("We can be their eyes and ears," Krassner said.) They get a return slightly above the five-year Treasury rate, currently around 6 percent. And, finally, the centers get loans for 10-year terms and low rates generally available from local and regional banks.

By the spring of 1993, three years after the program began, the pool had made seven loan commitments to centers from Boston to Phoenix, releasing money to five. One, a $1.4 million loan, went in 1992 to the Great Brook Valley Health Center in Worcester, Massachusetts, which provides primary health care—ranging from physical exams and family planning to dental care and mental health services—for 40,000 clients a year. The loan helped the center build a $3.6 million facility across from the housing project where it had been located in cramped quarters for almost two decades.

At first, operating on the theory that local development ought to be financed locally, the center tried to form a consortium of local banks to finance the new building. Such a network would have spread the risk, said

Zoila Torres Feldman, Great Brook Valley's executive director, but the banks, like many in the Northeast, were in such financial distress that "they did not seem very excited about it." Through the NCB program, the center received a 10-year loan with a fixed rate of 7.6 percent over five years. At that point, the rate will be repriced according to the five-year index.

With the loan and grants from local corporations and the federal government, Great Brook Valley opened a building that is entirely accessible to the handicapped, tripled the number of examining rooms to 18, and provides private office space for its physicians. More important, the physical improvements enabled the center to concentrate on caring for its clients, most of whom are poor blacks, Hispanics, or Southeast Asians and nearly 80 percent of whom are uninsured or on Medicaid, Torres Feldman said.

As much of a boon as the new facility has been to Great Brook Valley, it is also a burden. Torres Feldman said the center is "running a pretty tight budget" to pay off the loan, a financial condition that points out the risk that accompanies the reward in many social investments.

NOTES

1. *Social Investing in the Life and Health Industry* (Washington, D.C.: Center for Corporate Public Involvement, 1989), p. 11.
2. Josh Hoyt and Maria Choca, *The Silent Partner: The Life and Health Insurance Industry's Potential for Community Reinvestment* (Chicago: Woodstock Institute, 1989), p. 16.
3. *1992 Social Report* (Washington, D.C.: Center for Corporate Public Involvement, 1993), p. 8.
4. An Allstate Insurance Company spokesman said: "Being a major insurer, we have a vested interest in improving these neighborhoods. If you improve the housing stock and bring some life back into these communities, there's a better market for insurance products as well as a lower claim experience." ("Allstate: A Full Partner in Neighborhood Revitalization," *Response,* July 1992, p. 5.)
5. Sentiment for federal regulation is strong in some quarters. A report on the 1992 Conference on Community Investment and Renewal, sponsored by the Interfaith Center for Corporate Responsibility and the Evangelical Churches in America, stated: "Community reinvestment is demonstrably profitable, yet experience demonstrates that a combined carrot-and-stick approach is necessary to make it happen. Unfortunately, the present level of regulatory enforcement has not created a significant move toward community reinvestment. The Community Reinvestment Act should be extended to the insurance industry." Two pending bills in the U.S. House would require insurers to report in which neighborhoods they sell automobile and home insurance. (Ana Puga, "Lawmakers Are at Odds on Redlining," *Boston Globe,* Sept. 21, 1993, p. 18.)
6. *Standard & Poor's Industry Report,* Dec. 3, 1992.

7. *Social Investing,* p. 5; and *1992 Social Report,* p. 8.
8. *1992 Social Report,* p. 8.
9. *Social Investing,* p. 9.
10. Edward Skloot, *Social Investment and Corporations* (Washington, D.C.: Council on Foundations, 1989), p. 27.
11. *Social Investing,* pp. 55–56.
12. Bob Howard, "Investors Looking for Broader Returns in the 1990s," *Los Angeles Business Journal,* Jan. 25–31, 1992.
13. Steven M. Yeary, *Value Line Investment Survey,* Feb. 5, 1993, p. 1196; and *Standard & Poor's Stock Report Index,* Jan. 19, 1993.
14. "Joining Forces to Remedy the Shortage of Low-Income Housing," *Response,* July 1992, p. 4; and "After Releasing Report, Housing Task Force May Regroup as Permanent Body," *Responsive Investing News,* June 22, 1992, p. 5.
15. *1992 Social Report,* p. 12.
16. "1992 Minority Banking Program Contribution Equivalent Report," Prudential Insurance Company.
17. Ibid.
18. *1992 Social Report,* p. 12.
19. "Allstate: A Full Partner in Neighborhood Revitalization," *Response,* July 1992, p. 5; and Neighborhood Housing Services of America, Inc., 1993 report on programs.
20. Brody & Weiser, *Program Related Investment Primer* (Washington, D.C.: Council on Foundations, 1993), p. 50.
21. "Prudential Investment Brings Supermarket to Newark's Inner City," *Response,* March 1992, p. 14.
22. *1992 Social Report,* p. 12.
23. Ibid.

6

The Campuses:
Hotbeds of Social Rest

In May 1993, negotiators representing South Africa's main political factions agreed to hold the nation's first one-person, one-vote election on April 27, 1994, thus opening democracy for the first time to all racial groups.

The accord caused Cyril Ramaphosa, secretary general for the African National Congress (ANC), to declare: "We have taken a really gigantic step for millions of people in our country. . . . [W]e are poised to take dramatic steps forward to ensure we reach a solution to this country's problems in a short time."[1]

Within months, Ramaphosa was proved correct. In September, the white Parliament created the Transitional Executive Council, which gave blacks a role in governing the country; ANC leader Nelson Mandela urged the end of sanctions against the country; and South Africa was admitted into the United Nations. And, in October, Mandela and President F.W. deKlerk were chosen for the Nobel Peace Prize for their leadership in guiding their racially divided nation closer to the end of apartheid.[2]

Thousands of miles away, American college and university officials have watched the events in South Africa closely. Academic institutions placed South Africa at the forefront of the nation's political consciousness in the 1970s and 1980s, albeit reluctantly, by severing investment ties with South Africa and acting as the center for anti-apartheid activism (see Table 6-1). Today, years after South Africa ceased to be a burning issue on campus, investment officials must decide how to deal with the issue. Are they poised to take a dramatic step of their own? Yes and no.

153

TABLE 6-1   Institutions Ranked by Market Value of Endowment Assets*

Institution	Endowment Assets (In thousands)
1. Harvard University	$5,118,118
2. University of Texas System **	3,655,151
3. Princeton University	3,003,122
4. Yale University	2,833,100
5. Stanford University	2,428,491
6. Columbia University	1,683,014
7. Emory University	1,658,216
8. Massachusetts Institute of Technology	1,589,261
9. Washington University	1,533,445
10. Texas A&M University System **	1,483,179

* As of June 30, 1992, with exception of Stanford University, for which figures of April 30, 1992, are cited.

** Permanent University Fund serves the University of Texas and Texas A&M University systems, with two-thirds of income going to the former, one-third to the latter.

Source: NACUBO Endowment Study, 1992, by the National Association of College and University Business Officers.

Less than a month after Mandela's appeal in September for reinvestment in his country, a number of schools, including Wesleyan and Notre Dame, ended or were considering ending their investment bans. The University of Connecticut's trustees decided to rescind the school's investment ban five minutes after the proposal was made.[3]

But most colleges and universities have responded more cautiously. Fearful of stirring docile students, or of returning to South Africa before a peaceful transition of power is made, they are waiting until a full transition to majority rule is completed.

The Investor Responsibility Resource Center (IRRC) in September published the results of a survey of nearly 400 colleges in which, of 194 with investment guidelines on South Africa, only 17 had plans to change them.[4] "We certainly haven't gotten a lot of colleges and universities that are eager to jump back into the issue, even though Nelson Mandela said, 'Please do,' " said Carolyn Mathiasen, director of the IRRC's social issues service. "The campuses went through hell on this issue and they don't want to do it again."

SCREENS AND DIVESTMENT

Given the length of time apartheid was in existence, it was a long time before American colleges "went through hell." South Africa's racial caste system existed in various forms for centuries before the National Party, after its electoral victory in 1948, made it official policy. The party's win launched a modern South Africa, one built on the systematic denial of rights by the white minority to the majority population, blacks, "Coloureds," and Indians. The new parliament quickly approved or amended the "three pillars of apartheid:" the Population Registration Act (which required residents to record their race with the government); Group Areas Act (which segregated the races and relegated blacks to a small percentage of the land); and the Mixed Marriages Act (which banned interracial marriages). New laws also required non-whites to carry passes, which gave white authorities further control over where they lived, traveled, and worked.

After the Sharpeville massacre in 1960, in which 69 blacks were gunned down by police during what began as a peaceful demonstration against the pass law, all forms of opposition were silenced. Groups including the ANC and its offshoot, the Pan-Africanist Congress, were banned and their leaders and thousands of followers imprisoned. Security forces given free reign to enforce the racial policy, often did so brutally, as during the Soweto uprising of 1976, in which hundreds of blacks were killed.[5]

From 1948 to the early 1970s, as South Africa's progressively heavy-handed tactics made it an international pariah, closed off from diplomatic, economic, political and cultural relations, U.S. colleges and universities were only peripherally engaged in the issue. When religious institutional investors began introducing resolutions on South Africa, Namibia, Rhodesia (now Zimbabwe), and the then Portuguese Angola, a few schools formed committees to review proxy resolutions. But it took nearly three decades after the National Party came to power—and after the Soweto rioting and after the death of Steven Biko, the black consciousness leader, at the hands of police—before apartheid become a major issue on U.S. campuses.[6]

And even then, colleges acted in a limited fashion—rarely engaging in dialogues with corporations as shareholder activists, less often turning down grants from tainted companies, almost never sponsoring resolutions. Their primary involvement was to sell off assets in companies tied to South Africa.

The mechanism allowing them to divest came into being in 1977, when the Reverend Leon Sullivan, a black Baptist minister from Philadelphia who sat on General Motors' board of trustees (he was appointed in 1970 after Campaign GM), devised guidelines for investment in South Africa. Known as the Sullivan Principles for Fair Employment in South Africa, the rules urged American corporations to desegregate their operations, train and promote blacks, and press for better health care, housing and education. Sullivan hired the consulting firm Arthur D. Little Inc. to monitor the companies' compliance with the code. Those report cards gave investors, for the first time, a way to measure whether their money was contributing to the betterment of life in South Africa or tacitly supporting apartheid.

In 1977, Hampshire College in western Massachusetts became the nation's first to divest its holdings in South Africa. It was followed by two neighboring schools, Smith College and the University of Massachusetts at Amherst.[7]

In 1978, Harvard University adopted more cautious guidelines calling for a case-by-case review of its holdings in companies doing business in South Africa. The policy, drafted by its Advisory Committee on Social Responsibility—a panel of students, faculty and administrators—and later approved by the school's president, Derek Bok, contained four main characteristics. The code ruled out investments in corporations that did most of their business in South Africa, not a difficult task given that Harvard, like most U.S. universities at the time, held a negligible amount of international stocks. In addition, it prohibited investments in banks making loans to the South African government, called on the university to encourage companies to either improve the lives of black residents by following general outlines resembling the Sullivan code or get out of South Africa entirely, and asked the university, if all else failed, to divest.

Harvard said it would consider divestment when a company failed to "implement reasonable ethical standards," when its efforts to change corporate behavior were unsuccessful, and "where there is clearly no hope of improvement. The philosophical basis for this aspect of the policy is that it is far more appropriate to try to persuade management to abandon unethical practices than to simply dissociate itself from the company. Such dissociation leaves the institution with no influence whatsoever."[8]

Many other schools divested in the late 1970s, or, like Lehigh University, adopted proxy voting guidelines on issues concerning South Africa. But often in the 1980s, interest in the issue ebbed and flowed. In the early 1980s concern was at a low ebb. According to a 1989 IRRC study, four schools adopted new investment restrictions from 1980 to 1983. Another, the University of Michigan, updated a policy its board of regents adopted in 1978, divesting of all stocks except those of companies headquartered in or employing more then 500 people in Michigan.[9]

By the mid-1980s, as conditions in South Africa worsened and American interest groups organized, apartheid became the foremost moral and political issue on campus. Mock shantytowns, symbolizing the oppression of South African blacks, sprung up on quadrangles. The campus green at Dartmouth College became a well-known battleground, as anti-apartheid activists built a shantytown that was destroyed by a group of conservative students and later rebuilt. At Colorado College, as elsewhere, students interrupted a trustees' meeting to urge the board to divest. The public and media attention given to student activities fueled the anti-apartheid movement across the country.

Off campus, protests outside the South African embassy in Washington led to hundreds of arrests and put the issue on the front pages of newspapers and the covers of news magazines. Sullivan said he would abandon his code if no progress toward racial equality was made in South Africa. More than 175 cities, counties, and states adopted divestment policies. And, finally, in 1986, Congress approved trade sanctions against South Africa, overriding the veto of President Reagan.

The "veritable crescendo" over South Africa led the Common Fund, a pooled-asset fund that is the nation's largest manager of college endowment money, to create the South Africa Free Equity Fund in 1986, said Daniel A. Wingerd, vice president for investor relations. The pool proved instantly popular with schools that needed a vehicle that matched their new-found anti-apartheid convictions. In its first six months, a dozen schools placed $43 million in the fund; at its peak, it topped $490 million.

The pressure led even more colleges to divest, either partially or totally. For example, in 1985, the University of Virginia began reviewing stocks on a case-by-case basis. Under the policy, which stated that the university may "decide to disassociate from a particular company because the nature of that company's activities in South Africa is judged to involve the support of the apartheid system," investments in companies that had not signed the Sullivan Principles, received poor ratings from Arthur D. Little, or whose primary business was in South Africa were to be reviewed by an advisory committee and reported to the governing board. Within four years, the school divested itself of $400,000 in South Africa–related stocks and retained $21 million.[10]

A number of schools with divestment plans revised them. Harvard put more teeth in its policy, effectively barring investments in companies others than those listed as Category I ("making good progress") or Category II ("making progress") in the Sullivan Principles. The school's Corporate Committee on Shareholder Responsibility, the investment committee of the board of trustees, voted to divest in companies that "persist in selling significant quantities of an important good or service used in the direct enforcement of apartheid." The policy also required the school to monitor companies making or selling goods of strategic importance—those in the oil, computer, automotive, and mining industries—"with the expectation that [those companies] will be willing and able to achieve the highest Sullivan rating, and to demonstrate that its presence results in more good than harm within South Africa."

In the first 18 months of the policy, Harvard divested itself of $158.9 million in South Africa–related securities, including those of Ford and Exxon. The middle-of-the-road policy won the school few admirers in Cambridge, where demonstrations and newspaper columns repeatedly demanded complete divestment; in 1986, a plane flew over commencement with a banner reading, "Divest now."[11]

Smith College, which had an informal policy of selective divestment since 1977, formalized and strengthened the program in 1986. First, it divested of companies that did not achieve Category I or II. Then it gave its managers until 1988 to dump securities of companies in South Africa. Few securities were actually sold, however, since many corporations that had operations in South Africa began divesting from the country in the mid-1980s. (From 1984 to 1990, 214 American companies sold or closed their South African operations, dropping the total to 106; it later fell to less than 50.)[12]

In the late 1980s, few schools instituted new restrictions or tightened existing ones. That was due in part to the disintegration of the student movement, a victim of its earlier successes. Calling on schools that had already divested of companies with direct operations in South Africa to end investments in firms with non-equity ties in South Africa (licensing, franchise, and other agreements) didn't have the pizzazz of calling the trustees racist. Student activists also fell prey to bickering between black and white leaders over tactics and disagreement over their central mission.[13] By the time Sullivan, in 1987, removed his name from his principles, in the conviction they could not help bring an end to apartheid, it was as if an unheard tree had fallen in the woods. Fewer and fewer students took up the cause. Said Richard Smith, vice president for finance at Earlham College in Richmond, Indiana, "South Africa disappeared from student consciousness."

The lack of action by schools was also partly due to developments in South Africa. DeKlerk's election as president in 1989 ushered in a relatively enlightened era of white leadership. During his tenure, many onerous apartheid laws, the Group Areas Act and Population Registration Act among them, were lifted; restrictions were lifted on anti-apartheid groups, including the banned African National Congress; Mandela was released from prison after 27 years; the government, the ANC, and the Inkatha Freedom Party, the ANC's putative rival for black leadership, announced a peace agreement; and the Convention for a Democratic South Africa (CODESA), the all-party negotiating council, began laying the groundwork for a transitional government. In this atmosphere, President Bush lifted U.S. sanctions against South Africa.[14]

The combination of apathy at home and action abroad eased pressure on college trustees. From 1989 to 1992, fewer schools, among them Wesleyan, where one student takeover of a building resulted in 50 arrests, and Connecticut College, enacted partial or total investment restrictions. Others, such as Dartmouth College and Virginia, upgraded their policies, each opting for full divestment. In Virginia's case, the school's board of governors and, later, the state legislature approved divestment resolutions in 1990 after L. Douglas Wilder, a divestment proponent, became the first black to be elected governor of a state since Reconstruction.

At the end of this divestment period, the pool of socially screened investments by colleges and universities was vast. In 1989, according to the Council on Economic Priorities, 144 schools placed restrictions on $34.6 billion in holdings, nearly 40 percent of endowment assets at the time. Also in 1989, the IRRC found that 77 of 164 North American colleges surveyed had policies restricting South Africa–related investments. Three years later, an IRRC follow-up study of 50 of the largest of those schools showed that all had kept or toughened their policies.[15]

For several years, Jean Mayer, the longtime president of Tufts University, encouraged other schools to reinvest in South Africa. His arguments had little apparent effect, on his campus or elsewhere. As CODESA opened in 1991, Mayer said that South Africa had made enough progress toward democracy to warrant new investment. And he warned that violence, fueled by unemployment levels that reached 30 percent, would be a greater threat to negotiations than reinvestment. "Unless there is reinvestment soon, then all the political progress is going to be wiped out," Mayer told *The New York Times*.[16] Tufts officials reportedly made repeated overtures to other schools, seeking partners in an open reinvestment campaign, but got no takers.

After Mandela's 1993 call for Western institutions to lift sanctions, though, many schools jumped at the chance to reinvest. Wesleyan voted within a week of the announcement to allow managers to invest the $325 million endowment with companies doing business in South Africa. Other colleges quickly voted to reinvest or were considering doing so. They included Connecticut College, Smith College, Trinity College, the State University of New York in Stony Brook, University of Hartford, and the universities of Illinois, Vermont, and Washington.[17]

In 1991 and 1992, prior to Mandela's request for sanctions to be rescinded, two divested schools publicly identified when they would reinvest in South Africa: Clark University in Worcester, Massachusetts, and Oberlin College.

Clark voted to wait until the Transitional Executive Council was formed. Oberlin worried that standard wasn't enough. Its trustees, who in 1987 banned investment in companies with more than 25 employees in South Africa, voted for a two-step transition. First, they said, Oberlin could invest in companies rated highly under the Statement of Principles or State Department Fair Labor Standards when the United States recognized the transitional government. And second, when free and fair elections are held for a permanent government, the school will remove all restrictions.[18]

Also before Mandela's plea, other colleges ended their divestment policies silently. Six schools pulled nearly $47 million in holdings from the Common Fund's South Africa–free equity accounts in the year ended in June 1993. All of the schools—which the Common Fund's Wingerd described as small, private liberal arts colleges—changed their South Africa policies, but none made the information public.[19] When some were asked by the Common Fund if the information could be released, the schools agreed—but only if the other schools were named as well, Wingerd said.

While for these schools change appeared inevitable in South Africa, for others progress is by no means assured. At a spring 1993 meeting of the College and University Research Committee on South Africa, schools affiliated with the IRRC, officials expressed uncertainty about what would be a safe time, politically and financially, to reinvest in South Africa.

"Their feeling was 'It's sort of hands-off,' " said Jennifer Kibbe, a former IRRC senior analyst who wrote two studies on college divestment. Although they hoped the political situation in South Africa would change soon, "they feel like some colleges were stung pretty badly. . . . It was a difficult issue for them."

The fear of awakening the dormant campuses is a key consideration. A. Reid Weedon Jr., who for 17 years has monitored compliance with the Statement of Principles for Arthur D. Little, said schools worry about unfavorable reaction from students if they were to break ranks. Mostly they are worrying about a past time, the mid-1980s, when feelings on the issue were strong. Still, gauging student reaction is a tricky business. Even after Mandela's call for reinvestment, leaders of black student groups at Wesleyan had two immediate reactions to the university's plan to end restrictions: disappointment that they had not been consulted beforehand and concern that the school was moving too quickly.[20]

Aside from campus politics, some trustees are skittish about the potential for violence in South Africa. They don't want to have lifted investment restrictions, only to have to reimpose them if bloodshed or white recalcitrance threatens the move to black majority rule. There are good reasons for concern. More than 11,000 South Africans have fallen victim to violence since 1990, among them the 50 victims of the 1992 Boipatong massacre and Chris Hani, a charismatic black leader killed by white extremists. The possibility of further violence is strong.[21]

If a peaceful transfer of power is made, however, colleges are going to have to act fast, the IRRC's Mathiasen said. More than two dozen U.S. companies—sensing the move toward full democracy and normal economic relations, and to protect their products—have already moved into South Africa since 1991. Lotus Development and Microsoft were among the first. And as larger corporations move in, Mathiasen said, college trustees will be faced with the choice of changing their policies or selling off large segments of their portfolios. Clearly, she said, they will vote to reinvest.[22]

When reinvestment occurs, it may be considered a triumph for the colleges and universities that divested. Their actions, after prodding from student activists, helped move American public opinion.

"The college campuses helped lead the way in the sense that it [the divestment movement] was very visible, very public, and very strong in its demands," said Richard Knight, a research associate with the American Committee on Africa. "It was very important in setting up the whole mood in this country."

Kibbe said it would be "incredibly hard to quantify" the effect of divestment in South Africa, but "I think there was a political impact, because when a Harvard or a Columbia said, 'We're going to do this because we don't agree with what's going on in South Africa,' that was news." Smaller schools that divested helped keep the issue in the headlines and rally American opinion, she added. Even Pretoria has implicitly recognized the importance of campus divestment; since 1990, the South African consulate wooed some of the largest universities ("names you would recognize") to persuade them to reverse their policies, Kibbe said. Any reversal, especially by a large school, would have been a coup for the government.

Critics of divestment contend that colleges are not entitled to congratulations, for they failed to take the moral high ground on apartheid. Many, Harvard among them, continued to receive research grants from corporations in which they refused to invest, justifying their acceptance of grants by saying their passive role as a grant recipient was independent of their active role as an investor. Few followed the example of Princeton, which explained the purpose of its selective divestment policy in 1987 as separating "the university from companies whose conduct contravenes the values of the university; the purpose is not to censure governments, or to pressure companies or governments to adopt particular policies." It added that a "decision to exclude the securities of a company carries with it a decision not to solicit gifts from that company."[23]

Furthermore, activists have been accused of overstating colleges' roles in producing political change. David Salem, president and CEO of the Investment Fund for Foundations and a longtime money manager for colleges and foundations, said there is "absolutely no evidence" that higher education's divestment had any political effect on South Africa. And, he said, the cost to investment return, in time spent on divestment and of transaction costs associated with divestment "could have been spent on other issues," say, scholarships for minority students, in which schools had a more direct influence.

It might be overstating the case to say reinvestment in South Africa would be the death knell for widespread socially screened investing by colleges. But not by much. The anti-apartheid cause was the single most compelling investment issue ever on campuses, surpassing even the campaigns against weapons and chemical investing during the Vietnam War. And most schools that adopted South Africa policies abandoned their strict fiduciary principles for only one reason: pressure. The unrelenting scrutiny of students, faculty, alumni, governments, and other interest groups—and the implication that the schools' were profiting from an unjust regime—was not worth the money made through investments linked to South Africa.

There is no comparable social investment cause on campus today. Aside from isolated cases like Yale University—where a group called Students for Business Ethics, in the spring of 1993, called for the ouster of Baxter International chairman Vernon Loucks from the board of trustees after Baxter admitted complicity in the Arab boycott of Israel—the issue of corporate links to colleges is not under debate.[24] The argument has shifted to social issues (multiculturalism and speech and sexual behavior codes) that have no financial element, and to economic issues (finding jobs) that are more individual than institutional.

"The campuses are pretty dead these days," observed Mathiasen, of the IRRC. Indeed, a survey by the IRRC, in cooperation with the Common Fund, found that, after South Africa, there is no one issue that has captured the attention of college campuses.[25]

The IRRC believed in the late 1980s that the demonization of smoking would make tobacco the hottest social investment taboo on campus. All the factors seemed to be in place: universities, the centers of health education and research, have produced some of the most devastating studies on the effects of cigarette smoking; young people, including college students, are the targets of ad campaigns promoting tobacco smoking and chewing; and colleges have been closing off dorm rooms, classrooms, and buildings to smokers. A sense of moral outrage seemed to be building. And yet, according to an IRRC study on college investment policies, only 49 schools have a formal policy on tobacco investment.[26]

Mathiasen said: "We've been surprised that the tobacco issue hasn't taken off."

A few schools have prohibited investments in tobacco products for decades. In the 1950s, Earlham College officially ended investments in companies that derive most of their income from tobacco—as well as alcohol and gambling. (The school also avoids defense-related stocks, a standard imposed during the Vietnam War, and limits South Africa–related investments to Category I and II companies. Earlham believes that the policies are in keeping with its Quaker heritage; the school's investment standards are also among the most restrictive in the nation.) Tufts, under the tenure of Mayer, a noted nutritionist, banned tobacco and alcohol holdings in the mid-1980s. And Clark, which had made several campus buildings smoke-free and banned cigarette sales at its campus store, outlawed tobacco investment in 1989.

And, in 1989–90, there was a flurry of activity. Four institutions—Harvard, Johns Hopkins University in Baltimore, City University of New York and Wayne State University in Detroit—dumped tobacco holdings worth a combined $70 million. Harvard was miffed at the tobacco companies' lack of repentance, in correspondence and meetings with university officials, about challenging the evidence that links smoking and disease. Bok, then Harvard's president, wrote that the university refused to be associated "as a shareholder with companies engaged in significant sales of products that create a substantial and unjustified risk of harm to other human beings." Similarly, Ria Frijters, a senior vice president at Wayne State, said the university found its ownership of tobacco stock inconsistent with its commitment to "research the prevention and treatment of cancer."[27]

The University of Texas system has not invested in tobacco since 1990, reasoning that the potential cost of litigation and jury awards would injure the performance of those stocks, a university spokesman said; it continues to own tobacco stocks that were in the portfolio before then. The University of Texas Board of Regents in 1991 adopted a strict program that banned smoking in all university facilities, phased out on-campus tobacco sales, and created an education campaign to help student smokers quit. The policy satisfied those who had been calling for divestment.[28]

It appeared that a number of other universities would restrict tobacco investments. Most resisted. Yale's Advisory Committee on Investor Responsibility, which consists of faculty, students, administrators, and alumni, has recommended against divestment, a decision support by the corporate board's investment subcommittee. Its Ivy League counterpart, Cornell University, rejected divestment, despite a plea by one alumnus to show "our disapproval of tobacco companies and ending our complicity in a public health crisis of staggering proportion." But the school's board agreed with the opinion of Stephen Weiss, managing partner in Weiss, Peck & Greer, a New York investment house, that "the first objective of the university is to grow its endowment and that moral impediments to that are judgmental and difficult to apply on a consistently intelligent basis." Placing restrictions on money management, Weiss wrote, "really does affect performance and injure returns."[29]

The Tobacco Divestment Project, an activist organization buoyed at the time of its founding in 1990 by Harvard's divestment, has since had little encouragement from universities. In 1992, the group, based at Boston's Northeastern University, wrote to the presidents of 100 of the largest universities, asking them to divest. The effort got the attention of students newspapers, but failed to change a single policy.[30] The group dropped a plan in 1993 for a similar letter-writing campaign to 100 church-affiliated schools.

In the IRRC survey, schools said they adopted investment restrictions on a number of other issues. Forty-one colleges restrict investments in companies making alcoholic beverages; 25 have policies on gambling and equal employment opportunities; 23 on weapons; 20 on the environment; and 11 on contraceptives. Other issues on which there are policies include human rights, animal testing, nuclear power, Northern Ireland, pornography, the Arab boycott, and abortion funding.[31]

Besides asking what formal policies existed, the survey sought to find out whether schools had considered policies on other issues. While South Africa and tobacco topped the list, the environment, mentioned by 49 respondents, came in third. Interestingly, the survey showed the impetus for the first two issues came from trustees; most on-campus pressure for environmental policies comes from students.[32]

Some observers say that attention could make the environment the issue that replaces South Africa as the top investing issue on campus. Joseph Pickle, a religion professor at Colorado College and member of the school's proxy voting advisory committee, pointed to growing support on that campus for the CERES Principles, the code that requires signatory companies to report on their environmental performance. And another Colorado College professor's campaign to persuade the College Retirement Equity Fund to drop its holdings in Battle Mountain Gold Company, which has operations in Colorado's San Luis Valley, has had some resonance with students.

"The interest in the environment is high," Pickle said, "but it's diffused." Pro-environment sentiment is a potentially potent force but will reach its promise only if, like anti-apartheid feelings, it can be focused on a single, well-defined issue, he said.

Resistance from administrators and money managers will be the prime barrier to any new socially screened investing by colleges. Many are wary of limiting the investment universe, saying it harms return—and why bother limiting income unless there's strong political pressure to do so?[33]

Some studies support that contention that screens harm return; one claimed unrestricted endowments performed 1 to 2 percent higher, on average, than restricted funds.[34] But they often fail to account for situations unique to individual funds. For most schools, South Africa screens have tended to exclude large capitalization firms, forcing them to favor smaller, growth-oriented companies. Divested funds have had relatively poorer performance, it appears, when they have overcompensated for the shortage of value stocks, or when value has done well. But an emphasis on growth stocks generally helps divesting schools in the long run, said Norman G. Herbert, chief investment officer at the University of Michigan, and "recent numbers show that to be the case."

The Common Fund's South Africa Free Equity Fund is a case in point. It has lagged the S&P's South Africa Free Index since its founding in 1986.

In its first 6 $^1/_2$ years, the fund showed a 10.9 percent return, compared with 13.7 percent for the Standard & Poor's South Africa Free Index. In 1992, the Common Fund blamed the performance on "the S&P's heavy weighting of a very few large capitalization firms."[35] Adjustments in management were made in early 1991 and performance appeared to have improved. Through mid-1993, the South Africa Free Equity Fund showed a return on track with the S&P's South Africa Free Index.

Smith, Earlham's financial vice president, said screens "have an impact," but added that management is the determining factor in performance. Unlike many other divested schools, Earlham's $150 million endowment performs best when the market favors value stocks; its sin restrictions have hurt performance when growth stocks (a category that includes alcohol, tobacco, and gambling) have done well. In three-year performance figures through early 1993, Earlham's equity portfolio showed an annual return of 10 percent, compared with 13.5 percent for the S&P 500. The performance by its ongoing managers exceeded the S&P benchmark, however. And the managers who fell short were terminated and replaced. "It's hard to say its the social screens when it's the investment managers," Smith said. IRRC analyst William Moses agreed: "The main thing is not the restriction, it's the ability of the money manager."

A number of schools say South Africa restrictions have led to opportunity losses. Such losses are less likely to occur today than they would have been early in the divestment movement. In the early 1980s, South Africa–free investors were excluded from nearly 40 percent of the S&P 500; today, total divestment shuts investors out of less than 10 percent of that market. That still leaves some attractive industries beyond reach, however. Swathmore College estimates it lost $1 million since totally divesting in 1986, primarily because it could not buy high-performing pharmaceutical stocks.[36]

There is another side to that coin. James Collins, treasurer of Clark University, said one of the school's managers complained that his portfolio suffered in the late 1980s from being shut out of the pharmaceutical boom. More recently, Collins pointed out, the industry has fared less well: "He probably wouldn't say he wished he had the pharmaceutical companies when they had the hell kicked out of them."

INVESTING IN THE LOCAL COMMUNITY AND ECONOMY

Economically targeted investing, of the type engaged in by public pension funds and Taft-Hartley trusts, and community development investing, done by many foundations, insurance companies, and banks, are anathema to most universities, given their goals of maximizing endowment return in order to keep costs down. But a small number of schools have directives to invest in their states' economies. And others steer assets to the communities surrounding their campuses. For urban schools, in the latter case, aiding housing and commercial development enhances the safety and well-being not only of their neighbors but also of their campuses, thus paying them dividends beyond the immediate return.

One of the few endowment plans to become involved in a form of targeted investing is the $4.3 billion Texas Permanent University Fund, which serves the University of Texas and Texas A&M University systems. The fund has allocated $10 million in the Texas Growth Fund, a pooled economic development program for public pension funds and endowments. The TGF, authorized by a voter-approved amendment of the state constitution in 1988, is designed to create, retain, and preserve jobs by investing in Texas companies and those that relocate in the state. "The notion was, 'Let's use our domestic pension money for our domestic economy,' " said TGF principal Stephen Soileau.

Participating investors may devote up to 1 percent of assets to the TGF, which opened its doors in May 1992. The first investors were the Permanent University Fund and the Texas Teachers' Retirement Fund, which invested $42 million.

Although the TGF has a public policy element, it is not considered a targeted investing program, Soileau said: "It's a rate-of-return vehicle." He said the TGF does not see itself as an early-stage venture capital investor, but rather a fund that makes later-stage investments in "strong, forward-looking businesses," including cable television, distributorships, and retail propane. The fund, which will take a subordinate position in any investment, plans to make five to seven transactions each year for an average of $2 million to $3 million each. Thus far, it has made commitments to two companies for a total of $4.5 million. The anticipated yield is in the upper 20 percent range, Soileau said.[37]

A handful of schools have invested in community development, housing, and commercial development in their home cities. In 1985, Clark University invested $2.4 million in its neighborhood, Main South, on the edge of downtown Worcester. At about 5 percent of Clark's endowment at the time, the investment was one of the largest commitments, in terms of percentage of assets, by a university to its community.

Clark loaned the money to a subsidiary organization, which bought and rehabilitate residential and commercial real estate for non-university use. Apartments were renovated for low- and moderate-income tenants, and eight to nine commercial storefronts restored for businesses that serve the neighborhood rather than the university, Collins said. The university at first received a 10 percent return, market rate at the time; it restructured that to 8 percent when rates declined. The portfolio includes a small loan package with the Main South Community Development Corporation, a neighborhood non-profit group.

Yale has undertaken what is, on paper, perhaps the most ambitious community development investment by a college, the New Haven Initiative. In 1987, the university pledged to invest $50 million in its home city over a 10-year period. Benno Schmidt, then Yale's president, said: "New Haven is our home. No citizens have more to gain than we at Yale do from the city's economic development, cultural vitality, and sense of hope and confidence for the future."[38]

Six years into the program, to the dismay of the city, the pace of investment has been slower than expected; through 1993, the university had kicked in approximately $18 million. "Investments under the initiative are being made at a deliberate pace," Yale acknowledged in its annual report to the city government. "Activity has been constrained by the depressed New England economy, making it difficult to plan development projects on a sound financial basis. With unprecedented vacancy rates in New Haven, certain types of real estate projects, especially office buildings, may not make economic sense for many years."[39]

The cornerstone of the initiative is the $125 million Ninth Square Development Project, a long-delayed project designed to repair a "gaping hole" in the city's downtown. A mixture of 333 mixed-income housing units and commercial space, the project was announced in 1986, when the U.S. Department of Housing and Urban Development approved an $8.9 million grant. Yale came on board in 1990, chipping in $10 million to buy Connecticut Housing Finance Authority bonds.

But the project, which includes financing from the city, state, and HUD, was nearly killed in 1991 when the authority, at the urging of Governor Lowell Weicker, turned down a request for $48 million. With the help of Schmidt, the city government persuaded Weicker in 1992 to permit the issuance of the bonds. Yale also pledged to invest another $2.25 million, bringing its total stake in the project to $12.25 million. Ground was finally broken on the project in May 1993.[40]

As another part of the initiative, the university has targeted emerging companies. It invested $1 million in Connecticut Seed Ventures, a private-sector venture capital partnership with support from the state. The $15 million fund has invested in 11 start-up projects in high-tech and medical industries, including a company developing a drug to treat glaucoma. Several of the companies are located in New Haven.

In addition, Yale was part of a consortium of investors that made a $1.7 million investment in the Science Park Development Corporation, an incubator project specializing in high-tech firms, many involving faculty members. A faculty-researched neuroscience project won a $4.37 million state investment in 1991. The development has also received $76 million in state and federal capital.

In the area of housing, Yale has invested $1.45 million for the rehabilitation of buildings that created 84 units of low- and moderate-income housing, and, in one project, provided tenant support services such as child care and job training. "We remain committed to pursuing investments of this nature despite current economic difficulties in real-estate and development sectors," wrote Sheila W. Washington, secretary of the university.[41]

NOTES

1. Ellen Bartlett, "South African Negotiators Agree to Hold Majority-Rule Elections," *Boston Globe*, May 8, 1993, p. 2.
2. John Daniszewski, "South Africa Votes for Black Role in Governing During Transition," *Boston Globe*, Sept. 24, 1993, p. 1; and Chris Reidy, "From Divest to Reinvest," *Boston Globe*, Oct. 17, 1993, p. 73.
3. Katherine Farrish, "Colleges Ending South Africa Ban," *Hartford Courant*, Oct. 13, 1992, p. A-1.
4. "Social Investing Widely Accepted on Campus; South Africa–Related Policies Remain in Place," *News for Investors*, Sept. 1993, p. 1.
5. Steven Anzovin, ed., *South Africa: Apartheid and Divestiture* (New York: H.W. Wilson Company, 1988), pp. 12, 16. (Chapter by Roger Ormond. Also see Ormond's *The Apartheid Handbook: A Guide to South Africa's Everyday Racial Policies* [New York: Penguin Books, 1985].)
6. "Harvard University Committees on Shareholder Responsibility, 1972–1982: An Historical Perspective," 1982, p. 60; and Lauren Talner, *The Origins of Shareholder Activism* (Washington, D.C.: Investor Responsibility Resource Center, 1983), p. 27. Harvard, Stanford, and Oberlin were among a dozen schools and foundations that, in an effort to gather impartial information on corporate social responsibility, founded the IRRC in 1972.
7. Joan Vennochi, "Mass. Firms Still in S. Africa," *Boston Globe*, June 24, 1990, p. 65; and Jennifer D. Kibbe, *Divestment on Campus: Issues and Implementation* (Washington, D.C.: Investor Responsibility Resource Center, 1989), p. 50.
8. "An Historical Perspective," p. 64.
9. *Divestment on Campus* (1989), pp. 50–51; and Christine Kole, "Universities Grapple with Social Investment Pressures," *Responsive Investing News*, June 10, 1991, pp. 4–5. (The University of Michigan's divestment decision was challenged by the state, which in the 1980s enacted a law prohibiting any school from investing in companies operating in South Africa and the Soviet Union. The state Court of Appeals ruled in favor of the regents, the school's governing board, in 1988.

The school sold its remaining South Africa–related stock. From 1983 to 1988, the university divested itself of $52 million.)

10. *Divestment on Campus,* p. 64.
11. "Harvard University Corporate Committee on Shareholder Responsibility Annual Report, 1986–1987," pp. 29–31.
12. *Divestment on Campus* (1989), p. 59; and Jolie Solomon, "Back in Business in South Africa," *Boston Globe,* Feb. 12, 1991.
13. Jennifer A. Kingson, "Divestment Efforts Fade in the Face of Success," *The New York Times,* Dec. 13, 1987, p. E-26; and Matthew Countryman, "Lessons of the Divestment Drive," *The Nation,* March 26, 1988, pp. 406–409.
14. Jennifer Kibbe, *Divestment on Campus: Update on the Top 50 Schools* (Washington, D.C.: Investor Responsibility Resource Center, 1992), pp. 1–2.
15. Myra Alperson, Alice Tepper Marlin, Jonathan Schorsch, and Rosalyn Will, *The Better World Investment Guide* (New York: Prentice Hall Press, 1991), p. 1.; *Divestment on Campus* (1989), p. 4; and *Divestment on Campus* (1992), pp. 11–14.
16. "Colleges Wary of Easing Curbs on South Africa," *The New York Times,* Dec. 25, 1991.
17. "Colleges Ending South Africa Ties," *Hartford Courant,* Oct. 13, 1993, p. A-1.
18. *Divestment on Campus* (1992), p. 9.
19. Holdings in the South Africa Free Equity Fund dropped from $492 million on June 30, 1992, to $490 million in April 1993; the South Africa Free Equity Allocation Pool dropped from $126 million in June 1992 to $81 million 10 months later. Figures from the Common Fund's 1992 annual report and from interviews with Daniel Wingerd.
20. "Colleges Ending South Africa Ties," *Hartford Courant,* Oct. 13, 1993, p. A-1.
21. "Action News," American Committee on Africa, Summer 1992; and Bartlett, *Boston Globe,* May 8, 1993, p. 2.
22. Emily Martinez, "Pension Fund Headache: U.S. Companies Re-enter South Africa," *Investment Management Weekly,* March 8, 1993, pp. 1, 5.
23. Robert L. Payton, "Tainted Money: The Ethics and Rhetoric of Investment," *Change,* May/June 1987; and *Divestment on Campus* (1989), pp. 22–24.
24. Simon Billenness and Patrick McVeigh, "The Social Ticker," *Franklin's Insight: Investing for a Better World,* Aug. 15, 1993, p. 4.
25. The Common Fund's Wingerd cautioned that the study was intended to "get educational institutions to tell us what they're thinking about" and does not imply that any screened-investment vehicles will be offered. Setting up an environmentally friendly fund, for example, would take several years because of the breadth and complexity of the issue, he said. "And we're not even close to thinking about such a screen."
26. Facsimile transmission from the Investor Responsibility Resource Center, July 28, 1993, p. 3.
27. Trex Proffitt, "Tobacco Divestment Debate Revives Philosophical Questions," *IRRC News for Investors,* Oct. 1991, p. 7, 9.
28. Ibid., p. 10.

29. Ibid., p. 13.

30. "Tobacco Divestment Activists Pursue 100 Universities," *Responsive Investing News,* March 2, 1992, pp. 1, 4–5.

31. "Social Investing Accepted Widely on Campus," *News for Investors,* Sept. 1993, p. 8.

32. Ibid., pp. 5, 8.

33. Schools have reason for concern. College endowments have risen from $15 billion in 1976 to $109 billion in 1992. But the costs of expanding campus facilities, attracting and retaining faculty, and, especially, paying growing administrative salaries have soared. Bigger endowments did not prevent tuition costs from rising 151 percent in the 1980s. (See "From Carter to Clinton: The Pension Market Explodes," *Plan Sponsor,* April 1993, and Gilbert Gaul and Neil Borowski's "A Tax Break Colleges Can Bank On," *Philadelphia Inquirer,* April 20, 1993. The latter is part of an excellent seven-part series on the growth of the non-profit sector.)

34. "Colleges Ending South Africa Ban," *Hartford Courant,* Oct. 13, 1993, p. A-1.

35. The Common Fund, "Annual Report, July 1, 1991–June 30, 1992," pp. 3, 22.

36. *Divestment on Campus* (1992), p. 5.

37. As a number of other endowment funds have, to demonstrate their commitment to diversity, the University of Texas System has committed $100 million to women- and minority-owned investment management firms. The investments were likely to be placed with small- and mid-cap and value equity specialists. See "University of Texas Allocates $100M to Emerging Manager Fund," *Investment Management Weekly,* July 26, 1993, p. 3.

38. "New Program an Investment in Elm City's Future," *Yale Weekly Bulletin,* May 25–June 1, 1987, pp. 1, 3.

39. "New Haven Initiative: Annual Report to the City of New Haven," March 16, 1993, p. 1. The $18.4 million figure does not include any investment the university may have made in a rehabilitation project in the city's Broadway section.

40. "Annual Report," pp. 2–3; and Stephen Higgins, "9th Square Finally off Square 1," *New Haven Register,* May 14, 1993, pp. 1, 9.

41. "Annual Report," pp. 3–4; and letter from Sheila W. Washington to New Haven Mayor John C. Daniels, March 16, 1993.

7

Churches:
Prophets Outside the Gates,
Pastors in the Boardroom

In 1742, John Woolman, a 23-year-old Quaker, had a crisis of conscience. His employer asked him to write a bill of sale for an African slave woman, and Woolman felt the pull between duty—his loyalty to and dependence on his boss—and living according to his religious convictions—which he thought rejected slavery. He later recalled, "The thing was sudden, and though the thoughts of writing an instrument of slavery for one of my fellow creatures felt uneasy . . . yet I remembered that I was hired by the year, that it was my master who directed me to do it, and that it was an elderly gentleman, a member of our Society, who bought her; so through weakness, I gave way and wrote it."[1]

The task was an epiphany. From then on, Woolman refused to participate in slave sales. And in the next three decades, he became the Quakers' preeminent anti-slavery crusader. He told Friends that they must, as he had not, conduct their business within their spiritual beliefs.

Until his death in 1772, he traveled widely, addressing Friends' meetings in the North, where he asked members to withdraw from the Triangle Trade, and the South, where he called on wealthy Quakers to give up their slaves. He was known for his gentle persuasion, for speaking to his subjects with such "tenderness and deep humility that they could not take offense, for it was clear he sympathized as much with them as with the slaves."[2] And by 1784, with Woolman's words still quietly resonating, all of the Quaker meetings in the colonies declared that members who persisted in owning slaves would be disowned, or dismissed from the society.

171

Shutting themselves off from the slave trade was an imperfect vehicle for change. The Quakers paid an economic price, for they were eliminated from a substantial segment of colonial commerce.[3] And their action failed to eradicate slavery, which survived nearly a century after Woolman's death.

But acting according to conscience accomplished two things. It removed the Quakers from a business that ran counter to their beliefs and it helped transform the debate on the most important issue of the time, laying the groundwork for state and federal anti-slavery laws and the stronger abolitionist movement of the 1800s.[4] In a sense, the Quakers' refusal to be a party to slavery was the first act in North America of social investing by a religious community.

In the last 25 years, religious institutional investors in the United States have followed Woolman's path. They have, through hundreds of small epiphanies, awakened to their moral and economic influence. They have asked whether, as investors, they should "give way" on such issues as South Africa, the environment, the defense industry, racial and sexual equality, fair access to capital, and the promotion of alcohol, tobacco and gambling—or whether they should use the means at their disposal to bring about social justice. Like Woolman, they have found their voice, and they have challenged themselves and others to develop an economy that works for justice.

Even as church pension funds grew and the assets of their endowments and foundations appreciated during the 20th century, churches were slow to recognize their role as modern institutional investors. They issued high-minded statements such as one by the National Council of the Churches in 1954, recognizing that "Christians should be guided by their ethic to seek such adjustments of economic institutions as will serve most fully the three positive values of justice and order and freedom." Another by the Episcopal Church, called on church leaders to exercise "responsible stewardship over the funds entrusted to their care" when they considered the "moral dilemma" of South Africa. Despite these statements, "the impact of church social policies on investments," Lauren Talner wrote, "were left largely unexplored."[5]

The civil rights campaign in the early 1960s began to shake those attitudes. Led by Southern black churchmen like Martin Luther King and Ralph Abernathy, the movement challenged political and economic power in provocative ways. It showed that church leaders had influence beyond the pulpit. And it drew established Protestant, Catholic, and Jewish institutions from the North into the cause, showing them that social activism was a means of conveying their moral message.

In 1966, the FIGHT movement, formed by clergymen after rioting in Rochester, New York, transferred that activism to the corporate stage. Angered by Eastman-Kodak's sorry record in hiring minorities, the group (whose name stood for Freedom-Integration-God-Honor-Today) brought community and labor organizer Saul Alinsky in from Chicago to persuade the company to hire 600 blacks. A Kodak vice president accepted a FIGHT proposal, but backed the company out, saying he acted beyond his authority. In 1967, FIGHT, which owned 10 shares of stock, convinced a few institutions (among them the Episcopal Church and the Board of the Homeland Ministries of the United Church of Christ) to withhold 40,000 shares from being voted with management on routine matters at its annual meeting in Flemington, New Jersey. With more than 80 million shares under its control, Kodak overwhelmed FIGHT on the meeting floor. But, having won the battle, it lost the war. The meeting proved the biggest media event in Flemington since Bruno Hauptmann's 1935 trial for the Lindbergh baby kidnapping. The pugnacious Alinsky promised to keep the pressure up, saying the churches would "put their money where their sermons are." The threat petered out, as church leaders retreated from the unfamiliar territory of confronting a big-time corporation. Still, Kodak was so concerned about its public image that it agreed to hire more minority workers. FIGHT's victory opened new possibilities for shareholders wishing to hold a corporation publicly responsible for its policies.[6]

Three years later, the Project on Corporate Responsibility, backed by consumer advocate Ralph Nader, launched Campaign GM, which filed nine resolutions to be included on the General Motors' shareholder proxy statement. The automaker asked the Securities and Exchange Commission to exclude all nine, saying they were either ordinary business or overly broad. The SEC permitted two to stay on the ballot: one challenging the white male insider makeup of the board of trustees, the other requesting the appointment of a shareholder committee on corporate responsibility. As a result of the ruling, a social issue question went to stockholders for the first time. The resolutions got less than 2 percent of the vote.[7]

But, as with FIGHT, the immediate result was less important than the long-term outcome—the development of the leadership role of religious institutions in the corporate responsibility movement. Within a year, GM appointed the Reverend Leon Sullivan, a black minister from Philadelphia, to its board; in the 1970s and 1980s, Sullivan was a leading figure in the U.S. antiapartheid campaign. In 1971, the Episcopal Church presented a resolution on South Africa to GM's shareholders, the first of thousands of resolutions sponsored by religious institutions over the next 22 years.

The most important religious institution has been the Interfaith Center for Corporate Responsibility. The ICCR has injected passion, righteousness, and a clear sense of moral purpose into the discussion of corporate responsibility. The center claims 250 Catholic and Protestant member organizations— foundations, endowments, dioceses, congregations, and pension and denominational funds. It is small; it has a staff of nine, and much of its work is carried out by staff members of the member organizations and volunteers. ICCR members have only $35 billion in assets, less than the New York State Teachers' Retirement System alone. But, as in the parable of the mustard seed—in which Jesus compares his kingdom to a tiny seed that grows into a great tree— they have used a small base of resources to leverage social justice.

Over the last two decades, churches have expanded the roles played by Alinsky and Woolman. Timothy Smith, executive director of the Interfaith Center for Corporate Responsibility, described the churches' role as being "prophets outside the gate"—outsiders calling for social justice—and, simultaneously, as pastors in boardrooms—urging corporate leaders to exercise responsible stewardship.

"I think the strengths we bring to this effort are our history as religious bodies [and] the moral values that we stand for," Smith said. "For some companies . . . they would talk about the public credibility that the church has, and that's a strength that can be brought to the discussion table. Certainly, the fact that we are shareholders [and] that we can influence a constituency, that is of concern to a company."

As actively as they have promoted proxy issues and exercised moral suasion, religious investors recognize that social problems cannot be solved by those means alone. In the last five years, they have devoted more attention to so-called alternative or creative investments. These programs put money in high-risk investments such as housing for the poor, loans for minority and cooperative businesses, and microlending in the Third World. They fill gaps in the capital markets, demonstrating that the economic system can work for many more members of society. In the coming years, alternative investing offers church groups their best opportunity of addressing the needs of the people and showing that their money is, indeed, where their sermons are.

SHAREHOLDER ACTIVISM

Why do religious organizations introduce proxy resolutions and hold talks with corporations? Marian Nickelson, director of corporate social responsibility for the Evangelical Lutheran Church in America, said: "Corporations have so much influence and impact that we as a church want to provide a moral and ethical voice in their practices."

Smith said that access to proxy statements and ballots enables activists to shape corporate and social policy in ways they never could otherwise. Asking corporations like General Motors and IBM, which have large workforces and heavy constituencies of stock owners, to consider social issues is of huge practical and symbolic importance. On key issues like pollution and South Africa, shareholder activists can capture a good deal of attention for their cause.

Religious groups and corporations have come a long way from the early years of shareholder activism, when they viewed one another with mutual fear and loathing. Both sides have become less confrontational, more pragmatic. "[Shareholder resolutions] can be used very creatively by both a company and us for meaningful dialogue and moving forward on win-win situations," Smith said.

Brother Gerard Frendreis, director of social investing for Christian Brothers Investment Services, a financial advisor and manager for Catholic institutions, agreed, saying the first instinct of religious investors has turned from filing resolutions for their own sake to seeking dialogue with companies.

"In some important sense, we view a resolution that actually reaches the proxy stage as a failure on our part. We have a goal of changing a company's policies and practices, and that is best accomplished through negotiations," he said. More than one third of social issue resolutions are withdrawn because of agreements with companies.

Following are descriptions of several of the important social issues religious shareholder activists have been involved in for the last quarter century; a look at the difference, if any, their efforts have made; and the outlook for future action.

South Africa

More than any other issue, South Africa defined the corporate responsibility movement. As the first group of investors to challenge U.S. corporations with divestment campaigns, boycotts, and shareholder resolutions, the ICCR shaped America's agenda in South Africa. "We had both an early role and a leadership role," said Timothy Smith. "We helped define the issue." Today, the churches continue to have influence, and have positioned themselves to set the terms for U.S. corporate conduct in post-apartheid South Africa.

The churches' efforts had a significant impact. They formed public opinion about acceptable corporate behavior, and they plowed the ground for other anti-apartheid actions. After religious activists began their campaign: more than 130 corporations divested, removing more than $1 billion in U.S. assets from the South African economy; over 140 colleges and universities divested; about 175 cities and states stopped doing business with companies linked to South Africa; and the federal government, from 1986 to 1991, slapped sanctions on Pretoria. This economic pressure did more than any other external force to press the white government to free Nelson Mandela, lift the ban on the African National Congress, and join negotiations pointing the way toward free elections. It is traceable to the initial effort of the American churches.

The ICCR was mainly "a meaningful supporter. What's going on over there, people of conscience [in South Africa] have . . . brought it to the place in history where it is now," Smith said. "But in doing that, they asked for support from Western institutions to put pressure on the South African government. We were a part of that pressure and, I think, played a very important role in it."

The mainline Protestant and Catholic churches, too, had to be shown the light. After the Sharpeville massacre in 1960, domestic civil rights leaders and South African clergymen made them aware of their real and symbolic links to apartheid. U.S. church foundations, endowments, and mission boards invested in international corporations that profited from close relationships with the white South African government; and churches, therefore, were making economic gains from the kind of practice they preached against. If churches were complicit, even in an indirect way, in the apartheid system, the possibility of changing other investors perspectives was remote.

One of the first church groups to see the connection, the United Methodist Board of Missions, withdrew a $10 million portfolio managed by First National City Bank in the late 1960s because the bank (now Citibank) extended a line of credit to the South African government. In 1969, the United Church of Christ and the Presbyterian and Episcopal churches threatened to do the same, relenting only when South Africa did not renew the credit line. (Eventually $1000 million in church money was removed from Citibank.)

The Episcopal Church's success in gaining access to the shareholder ballot at General Motors opened the door to a new form of protest: the proxy resolution. In 1971, the first year in which churches brought sponsored resolutions, the Episcopals asked GM to withdraw from South Africa. The proposal caused a stir when board member Leon Sullivan, speaking against the company line, supported it, but it won only 1.29 percent of the vote.[8]

The Christian Brothers' Frendreis said religious investors "tend to front-run an issue"—meaning they often take an issue that has no champion, that is not well-known to the general public, and bring it to the attention of corporate shareholders because it presents moral and ethical questions that demand answers. In the 1970s and early 1980s, South Africa was one of those issues. ICCR members, led by the American Baptist Churches, the Lutheran churches and, before they divested, the Episcopals, were the only institutional investors consistently sponsoring anti-apartheid resolutions.

The Baptists, whose church is the descendent of the Northern Baptist Convention, split with its Southern branch following a 19th century dispute over slavery. At its peak, the church—through its pension funds and national and international ministries boards—introduced 80 resolutions a year, most having to do with South Africa, said J. Andy Smith III, director of the denomination's social and ethical responsibility in investments program.[9]

Some resolutions wanted corporations to divest from South Africa; report on their operations; or cut franchise, contract, and other non-equity ties. Others called on banks to halt lending to the white-minority government and stop offering vehicles like American Depository Receipts to domestic investors. Still others asked companies to abide by the Statement of Principles or refrain from selling materials and services to the South African security forces, and such key institutions as Escom (the South African Electricity Supply Commission) and SASOL (the former South Africa Coal, Oil and Gas Corporation).

As is true of proxy actions generally, they fell well short of approval. But after the Sullivan Principles were issued in 1977, interest in South Africa began building. And by the early 1980s, two public pension giants, the New York City Public Employees' Retirement System and the California state retirement system, began introducing South Africa proposals.[10]

In 1985, the ICCR launched its Partners in Apartheid campaign, which identified the top U.S. corporate presences in South Africa. The companies included American Cyanamid, Chevron, Citicorp, General Electric, General Motors, IBM, and Mobil. The companies were targeted with "selective buying" and concerted shareholder pressure unless they withdrew from South Africa or actively moved it away from apartheid by the end of 1986.[11] Many churches didn't wait for them. Frustrated by the lack of progress, they divested themselves of holdings in all companies with operations in South Africa.

But the Baptists, Lutherans, and public pension funds continued with their resolutions, and consistently won victories, even if they were not be attributed directly to their actions. In 1983, BankAmerica suspended loans to South Africa and American Express stopped advertising Krugerrands; each cited shareholder pressure. In the mid-1980s, Ford and Eli Lilly issued reports to their shareholders on their operations in South Africa. In 1986, after 15 years of shareholder pressure begun by the Episcopals, General Motors sold its South African operations. In 1987 and 1988, Black & Decker, Cigna, Sterling Drug, and Marsh & McLennan agreed, after dialogue with shareholders, to divest. American Cyanamid stopped shipping toxic waste to South Africa in 1989, and Mobil Corporation sold its assets there in the same year. The Bank of New York cut ties with the country in 1990.[12]

Mobil's departure from South Africa was an especially instructive one. The oil giant—a driving force behind the formation of the Sullivan Principles and the most vocal opponent of corporate withdrawal—sold its operations there to a South African industrial firm. Mobil chairman Allen E. Murray brushed off a suggestion that shareholder pressure compelled the company to make the sale. Instead, he attributed it to "very foolish laws" preventing the company from writing off South African tax payments from its U.S. tax bill. The measure effectively raised the tax rate on corporate earnings in South

Africa from 57.5 percent to 72 percent. The ICCR's Smith called the sale "a very significant victory for the anti-apartheid cause," telling the *Africa News:* "The 'foolish laws' are the result of concern and pressure form many Americans who want tax disincentives for U.S. companies choosing to remain in South Africa."[13]

In the last two years, anticipating a new investment climate in South Africa, the churches have been planting seeds for positive change in the country. In the 1992 and 1993 annual meeting seasons, the resolutions sponsored by the ICCR and its partners, the New York state and city pension plans, changed emphasis. Instead of calling on companies to withdraw, several proposals asked them not to expand operations until South Africa adopted a new constitution. (The sponsors exempted food, health care, and pharmaceutical companies, provided they could demonstrate that their products were reaching South Africa's black majority.) And others asked companies to review a code of corporate conduct drafted by the South African Council of Churches, in consultation with the ICCR, and to tell shareholders whether they planned to implement it once a multi-racial democracy was established.

While the resolutions were intended to smooth the transition between the apartheid and post-apartheid eras, they received less shareholder backing than the get-tough proposals of the mid-1980s. In 1993, the top showings of the 42 resolutions filed were with Union Carbide (17.3 percent for a proposal to halt expansion) and IBM (15.2 percent for a proposal to end computer sales to the South African military), but the votes overall were several percentage points short of the 1992 proxies. Analysts said support from institutional investors, many of which are locked into anti-apartheid policies, held steady. But individual investors drifted. That may be attributed to the "out-of-sight, out-of-mind syndrome": voters lost interest in the issue when it disappeared from headlines.[14]

In the 1993–1994 shareholder season, the churches are sponsoring new resolutions promoting a code of conduct—this one designed by the South African Council of Churches to set the tone for corporate behavior in the post-apartheid era.

The code states that "businesses can play a constructive and creative role in partnership with workers, communities, and other members of civil society, to lay the foundations for a stable and prosperous South Africa." It identifies 10 broad goals for corporations and, indirectly, investors to meet. Among them: supporting equal opportunity; developing education and training opportunities for blacks; improving living and working conditions; and promoting black-owned businesses. The new ICCR resolution was scheduled to have its first test in January 1994 at the annual meeting of Baker Hughes.[15]

A successful move to democracy, along the lines of the South African church code, would transform U.S. religious investors from naysayers to brokers for positive change, Timothy Smith said: "South Africa will not fall off our scope when sanctions are lifted, but we will turn from a group that called for economic pressure and ran campaigns against companies to a group that encourages investments." Added Andy Smith of the American Baptist Churches: "Clearly there is a role that church investors will emphasize. . . . I see a new day dawning there."

Other Oppressive Regimes

Religious investors often pressure U.S. companies operating in nations under dictatorial regimes. But they don't see themselves as the world's moral policemen. "Rather than just deciding what country has the worst human rights abuses," Timothy Smith said, the investors ask two key, pragmatic questions. Can corporations be agents for change in the nation? And do religious, labor, and human rights groups on the inside advise activism? When the answers are yes, the ICCR introduces resolutions supporting human rights. It has done so in Chile, the Philippines, El Salvador, and Myanmar, the former Burma. Using the same criteria, the group has, with one exception, stayed away from addressing abuses in China.

For two years, the ICCR has urged Amoco, which has a drilling contract with a Myanmar state-owned oil company, and PepsiCo, which owns 40 percent of a bottling plant in the capital, to suspend operations until political prisoners are released and a transition is made to the elected government. Church groups were set to bring resolutions to the shareholders in 1993, but the companies agreed to publish reports on their operations, a result the ICCR regards as progress.

China has been the subject of one post-Tiananmen shareholder action by religious investors. After the Food & Allied Services Trade Department of the AFL-CIO accused Wal-Mart, through a shareholder resolution and an NBC-TV news report, of relying on suppliers who used Chinese prison labor, the ICCR entered a dialogue with the company. It resulted in Wal-Mart's adoption of international business standards similar to Levi Strauss'. The code includes renunciation of the use of prison and child labor.[16] (For a fuller account, see Chapters 1 and 4.)

Environment

Churches increasingly regard the Earth as a sacred trust, a resource over which God's people have stewardship. But, as shareholders, they haven't consistently and vigorously championed what Marian Nickelson, of the Evangelical Lutheran Church in America, called "care of creation." For certain, some of the very first resolutions sponsored by religious groups were related to the environment; in 1971, a year after the first Earth Day, the Episcopal

Church unsuccessfully sought to have stockholders block two corporations from mining copper in Puerto Rico. During the 1970s and 1980s, religious institutions took on a relative handful of environmental issues, such as nuclear plant operations and the Bhopal tragedy. But most of their energies were directed elsewhere.[17]

On February 10, 1993, Sun Oil Company, the nation's 12th largest petroleum company, became the first Fortune 500 company to sign the CERES Principles. Nickelson described the agreement as one of the most significant moments in the history of the corporate social responsibility movement, since it marked a recognition by corporate America that it could work with environmental activists—and vice versa. "People realize that it is good business to be environmentally responsible," she said. "It really does affect the bottom line, which is what we've been saying all along. That has been part of our premise."

Another victory came in 1990, when McDonald's stopped using styrofoam hamburger boxes. The decision occurred a year after the Evangelical Lutherans introduced an anti-styrofoam resolution. The church pulled the resolution before it went before shareholders and spent several months talking to the company about making the change. In 1991, after talks between with the Environmental Defense Fund, the corporation agreed to further recycling of its packaging.[18]

Shareholder resolutions and dialogue forced Chevron and DuPont officials to meet residents of Panna Maria, Texas, where their jointly run uranium mill polluted groundwater and threatened the community's health. The meetings in 1989 and 1990 resulted in the company's agreeing to clean up the site and continue meeting with community leaders, the ICCR said.[19]

Religious shareholders have also persuaded corporations to report on specific, non-CERES aspects of their environmental performance. In 1991, six corporations stepped up their efforts to eliminate their use of chlorofluorocarbons, the ozone-depleting gases, and reported on their projects; and two auto makers agreed to report on fuel efficiency of their fleets and on their congressional lobbying against efficiency standards. In 1993, six Midwest utilities consented to report on their efforts to reduce carbon dioxide emissions from burning coal, oil, and gas, and to detail their conservation efforts.[20]

The ICCR plans active campaigns against environmental racism (including work with community-based groups), food irradiation, nuclear power, and toxic waste disposal. Its top priority will continue to be the CERES Principles.

Maquiladoras

In Mexico, from Matamoras, near Brownsville, Texas, to Tijuana, south of San Diego, there are more than 2,000 foreign-owned factories known as maquiladoras, or "golden mills." Ninety percent are owned by U.S. corporations. In some, workers produce cars or carburetors, assemble batteries, mix chemicals, or sew clothing. In others, they make machinery or sort coupons clipped by American shoppers. The plants employ 400,000 Mexican workers, who, for the opportunity to do jobs once done by Americans, are paid as little as 55 cents an hour.

The influx of jobs has come at a huge cost to the Mexican workers and their families, according to the Coalition for Justice in the Maquiladoras, a group of 60 organizations including labor, environmental, women's, religious and public policy groups. The coalition charges that there have been massive environmental, human rights, and labor abuses in the region, all for the profit of what Benedictine Sister Susan Mika, president of the coalition, calls the "Who's Who of the Fortune 500."

The maquiladoras were begun in 1965, under a program allowing U.S. companies to set up finishing shops in northern Mexico. The plants take parts made in the United States for assembly by Mexican workers. In addition to lower wages, the corporations get to take advantage of tremendous tax breaks; items are taxed only for the value added in Mexico.

The coalition's shareholder activism has had limited success. Two chemical companies in Matamoros closed their plants (one, New York–based ASARCO, after a shareholder resolution in 1992), and others have improved worker safety, posted warning signs in Spanish, or agreed to conduct "market basket surveys" to determine whether workers can actually live on the wages the companies pay. The coalition has also won cooperation from companies—including General Motors, the largest U.S. presence in the region with 37 maquila sites—that have agreed to provide detailed information about operations and permit monitors to visit their plants.

"And while no company officials will say so in public, they admit off the record that our efforts made them really sit up and notice what is going on in their factories," Mika said. But so far, no corporation has formally agreed to abide by the Maquiladora Standards of Conduct, a code designed to promote environmental, health and safety, fair employment, and infrastructure standards.[21]

In the last two shareholder seasons, the ICCR has sponsored 23 resolutions, with two coming to a vote. In 1993, shareholders with Zenith, the television and electronics company, gave a pro-coalition proposal 10 percent support, and those with Stepan Chemical, 13.9 percent. Zenith and 16 other companies are involved in dialogue, have issued reports, or agreed to visits by social investors.[22]

Further progress will be an uphill climb. The coalition fears ratification of the North American Free Trade Agreement (NAFTA), which would set up a free-trade zone in Canada, Mexico, and the United States. It is concerned that even more U.S. companies will gravitate toward Mexico's cheap labor and loose environmental laws, further degrading workers and the ecosystem. And the ICCR worries that NAFTA would make corporations less accountable to shareholders. Said the ICCR's Valerie Heinonen: "Overall, if the analyses I've been reading are accurate, then it's going to make it much harder for us to make the requests we do and see results."

Militarism

Due to concerns about defense cutbacks at Texas Instruments' 1993 meeting, shareholders were asked to vote on resolutions requiring the company to tell what plans, if any, it had to retrain workers and convert its plants to civilian production. Another question sought a company report on defense-related sales to foreign governments. The proposals got 17 percent and 14 percent of the vote, respectively, an astonishing level of support. When the results were posted, Heinonen said, "there was actually a gasp."

No one was more surprised than the sponsors. Since the Vietnam War, religious activists have put more than 220 defense-related resolutions on corporate ballots. The proposals called on companies to stop competing for weapons contracts that supplied the United States in the arms race with the Soviet Union and destabilized the Third World. Or they asked for the end of production of the B-1 bomber; MX missile; Strategic Defense Initiative; chemical, biological, and nuclear weapons; and war toys.

But working for peace—described by Frendreis as, along with South Africa, one of the "twin pillars" of the corporate responsibility movement— has been largely a futile pursuit. Investors in defense companies are not naive. By and large, they own the equities for their profitability and they believe in the military purposes the companies serve. And it would not be hard to imagine most agreed with writer Patrick Glynn's tart 1983 assessment of religious anti-nuclear activists:

> The clerics directing the corporate responsibility campaign are remark-
> ably untroubled by the prospect that their efforts could have a one-sided
> impact, curtailing U.S. weapons production without affecting similar cut-
> backs in the Soviet Union. They act with the assurance that only the
> Holy Spirit should provide. . . . To hear [these clerics] discuss these mat-
> ters so simplistically is to long for the days of Wolsey and Richelieu,
> when the Church's immense power fell into the hands of men who, while
> ebulliently corrupt, were nonetheless shrewd and prudent.[23]

Unsurprisingly, the proxy proposals languished in the single digits through the mid-1980s. In the early 1990s, though, they have gotten a somewhat better hearing. Massive layoffs by defense contractors and "maybe just general disgust" with corporate management have led to higher support in 1993, Heinonen said.

As hard as it has been to interest shareholders in their cause, church activists claim some successes. In 1988, ITT agreed to provide a conversion report.[24] Companies including AT&T, Union Carbide, and Monsanto eased away from defense contracts, in part because of liability concerns. The ICCR raised the same issues in the 1970s, Smith said, and the companies denied that to be the case.

A big win occurred in 1993, when General Electric, the Defense Department's fifth largest contractor, sold its aerospace division to Martin Marietta. The sale ended GE's production of nuclear weapons. GE had been edging away from the industry for several years, and withdrew in 1990 from its 37-year contract to make nuclear bomb triggers. The period of withdrawal coincided with a seven-year boycott of GE products led by INFACT, a corporate responsibility group allied with the ICCR.

Elaine Lamy, INFACT's executive director, lauded the sale, telling *The Corporate Examiner,* "With the most powerful corporation in the United States out of the nuclear weapons business, the nuclear weapons industry will no longer wield the kind of influence over government decision-making that it has in the past."[25]

The victory may have been Sisyphean, however. Martin Marietta, which was the tenth largest military contractor before the sale, remains in the nuclear arms business, producing the components formerly made by GE. Smith acknowledged: "If a company gets out of a business you disagree with and passes it on to somebody else, I still think it's a considerable victory. But you can't pretend it's an unqualified success."

MacBride Principles

Since 1985, the Irish National Caucus has asked U.S. corporations to adopt the MacBride Principles, a code based on the notion that sectarian violence and the Unionist-Republican dispute are exacerbated by economic and human rights problems, one of the most striking of which is rampant job discrimination against Catholics.[26]

As an ecumenical organization, the ICCR sees itself as ideally situated to bringing about change in Northern Ireland. "I think we see our role not as a political-legislative role. We are a corporate responsibility organization, trying to enhance the role that companies do and can play there," Timothy Smith said. We are "actually supporting investment in Northern Ireland, in contrast to South Africa . . . and to encourage companies to try to eradicate discrimination from their plants and to try to eradicate the pattern of discrimination in society."

Twenty-three U.S. companies have agreed to abide by the MacBride Principles. IBM, which was engaged in dialogue with three U.S. Catholic orders, was among those pledging in 1993 to accept MacBride. GATX and Unisys, which were tracked by the New York and Minnesota pension funds, were the others. Interestingly, while they live by the spirit of the code, U.S. corporations operating in Northern Ireland are leery of formally signing them, as dozens of firms have with the Statement of Principles. By not signing, they hope to avoid the appearance of taking sides in the conflict.

As for future action, religious investors and their allies have set their sights on firms based outside the United States. Since most American firms in Northern Ireland accept the principles, attention will turn to Australian, Canadian, and European companies that have not implemented the code.[27]

Tobacco

On the issue of cigarette smoking, shareholder activists have captured the mood of a nation that has exiled its workers outdoors for a few furtive puffs; and yet they have made little headway in persuading institutional investors to give up tobacco stocks or in making the companies change their policies and practices.

During the 1980s, investors led by Michael Crosby, a Franciscan Capuchin who advises 25 Midwestern ICCR members on social investing, introduced proxy issues that would have forced the tobacco companies to go out of business. When they weren't removed from the ballots by the Securities and Exchange Commission, stockholders greeted them with indifference.

More and more, ICCR members are reaching out to companies in other industries—insurers, retailers, restaurant chains, advertisers, and suppliers— that reap revenue from tobacco, to end their business relationships with tobacco companies.

Insurance companies recognize that smoking is harmful to their policy holders and to their own bottom lines; they often charge lower premiums to non-smokers on life and health policies. But, according to a study by Dr. Gregory Connolly of the Massachusetts Department of Public Health, a major figure in the anti-smoking movement, they are also big investors in tobacco. In recognition of the fact, religious investors have aimed shareholder resolutions at insurers, asking them to report on their tobacco holdings. A few companies, Aetna Life & Casualty and Travelers Insurance, have demonstrated they reduced their tobacco investments. Still, the activists "do not yet have a clear strategy" for dealing with insurers, according to a 1993 ICCR report. And, given the continuing financial pressures on the insurance industry and the fine performance of tobacco equities, convincing other companies to sell their stock will be difficult.[28]

As for retailers, Christian Brothers Investment Service is involved in dialogues with two drugstore chains, Melville, the parent company of CVS, and Walgreen's, over the sale of tobacco products. The negotiations have a long way to go, as Christian Brothers would have to persuade the companies to forgo a substantial portion of their business.

In other industries, the activists have had difficulty getting past the SEC. In 1993, anti-smokers asked two restaurant giants, McDonald's and PepsiCo—owner of KFC, Pizza Hut, and Taco Bell—to make their facilities smoke-free. Both companies challenged the petitions before the SEC on the grounds that they infringed on the conduct of ordinary business. McDonald's, which as an experiment has already made some of its franchises smoke-free, was successful; the sponsors withdrew their petition with PepsiCo before the SEC reached a decision. The publishing giant Gannett blocked a proposal that would have prevented it from displaying cigarette ads on its billboards. And in 1991, the SEC, again citing the ordinary business rule, let Mobil Oil remove from the ballot a proposal that would have prevented it from making wrappers for cigarette packaging.[29]

Even as they targeted industries peripherally associated with tobacco, anti-smoking activists continue to confront the Big Six tobacco manufacturers directly. In 1993, for instance, they asked Philip Morris to put surgeon general-style warning labels on all merchandise, including logos and symbols displayed on clothing items and at sporting events. The vote at Philip Morris' meeting gave the anti-smokers their best showing of the season, 6.5 percent of the vote. The sponsors and Philip Morris are holding talks about the issue.[30]

Infant Formula

In the 1970s, infant formula manufacturers mass marketed their products in the Third World, using ad slogans claiming that formula was healthier for babies than breastfeeding. Religious investors, along with medical, women's, and consumer groups, concerned about infection and malnutrition they said was caused by improper bottle feeding, began a counter-campaign to end the sales campaign.

In 1975, religious investors affiliated with the ICCR filed their first resolutions on infant formula marketing. The following year, the Sisters of the Precious Blood sued Bristol-Myers on the eve of its annual meeting, alleging that it misled shareholders in a proxy statement. (The suit, settled out of court years later, helped establish the standard to which corporations could be held in addressing social issues on their shareholder statements.) The advocacy group INFACT, which led the GE boycott, started a worldwide boycott of Nestlé in 1977 with the full support of religious activists. Nestlé, a multinational company based in Switzerland, could not be touched by U.S. shareholder resolutions.

Four years later, the United Nation's World Health Organization (WHO) unveiled the Code of Marketing for Breastmilk Substitutes, a voluntary standard to which the five major formula-makers have selectively adhered. The Infant Food Manufacturers, their trade association, agreed to abide by a provision in the code that prohibits issuing of free supplies, as long as there was a level playing field, that all companies were made to follow the same policy. That required passage and enforcement of laws on a country-by-country basis. Today, 122 countries, at the urging of WHO and UNICEF have adopted the Baby Friendly Hospital Initiative, which forbids free samples.[31] "And that is moving ahead slowly but surely," Smith said.

Domestically, the ICCR has fought the increased advertising of formula. Since 1989, Gerber, Bristol-Myers Squibb, and Nestlé, through its Carnation subsidiary, have been advertising directly to the American public rather than to physicians. (American Home Products and Abbott have not joined in.) The companies argue that parents are fully capable of deciding whether to use formula or to breastfeed and do not need the advice of a doctor. The strategy, a break with industry tradition, has been condemned by the American Academy of Pediatrics, saying it undercuts doctors' efforts to encourage the healthier alternative of breastfeeding. However, after a court decision in 1992 that Abbott and Bristol-Myers Squibb engaged in price-fixing, a verdict that cost the latter $40 million, the Federal Trade Commission is reviewing whether advertising should be required, since that might open up competition and reduce prices.[32]

Smith said infant formula is no longer "a big issue in terms of staff time," but is one the organization carries on because of its long association with it. It is not clear what the religious investors' next move will be. Shareholder resolutions may have run their course; investors have filed and refiled so many proposals, especially with Bristol-Myers Squibb and Gerber, that they may not be able to follow that route any time soon. Other forms of action, from dialogue to a full-court press on other issues, such as resolutions on the environment and equal employment, may be considered.

Drug Pricing

In one of his first statements after his inauguration, President Clinton condemned U.S. pharmaceutical companies for price gouging. The ICCR, which has made more of an issue of prescription drug pricing in recent years, could not have agreed more.

In five resolutions in 1993, sponsors, many of them Catholic health care agencies, stated that federal government studies had found that the price of drugs increased at nearly three times the rate of inflation during the Reagan and Bush presidencies and that Americans pay 62 percent more for the same products as Canadians. The ICCR was also concerned that drug companies spend up to 20 percent of their budgets on advertising, and that they claim a great need for research and development dollars, even though only 40 percent of new drugs were deemed significant advances over products already on the market. They said that the high prices were particularly onerous for the elderly, for whom prescription drugs are the highest out-of-pocket medical expense.[33]

The resolutions were withdrawn when all five corporations agreed to provide reports that were to have revealed their formula for pricing new drugs, the time it takes to recover research and development costs, and explained the difference in prices between the United States and other industrial countries. But Susan Vickers, director of advocacy for Catholic Healthcare West, which sponsored a resolution with Johnson & Johnson, called the reports unsatisfactory.

Community Reinvestment

In the most recent annual meeting season, an issue reemerged after virtually disappearing from the social investment agenda for 15 years. The issue was redlining, the systematic racial discrimination in lending. The enactment in 1977 of the Community Reinvestment Act, which requires banks to meet the financial needs of their communities—including low-income areas— appeared to have addressed the issue. But evidence gathered in the early 1990s showed that financial institutions were again, in effect, drawing lines around minority areas. Using data obtained from Home Mortgage Disclosure Act reports, the Association of Community Organizations for Reform Now, and the Federal Reserve Board showed in 1992 that banks across the country rejected blacks at a rate 2.4 times higher than whites. A similar study by the Federal Reserve Bank of Boston revealed that, even when data for factors such as credit-worthiness were taken into account, black applicants in Greater Boston face a 60 percent higher rejection rate from banks than whites.[34]

Religious investors co-sponsored eight resolutions aimed at multi-bank holding companies, asking them to report on lending to low-income areas and minority applicants for each subsidiary and for the company as a whole. The proposals also recommended the companies dedicate 0.75 percent of assets to community reinvestment and establish community development corporations. Seven agreed only to provide reports. The eighth, Bank One, successfully challenged the resolution with the Securities and Exchange Commission. The ICCR plans further dialogue with the banks, as well as with the Federal Home Loan Mortgage Association.[35]

Equal Opportunity

Increasingly, churches are making corporate behavior in the areas of equal employment opportunity and affirmative action part of their shareholder agenda. In the last two years, their efforts have resulted in two major court decisions that could advance the cause of equality. But they may be most notable for blunting the Securities and Exchange Commission's ability to keep social issues from coming before shareholders.

In the first decision, U.S. District Judge Kimba Wood ruled in April 1993 that the SEC was out of bounds in 1992 in allowing Wal-Mart Stores to exclude a resolution on its equal opportunity practices from the shareholder ballot. The proposal—whose sponsors included the Dominican Sisters of St. Catherine of Siena, the National Council of Churches, and the Unitarian Universalist Association—asked Wal-Mart to report on its hiring of women and minorities and describe its affirmative action and minority outreach programs.

Wal-Mart was prepared to strike the resolution from its shareholder report for the second straight year in 1993, but Wood's ruling prevented that action. The company has agreed to include that information in its 1994 report. Smith said:

> Judge Wood's decision is a highly significant victory for corporate social responsibility and the right of shareholders to hold their companies accountable for [equal employment opportunity] and affirmative action performance. . . . The SEC has been allowing companies to omit shareholder resolutions on employment issues, even though all of them had significant policy implications such as discrimination, minority contracting, fair employment in Northern Ireland, or workplace issues in South Africa. We hope this ruling makes it clear to companies that they must address these concerns.[36]

In the second case, Wood in October 1993 ordered that the SEC could not prevent shareholder activists from introducing a resolution asking Cracker Barrel to adopt a policy of nondiscrimination against gays. In 1991, the company, citing its commitment to "traditional American values," announced it would no longer hire homosexuals. Several workers were fired as a result of the policy. Cracker Barrel retreated from the position, saying it would "continue to employ those folks who will provide us the quality service our customers have come to expect from us" and would handle "disruptions in our units. regardless of cause, on a store-by-store basis." The New York City Employees' Retirement System introduced a gay rights resolution in 1992, but the company asked the SEC to keep it off the ballot, saying it dealt with employment issues, which are considered ordinary business. SEC staffers, and later the full commission, agreed.[37]

Gay rights is not officially part of the ICCR's agenda. But some members are actively working to eliminate discrimination against homosexuals in the workplace, seeing parallels to other civil rights and employment issues and shareholder rights. Connie Takamine, treasurer of the Women's Division of the United Methodist Church, a plaintiff in the suit against the SEC, told *News for Investors* that the division regarded that SEC ruling as "an onslaught on the rights of investors to summon shareholders to a vote on questions such as racial and sexual discrimination."[38]

Wood's decision meant that Cracker Barrel shareholders would vote on a resolution seeking an end to anti-gay discrimination, with the annual meeting set for November 1993. But it was a larger victory, a "big, big deal," said Diane Bratcher, the ICCR's communications director. "This is particularly a defining moment on gay rights issues because big institutions are going to have to say whether they support, deplore, or accept" anti-gay rights policies. (Greater church involvement on the gay rights issue is difficult to foresee. Most churches view homosexuality as a sin, and few denominations ordain people who are openly gay. "Success here will be no small feat," Bratcher has written.)[39]

Churches are most active in equal opportunity issues revolving around the workplace and corporate management. In 1993, they filed 12 resolutions asking for reports on EEO and affirmative action policies, similar to the one at the center of the Wal-Mart case, and eight "board of inclusiveness" proposals seeking to end the white-male hegemony on corporate boards.

Church sponsors withdrew a resolution asking Texaco for EEO reports in order to concentrate on a dialogue with the company. Texaco agreed to provide the reports. But the sponsors discovered during the process that Texaco was the target of 12 lawsuits alleging age discrimination, unlawful dismissal, racial discrimination, and sexual discrimination and harassment. Several church-affiliated speakers denounced the company at its annual meeting. The ICCR reports that Texaco workers and advocates of equal rights credit it with galvanizing resistance against the company's policies.[40]

The concept of inclusive boards is especially important to churches, who believe that the directors set the tone for the entire corporation. Women and minorities, a majority of the population, constitute only one in five top officers, directors, and board members in Fortune 500 companies, the churches said. So a number of institutions (the Episcopals, Methodists, Unitarians, and Christian Brothers Investment Services, among others) have encouraged corporations to conduct open searches for suitable women and minority board members. Sponsors withdrew four of the eight resolutions on inclusive boards in 1992, including one with Bristol-Myers Squibb, which named Louis Sullivan, the former health, education, and welfare secretary, to its board.[41]

LEFT AND RIGHT

A word needs to be said about the generally liberal nature of shareholder activism. Religious shareholder activists have remained true to their Social Gospel and Naderite roots, approaching virtually every issue from the political left. Conservative religious investors have chosen not to be shareholder activists, convinced (with some justification) that institutional investors are indifferent or hostile to their causes.[42]

It may also be that conservatives, because of their belief in the efficiency and fairness of the free market system (with its emphasis on freedom and reward for the individual), have found that corporations operate in line with their moral code, or are, at worst, morally neutral. Furthermore, many conservative religious institutions, including rapidly growing fundamentalist churches, are less established and less wealthy than those aligned with the ICCR. Having less economic clout than the religious left, they have, on the comparatively rare occasions they have disagreed with a corporation, used grass-roots methods such as boycotts, protests, and letter-writing campaigns.

The conservative avoidance of shareholder activism has also been due to the right's success in national politics. From the late 1970s, with the victory of Proposition 13 in California, through the Bush presidency, conservatives carried the day on taxes, social issues, the defense buildup, and the prosecution of the Cold War. If social investing is "politics by other means," as Peter Kinder has suggested,[43] conservatives had little need of it. They won politics by political means. Liberals, in suffering one electoral setback after another, had fewer avenues available.

Smith said: "Our agenda for the ICCR comes from our members of the communion. And if we're working on issues, we've been mandated to by our members. So I'm sure some of our issues seem to be more on the liberal end of the agenda, but there's an awful lot that sort of crosses the line. . . . I think in general the tone we take is not a kind of strident political tone. It's to raise up the basic moral and ethical issues in these questions."

ALTERNATIVE AND COMMUNITY INVESTING

The 1980s and early 1990s have been unkind, social investors point out, to the neediest in society. During the early 1980s boom, the lubricant that kept the rest of the economy running smoothly, access to capital, failed to grease the wheels of the poor. Later, during the recession, with bank and savings and loan failures and a squeezing of credit availability, the wheels fell off.

The ICCR has blamed the federal government, saying it "abandoned low-income communities, withdrew support for affordable housing and economic development, and unleashed a nationwide epidemic of homelessness, unemployment, hunger, and ill health."[44] In truth, private-sector investors—including religious institutions themselves—also failed these communities, bypassing them for more lucrative investments. Finally, in the late 1980s, members of the faith community renewed their commitment to such programs as low-income housing, cooperative businesses, and minority-owned farms.

In a sense, it was a return to their roots. Alternative investing was common in the 1960s. In hopes of redressing inequalities made evident by rioting and the reports of social scientists, churches handed out loans to and made investments with individuals and groups with negligible track records—almost "throwing money at a terrible situation," Timothy Smith said. Given the experimental nature of these investments, financial failures were abundant; the Episcopal Church poured $3 million into a "ghetto seed fund," a high-risk venture capital enterprise. It lost all but $25,000, an investment in

South Shore Bank that has never paid a dividend. Churches failed "mostly because they tried to do the lending directly and didn't have the financial knowledge or the community development knowledge to review the credit-worthiness, and the social and economic viability," Martin Paul Trimble, executive director of the National Community Development Loan Fund, told *The Wall Street Journal.* During the 1970s and early 1980s, with the exception of Catholic women's orders, the angels of the community development funds, religious institutions all but abandoned alternative investing.[45]

A number of factors turned that around. First, federal legislation such as the Low-Income Housing Tax Credit made investments in affordable housing sensible for big investors such as banks, insurance companies, and other corporations. These private sector investors could be induced to join investment consortiums—especially when churches, foundations, and other non-profit entities handled initial-stage financing, took lower returns, and carried a large share of the risk—since their returns would be financially sound and relatively low-risk. Second, and very importantly, some non-profit groups—such as Neighborhood Housing Services, the Ecumenical Development Cooperative Society, and members of Trimble's National Association of Community Development Loan Funds—matured and became more stable. In essence, these groups act as investment managers, bundling investments and parceling the funds out to carefully selected borrowers in low-income communities in the United States and abroad. In addition to spreading risk among investors, the intermediaries provide technical assistance to borrowers, helping ensure that the investments are paid back with an adequate return.

The presence of deep-pocketed co-investors and more sophisticated non-profit agencies gave religious investors something they never had previously: the chance to leverage social change beyond their means. "It's a piece of the puzzle that can make things happen," said the Reverend Gregory Johnson, president of the First State Community Development Loan Fund, a new housing and business development fund in Wilmington, Delaware.

Finally, there was Los Angeles. Riots frame the era of alternative investing. In the 1960s, the torching of Watts, Newark, and Detroit spoke inarticulate volumes about the depths of urban blight, despair, and rage. And again, in 1992, the riots in Los Angeles after the first Rodney King verdict showed that despite the passage of years since the Kerner Commission report, America had not succeeded in legislating an end to this nation's racial, social, and economic divide. The realization snapped religious institutions to attention—"embarrassingly," Smith said, since they should have been invested morally and financially in the cities all along. Their response since the conflagration of South Central Los Angeles—a combination of 1960s idealism and a "more prudent and business-like" attitude acquired in the 1980s—shows alternative investing has more promise than ever before, Smith said.

The Methodist Church

The General Board of Pensions of the United Methodist Church—the largest denominational pension fund in the country, with more than $5 billion in assets—is one of the relative newcomers to community development investing. But it has emerged as the largest and most important of the religious community's alternative investors.

In 1990, the board committed $25 million to low- and moderate-income housing development. In 1992, the board increased the allocation to $100 million, or about 2 percent of total assets.[46] Not all of that amount has been invested at this writing. Said Jerry Schmahl, the board's portfolio accounting manager: "This is really the beginning of our socially proactive investing."

The board has a number of requirements to protect its investments and meet its social mission, Schmahl said. The board places all investments with intermediaries. It requires that the projects it invests in comply with tenant guidelines set by the U.S. Department of Housing and Urban Development. And it mandates returns exceeding comparable-maturity Treasury certificates and hewing close to the real estate market rates. The board declined to disclose its rate of return.

The board's most significant relationship is with the Enterprise Social Investment Fund, the Columbia, Maryland–based community development fund. The Methodists have invested $30 million with the fund for low-income housing and housing programs for the homeless through the Corporate Housing Initiatives Fund. The Methodists have also invested $5 million with the Community Investment Corporation (CIC), a non-profit banking organization that, over 20 years, acquired and rehabilitated more than 12,500 housing units for low- and moderate-income residents in Chicago. Schmahl said the investment demonstrates the prudence the board exercises. CIC makes loans from a revolving pool of 37 investors, including banks, non-profits, and corporations. Each loan is made in proportion to the institution's investment, so if any single CIC project fails, the investors are on the hook for only a small portion of its investment.

"What we try to do is reduce risk as much as we can," Schmahl said. "We try to look for all the elements. I think we approach our investments as a fiduciary. And we take our fiduciary responsibilities very seriously."

The Methodists were among the first investors, along with Harris Bank of Chicago, in a complex program—started by the Local Initiatives Managed Asset Corporation (LIMAC) and the Federal Home Loan Mortgage Corporation (Freddie Mac)—that was intended to create a new secondary market for low-income, multi-family housing.

As part of the deal, LIMAC, a subsidiary of the Local Initiatives Support Corporation, bought $5 million in low-income, multi-family mortgages from Harris Bank's portfolio. (The mortgages financed eight properties with 219 units.) LIMAC swapped those loans with Freddie Mac for $5 million in that corporation's securities; the Methodists, in turn, bought those 20-year certificates from LIMAC, thereby freeing LIMAC to recycle the $5 million for more housing financing.

The secondary-market program was to have brought $100 million into affordable housing deals by early 1993, and a larger second phase was to have followed on its heels. The program landed other institutions, but LIMAC has found the going slow with investors who balk at any association with social investing. LIMAC has also had difficulty tying together a package of multi-family loans to create a pool of identical loans. If the overall program has not met expectations, it has proved satisfactory to the Methodists, who negotiated with LIMAC and Freddie Mac for two years before closing the deal; the combination of market rates and security proved too good to pass by.[47]

Money that the Methodists have not invested with specific organizations is placed in certificates of deposits with banks recognized for their work in community development and housing, including the Boston Bank of Commerce, a black-owned bank; Elk Horn Bank & Trust Company, an affiliate of South Shore Bank of Chicago; and Vermont National Bank, which offers social investment accounts.

The Evangelical Lutheran Church

The $2.5 billion pension fund of the Evangelical Lutheran Church is also involved in alternative investing. In 1989, a year after the merger between three Lutheran groups formed the current church, the Board of Pensions began offering a social purpose fund to employees covered by its defined contribution plan. The account covered three areas: stock, bond, and balanced funds. The stock fund and the stock component of the balanced account are covered by a strict set of screens. The bond portion of the account contains what Michael Troutman, senior manager of the investments program, calls "the most exciting" aspects of the church's program—alternative investments.

Church pension funds are governed by Section 403(b)(9) of the Internal Revenue Code, not ERISA, but are required to follow similar prudence requirements. Troutman said the Evangelical Lutherans begin, early in the process of evaluating potential investments, to seek a reasonable balance between risk and return.

The due diligence process has led them to two well-regarded funds, the Community Reinvestment Fund of Minneapolis, a secondary market for loans made by community development corporations, and the Enterprise Social Investment Fund. Troutman said the Community Reinvestment Fund, in which the Evangelical Lutherans invested $300,000 in 1992, has a reputation for careful underwriting. Foundations and other non-profits take subordinate positions, giving other investors first crack at the fund's assets should a large number of failures occur. That protection is essential for pension funds to meet their prudence requirements, he said. The Enterprise fund also provides recourse to the pension board to recover its investment.

While the investments are safe, they are also paying higher returns than comparable-term Treasuries, Troutman said. The safest of the fund's investments yield 10 to 20 basis points above comparable Treasuries; for the riskiest investments, the spread is 200 to 250 basis points.

Among pension fund participants, the social option accounts are growing in popularity, Troutman said. Of all the pension assets, $130 million is invested in social purpose funds; $60 million of that is in the alternative investing bond program. (Another $200 million is designated for South Africa–free funds.) In terms of current contributions, about one dollar in four is sent to accounts with social restrictions.

The Episcopal Church

The Episcopal Church, one of the religious investors burned in the 1960s alternative investment spree, began to reinvigorate its program in the mid-1980s. The church appointed an advisory board of clergy and lay people, investment advisors and lawyers to study the issue, and decided to commit 10 percent of non-designated funds in its endowment—or about $7 million—to program-driven, community development investments.

There are two pieces to the investment program: minority bank deposits and community development. Under the minority banking program, the Episcopalians increased sixfold the amount of money available for minority-owned banks. From $500,000, an amount set during the first incarnation of alternative investing in 1968, the church poured in $3 million. The church has opened $100,000 certificates of deposit in banks selected for socially responsible lending practices and solid financial standing. The CDs carry full Federal Deposit Insurance Corporation protection and provide the individual banks with an expanded deposit and loan base.[48]

In the $3.6 million community development program, about 60 percent of the money goes to community development loan funds, 25 percent in community development credit unions, and 10 percent in community development bank deposits.

At the same time in the 1980s that executives at the Episcopal Church's national offices were developing alternative investing guidelines—a top-down initiative—dioceses and parishes across the country were building a bottom-up case for more of a commitment to economic justice.

At the 1988 national General Convention, which became known as the Michigan Convention, delegates voted to set aside $24 million for investing in economic justice. In the five years since, members of the social justice committee have struggled to determine their investment criteria, and the grass-roots effort has not come close to meeting its ambitious goal. The program has been allocated $3.5 million to invest, and has, to date, invested $300,000.

The Presbyterian Church (U.S.A.)

The Presbyterian Church has been making what it calls creative investments since 1975. That year, the church's General Assembly adopted guidelines to use investment to promote the worldwide social concerns of the church's membership. According to a 1993 study of the program, "The intention . . . is to make low-interest loans to community-based organizations to assist the poor and financially disenfranchised across the country, as well as around the world. This effort is to assist facilitating hunger programs, low-income housing programs, and other community development programs by making available funds to those who may not be able to qualify due to either their financial circumstances or their racial and ethnic backgrounds."[49]

Initially, the General Assembly committed up to 3 percent of the assets of its foundation, about $1 million. After a review in 1983, it upped the amount to 5 percent; in 1988, it made the commitment 10 percent. As a result, the Presbyterians make about $8 million available to creative investments worldwide. At this writing, $5.5 million has been committed.

The foundation has strict collateral safeguards. It works closely with intermediaries, which spread risk, and often requires borrowers to assign it a liquid asset for the full amount of the investment. "We have to be a little careful on the collateral side," said Thomas A. Seel, the foundation's vice president and investment officer. "We would rather err to the side of safety than lose money for the church."

The formula seems to have worked. In a 10-year review of the program, completed this year, the foundation stated that the program had been a financial success. Of 69 investments made (at an average size of $233,469), it had only one partial default, a 99.6 percent success rate. Furthermore, the average annual return of 5.1 percent met the foundation's goal of reaching two-thirds the yield of the Lehman Brothers Intermediate Government/Corporate Bond Index, which was 7.5 percent for the same period. That same report noted, however, that the program can drain resources in other ways: "In all candor, the foundation staff was and still is very concerned about . . . [spending] an inordinate amount of time . . . on creative investment work, with minimal benefit to the foundation."[50]

Still, the foundation notes its successes, among them the East Central Federal Credit Union in Louisville, Mississippi. Through the mid-1980s, members of the Southern Woodcutters Association, a group of manual laborers, were effectively shut out of bidding for options on lumber projects that would have made them more self-sufficient. Intermediaries who acquired leases, through competitive bidding, for wood lots hired members of the association to clear them; the intermediaries then sold the wood to pulp and paper companies. As hired hands, the woodcutters could not scrape together the capital to make a successful bid. With the help of a $50,000 investment by the Presbyterian Foundation in 1985, the woodcutters created their own credit union, initially called the United Woodcutters Federal Credit Union. The pooled assets gave the woodcutters the means to bid for options. Acting on their own behalf, they reduced their reliance on intermediaries and used their profits to make further successful bids. "The circle of success began," the foundation's study said.[51]

The Presbyterians no longer have a stake in East Central. But they have increased their position in the Quitman County Federal Credit Union, in Marks in northwest Mississippi, which Seel called a "classic poverty-stricken area." With $50,000 already in the institution, the foundation planned this year to raise the amount up to $100,000, the maximum amount protected by the National Credit Union Administration, or 20 percent of non-member deposits, whichever is lower. The investment will enable Quitman County, like East Central, to make loans that will help make poor people self-sufficient, Seel said.

In 1992, the foundation made a five-year, $500,000 investment, one of its largest, with the Northern Ireland Innovation Programme, an embodiment of the MacBride Principles' stated goal to encourage enterprise in Northern Ireland. The program creates jobs in young, small businesses that bring Catholics and Protestants together. The money goes to manufacturers, dairy farms, and other businesses that have been in operation between two and four years; these companies are out of the throes of birth, but need extra capital to expand. While not a venture capital investment, which the Presbyterian Foundation avoids, "we expect a number [of companies] will fail, but hope that the couple that do make it will really kick in," Seel said. The favorable attention given the foundation's investment drew another $2 million from Catholic and Protestant investors, so "our money was able to be used in a way to leverage" more investment, Seel said.

In addition to the Presbyterians' $8 million pool for worldwide creative investing, they have set aside $4 million for Los Angeles. In a vote reminiscent of churches' social investing in the 1960s, the General Assembly decided in June 1992, just after the rioting in South Central Los Angeles, to invest in rebuilding the city. Following up on those impulsive good intentions has proved difficult. More than a year later, the first investment had yet to be made. Part of the problem is that few groups can meet the foundation's strict collateralization requirements. Seel said the standards may have to be reexamined, or waived, in order to get some money into the city.

The Unitarian Universalist Association

The Unitarian Universalist Association (UUA) has one of the longest associations with direct social investing of any religious organization. Described by financial vice president David Provost as a "big player" in alternative investing since 1969, the UUA has committed $1.3 million of its assets (an $80 million endowment) to community and economic development. Among its current projects is an $150,000 investment, 3.5 percent interest, with the Atlanta-based Federation for Southern Cooperatives. The federation works with about half of the African-American farmers in the United States, helping them retain their properties and develop markets for their products. Besides providing education and cooperative purchase programs, the federation helps farmers who have lost or are in danger of losing their property to retain control of their properties and restructure their debt.

In early 1993, the UUA made a challenge to member congregations, putting up $500,000 for community investments. The association will match up to $10,000 that any congregation invests in alternative investments. The program will encourage more social investing throughout the country, Provost said, and stretch the association's own assets even further. In its first few months, the challenge had gotten a few takers. The UUA planned to promote the program more vigorously in the fall and expected that participation would pick up greatly.

The ICCR's Timothy Smith said that examples such as these are likely to lead to more church investment in inner cities and rural areas deprived of access to capital: "There are many success stories. We're putting out money that we really watch, and [we] watch that money help rebuild communities and make a difference. So we really have a financial and social impact."

NOTES

1. Daisy Newman, *A Procession of Friends* (Garden City, N.Y.: Doubleday & Company, Inc., 1972), p. 66.
2. Ibid., p. 70.
3. Margaret Hope Bacon, *The Quiet Rebels* (Philadelphia: New Society Publishers, 1985), pp. 76–77.
4. Ibid., p. 102.
5. Lauren Talner, *The Origins of Shareholder Activism* (Washington: Investor Responsibility Resource Center, 1983), p. 28.
6. Sanford R. Horwitt, *Let Them Call Me Rebel: Saul Alinsky, His Life and Legacy* (New York: Alfred A. Knopf, Inc., 1989), pp. 493–500.
7. *The Origins of Shareholder Activism,* pp.15–19.
8. *The Origins of Shareholder Activism.* pp. 29, 31–32.
9. Don Lattin, "First Latino Elected President of American Baptist Churches," *San Francisco Chronicle,* June 25, 1993.

10. The ICCR was lukewarm about the Sullivan Principles, saying they lent legitimacy to corporations that did little or nothing to end apartheid. Religious leaders criticized them for being weak on job training and promotion into management for blacks. But when the Reverend Leon Sullivan withdrew his support for the code a decade later, ICCR executive director Timothy Smith said, "They played a terribly important role in getting fair wages, community outreach, job equity, and even limited political lobbying." (See David Clark Scott, "Rev. Sullivan May Scrap S. African Business Code, Back Pullout," *Christian Science Monitor,* June 3, 1987, p. 19.)

   The presence of public pension funds in the anti-apartheid movement added a new dimension to the church effort. The Baptists and the New York City Employee Retirement System also pushed in the late 1980s for meeting of Royal Dutch Shell shareholders to discuss the company's South African operations. (The Netherlands-based company is not subject to laws requiring regular owners' meetings). That effort proved unsuccessful. So the coalition led a boycott that held significant support from unions, public pension funds, and state and local governments, and, in the ICCR's estimation, cost the company millions of dollars in business.

11. "Church Group Mulls Sale of Stock Due to Apartheid," *Wall Street Journal,* May 21, 1985, p. 20.

12. "Churches Settle Social Issues with Corporations," United Press International, Dec. 21, 1983; Barnaby J. Feder, "Companies Face the Social Issues," *The New York Times,* April 12, 1988, p. D-2; "Taking Stock in Protest," *Chicago Tribune,* May 8, 1987, p. C-7; Mark Dowie, "Feel-Good Investing: Clean, Green and Guilt-Free Funds," *The Nation,* April 26, 1993, p. 553; and "Business Q&A," Gannett News Service, February 28, 1990.

13. "Annual Report," *The Corporate Examiner,* Volume 18, Number 4, 1989, pp. 1, 4; and "U.S., South Africa Union Slam Pullout Terms," *Africa News,* May 15, 1989.

14. "South Africa Shareholder Proposals Show Change in Emphasis," *Responsive Investing News,* Nov. 23, 1992, pp. 1, 7; "First Semi-Annual Review: 1992," *Responsive Investing News,* July 20, 1992, pp. 1–2; and "ICCR Highlights, July 1992 to June 1993," July 1993, pp. 7, 12. In 1993, churches also sponsored six resolutions aimed at banks making loans to and taking deposits from South Africa. Votes for the resolutions hovered around 10 percent. The sponsors' talks with Firstar, a Milwaukee-based bank, found reason for optimism in working with regional banks on community reinvestment in a democratic South Africa, the ICCR said.

15. "Code of Conduct for Business Operating in South Africa," South African Council of Churches, July 1993; and "New York State Ends South Africa Campaign, But Church Groups Write New Resolution for 1994," *News for Investors,* September 1993, p. 9.

16. Simon Billenness, "Franklin Research Dialogues with Wal-Mart," *Franklin's Insight: Investing for a Better World,* April 15, 1993, pp. 2–3.

17. *The Origins of Shareholder Activism,* pp. 30–31; and *The Social Investment Almanac,* p. 144. Chapter by Edgar G. Crane, Ariane van Buren, and Andy Smith on "Shareholder Actions and the Environment."

18. *The Social Investment Almanac,* p. 150. Chapter by Crane, van Buren, and Smith.
19. "Annual Report," *The Corporate Examiner,* Volume 19, Number 4, 1990, p. 8.
20. "Annual Report," *The Corporate Examiner,* Volume 20, Number 4, 1991, p. 5; and "1993 Proxy Season Update," *The Corporate Examiner,* Volume 21, Number 9, 1992, p. 1.
21. "Maquiladora Activists Withdraw Last Shareholder Resolutions," *Responsive Investing News,* April 13, 1992, p. 2.
22. "ICCR Highlights," Interfaith Center for Corporate Responsibility, July 1993, pp. 42–44. Stepan, a defendant in the suit brought by the Brownsville parents, informed the coalition in June 1993 that it was advised not to work closely with it. The company was to do a site assessment of its Mexican operations and forward the report to the country's environmental regulators, from whom the coalition has been unable to obtain basic information.
23. Patrick Glynn, "Pulpit Politics: In a Time of Doubt, the Church Turns to the Social Gospel," *The New Republic,* March 14, 1983, p. 11.
24. "Companies Face the Social Issues," *The New York Times,* May 11, 1988, p. D-2.
25. "INFACT Ends Boycott after GE Exits Nuclear Weapons Business," *The Corporate Examiner,* Volume 22, Number 1, 1993, p. 5.
26. Andrea Mackiewicz, "Environment Is Top Concern of Shareholder Resolutions," *Business International,* April 1, 1991. An overview of the resolutions sponsored by shareholder activists.
27. "MacBride Proponents Look Beyond U.S. Border; Start New Focus on International Corporations," *News for Investors,* April 1993, pp. 8–11; and "ICCR Action Plans," July 1993, pp. 36–37.
28. Ibid.; "1993 Proxy Season Update," *The Corporate Examiner,* Volume 21, Number 9, 1992; and "Tobacco Issue Group: Interfaith Center on Corporate Responsibility," memo, July 1993.
29. Ibid.
30. "Production and Marketing of Tobacco and Related Products," Investor Responsibility Resource Center, Jan. 25, 1993, pp. E1–E2.
31. "Annual Report: Infant Formula," *The Corporate Examiner,* Volume 20, Number 4, 1991, p. 12.; and "ICCR Highlights," pp. 38–39.
32. "ICCR Highlights," pp. 38–39.
33. "Church Proxy Resolutions," pp. 41–42; and "ICCR Highlights," p. 37.
34. "Bank Redlining Returns as a Proxy Issue," *Responsive Investing News,* Dec. 7, 1992, pp. 1, 5.
35. "Action Plans," p. 33.
36. "Federal Court Restores Shareholder Resolution on Equal Employment Opportunity to Wal-Mart Statement," *The Corporate Examiner,* Volume 22, Number 1, 1993, p. 1.
37. "Gay Rights Shareholder Resolution Gains Support in Philadelphia," *Responsive Investing News,* Feb. 17, 1993, pp. 1, 4; "NY Pension Fund May Sue to Reverse SEC's Cracker Barrel Ruling," *Responsive Investing News,* Oct. 26, 1992, p. 4; and "It's Official: NYCERS Sues over Cracker Barrel; Kimba Wood Accepts Case on SEC's EEO Stance," *News for Investors,* April 1993, p. 6.

38. "It's Official," *News for Investors,* April 1993, p. 7. The U.S. Trust Company of Boston joined the Women's Division and New York City pension system in filing the suit.

39. *The Social Investment Almanac,* p. 658. Diane Bratcher chapter on "Corporate Responsibility and Gay and Lesbian Rights." The Wall Street Project, a group of investment professionals active in the fight against Cracker Barrel, is compiling a database on the gay rights policies of the top 1,000 U.S. corporations. The information was expected to be available by late 1993.

40. "ICCR Highlights," p. 21.

41. Ibid., and *Church Proxy Resolutions,* pp. 34–35. Some church investors have a policy of voting against boards of directors that are not inclusive; the Unitarians withhold votes from white male board candidates.

42. "Pro-life, Pro-choice Activists Battle over Corporate Giving," *Responsive Investing News,* April 29, 1991, pp. 4–5. Perhaps the one exception in 1993 was an anti-pornography proposal brought before Kmart shareholders by the Women's Division of the United Methodist Church.

43. Comment on "Fresh Air," National Public Radio, July 6, 1993.

44. "Annual Report," *The Corporate Examiner,* Volume 21, Number 4, 1992, p. 11.

45. Dorothy J. Gaiter, "Churches Boost Inner-City Aid, Insist on Results," *Wall Street Journal,* Aug. 21, 1992; and "Alternative Investing," *The Corporate Examiner,* Volume 20, Number 4 (Annual Report, 1990–91), p. 17.

46. The General Pension Board has a total of $300 million, about 6 percent of its portfolio, in real estate. Of that, $200 million is invested in areas other than affordable housing.

47. "Freddie Mac, LIMAC Program Attracts Methodists, Harris Bank," *Responsive Investing News,* May 11, 1992, p. 3; Christine Philip, "Fund Invests in Housing Program," *Pensions & Investments,* May 11, 1993, p. 22; Barbara Grady, "Mortgage-Backed Securities Fund Affordable Housing," Reuters Business Report, March 30, 1993; and "Freddie Mac, N.Y. Group Team Up to Buy Low-Income, Multi-Family Mortgages," *Responsive Investing News,* May 13, 1991, p. 6.

48. "Episcopals Boost Deposits with Minority Banks," *Responsive Investing News,* April 13, 1992, p. 4.

49. "Ten-Year Creative Investment Study," Presbyterian Church (U.S.A.) Foundation, Feb. 9, 1992, p. 3.

50. "Ten-Year Creative Investment Study," pp. 9, 11–13.

51. Ibid., pp. 5–6.

8

Community Development Banking: The South Shore Bank Experience

By the early 1970s, by most accounts, the Chicago neighborhood of South Shore was ready to slide into urban decay.

The once-fashionable area, though still stable and viable, had changed in a single decade from a predominantly white, middle class community to a mostly African-American, working class one. As is too often the case, white flight begat capital flight and small businesses began to close or move out. According to conventional wisdom, South Shore had become a bad investment. It seemed only a matter of time before vacant lots, boarded-up buildings, and despair took over.

Fortunately, that didn't happen, thanks in large part to South Shore Bank, a relatively small but highly influential community development experiment that has been called Bill Clinton's favorite bank. Twenty years of growing pains and trial-and-error lessons later, this bank with a mission has been called the prototype for a string of community development lending institutions around the country.[1]

Ironically, the community of South Shore has been resurrected due to the efforts of an institution which, twenty years ago, was anxious to abandon the area in search of greener pastures. In 1973, having long since stopped making most of its loans in the neighborhood, The South Shore National Bank (as it was then called) had plans to sell out to investors who intended to move its operations to downtown Chicago. Only strong community opposition and action by the Office of the Comptroller of the Currency—which denied permission for the bank to leave the South Shore neighborhood—kept that from happening.

It was that action by the OCC which paved the way for the bank to be acquired, instead, by a group headed by four young, and highly idealistic bankers who cut their teeth at the nearby Hyde Park Bank and Trust Company, which serves the racially integrated neighborhood adjacent to the University of Chicago. The new managers were determined not only to keep the bank in South Shore, but also to make the institution a catalyst for the neighborhood's recovery.

Capitalized by funds raised from foundations, individuals, and the United Church of Christ Board of Homeland Ministries, Milton Davis, Ronald Grzywinski, and Mary Houghton took over as managers of the bank in August of 1973.[2] Davis is now chairman of South Shore Bank; Grzywinski is chairman of Shorebank Corp. and chairman of the bank's executive committee; and Houghton serves as president of Shorebank Corp. James Fletcher, the fourth member, who joined the management team in 1978, is president of the bank.

At the time of the takeover, the bank, which had assets of $42 million, including deposits of $40 million, was anything but fully committed to the development of the community. During the year prior to the takeover, it had made only two mortgage loans in South Shore, for a total of $59,000. The vast majority of the bank's loan activity was outside the neighborhood that gave it its name.[3]

The bank's new owners intended to change that. The heart of their plan was an emphasis on the oldest principle of banking: that a bank should provide capital to the geographic area where it is located and from which it takes deposits. In addition, there would be affiliated non-bank companies to round out a comprehensive development strategy.

Despite widespread prediction of failure, South Shore has been able to prove that, despite widely held assumptions about lending opportunities in the inner city, a strongly concentrated effort by a disciplined lending organization could not only help to revitalize a neighborhood, it could make money at the same time. While not wildly profitable compared to other banks in its peer group, the bank has been in the black every year since 1975. Despite the seemingly high-risk nature of its business, its low loan losses are enviable (see Figure 8-1).[4]

Since the acquisition in 1973, the bank and its holding company have not only survived, but have grown several fold (see Figure 8-2). In recent years, Shorebank has expanded its activity to include lending in four other targeted Chicago neighborhoods, and is involved in activities in Arkansas, Northern Michigan, and Poland. Plans are in the works for development-based initiatives in several other Midwestern cities.

FIGURE 8-1   South Shore Bank Net Loan Losses Compared to Peer Group

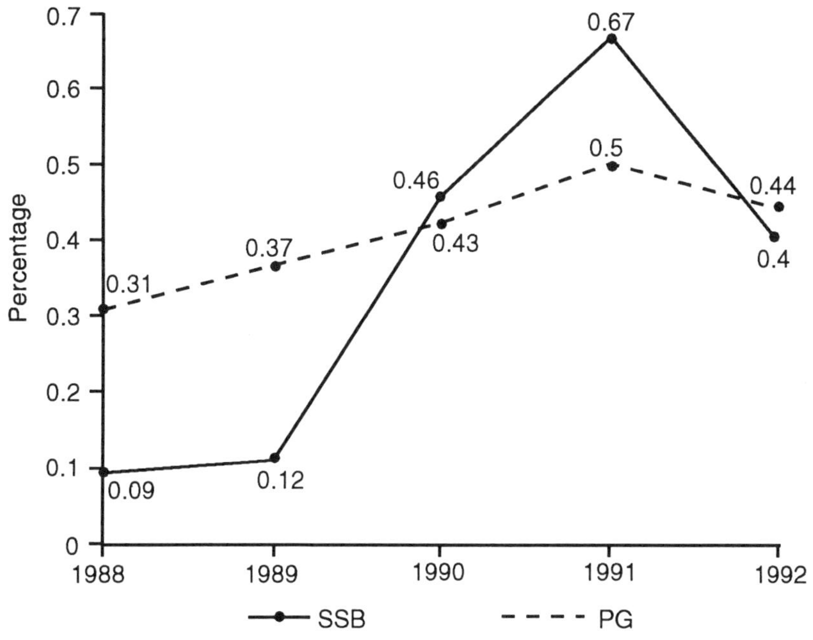

Source: Shorebank Corp. 1992 Annual Report.

Furthermore, the bank has been successful enough in revitalizing South Shore that it has attracted two competitors to the neighborhood. The First National Bank of Chicago announced in 1993 that it will open a branch office nearby, located in an area straddling South Shore and the more disinvested Woodlawn neighborhood.[5] Cole Taylor Bank opened a storefront office in 1992.

Assets of the bank had grown to $244 million by 1992, including $209.8 million in deposits according to Shorebank's annual report. Of those deposits, more than half come from so-called Development Deposits (Shorebank's service-marked term for deposits from outside its geographic service area), which are made by institutions and individuals nationwide. The vast majority of the bank's deposits are in federally insured accounts which pay market interest rates, but the bank also offers below-market-rate certificates of deposit. Called Rehab CDs, Community Jobs CDs, and TNI (The Neighborhood Institute) CDs, these deposits pay an interest rate set by the investor 1 percent or more below current market rates and are used to finance special housing and job retention programs. Such deposits totaled slightly more than

FIGURE 8-2   Growth of Shorebank Corp. Assets, 1988–1992

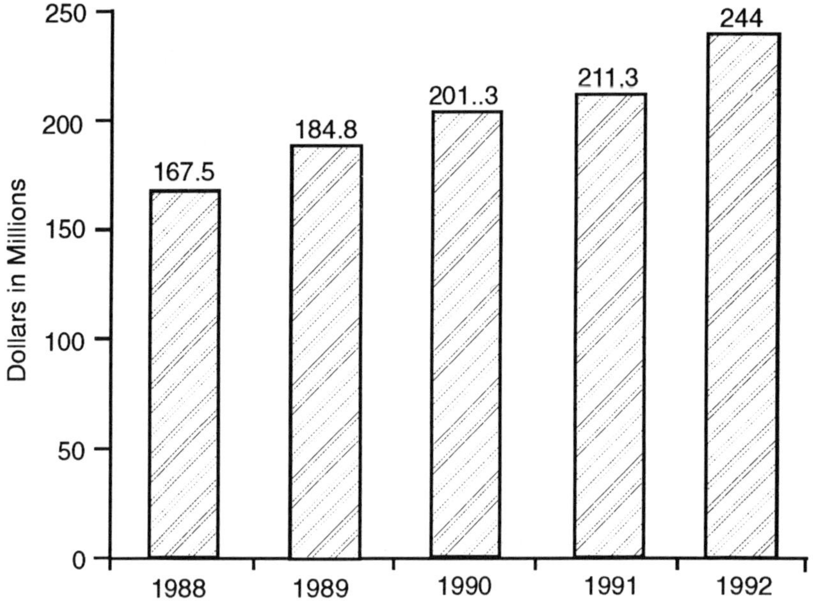

Source: Shorebank Corp. 1992 Annual Report.

$8 million, out of about $135 million in Development Deposits, as of August 1993, according to a South Shore Bank official.

Shorebank's net income in 1992 was about $1.6 million, or a 10.87 percent return on equity, compared with earnings of $866,000 in 1991. As Chairman Grzywinski recently told *USA Today,* many of South Shore's retail depositors maintain small accounts and make a large number of transactions. In addition, numerous other expenses, such as a larger-than-normal holding company, tend to drag down earnings.[6]

THE SOUTH SHORE BANKING PHILOSOPHY

According to Joan Shapiro, a senior vice president with South Shore Bank and its parent, Shorebank Corp., some of the important the goals of the bank and its affiliated companies have been:

✦   [To] reinvest in its neighborhood, according to prudent underwriting standards;

FIGURE 8-3   Shorebank Multi-Family Housing Rehabilitation

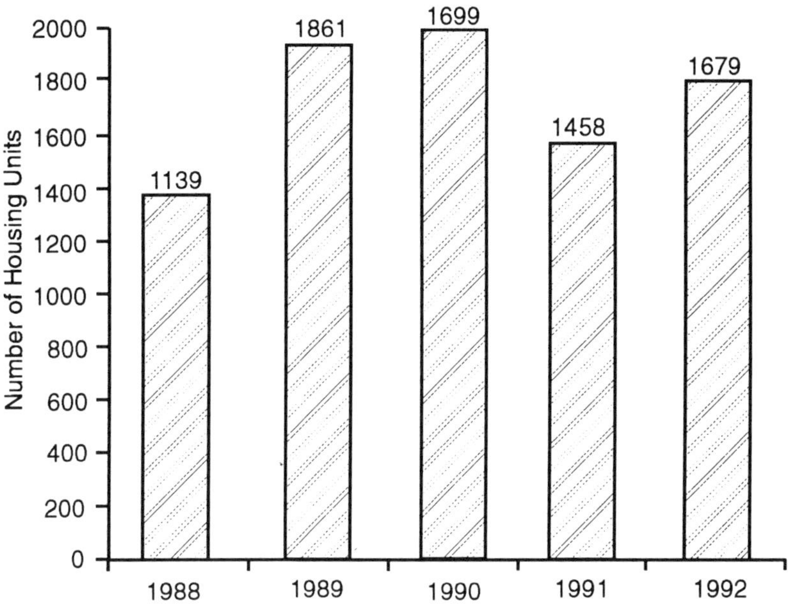

Source: Shorebank Corp. 1992 Annual Report.

+ be tough but fair with borrowers;
+ meet rigorous examination guidelines; and
+ renew the area without gentrifying it.[7]

To do that, the bank integrates its activity with a series of for-profit and not-for-profit affiliates. They include a real estate development company, called City Lands Corp., which buys and renovates properties, a venture capital firm, the Neighborhood Fund, which assists minority-owned small businesses; the nonprofit Neighborhood Institute, which offers neighborhood residents assistance in the form of housing, education, and jobs programs, and a development consulting firm called Shorebank Advisory Services.[8]

The idea, Shapiro points out, is to provide business-oriented solutions to urban problems while giving a nudge to the invisible hand that guides market and propels development.

According to its annual report, Shorebank Corp., made $29.7 million in development-oriented loans and investments in 1992 (slightly less than the $30.3 million loaned in 1991), of which about $16 million went to multi-fam-

FIGURE 8-4   Growth in South Shore Bank Deposits, 1988–1992

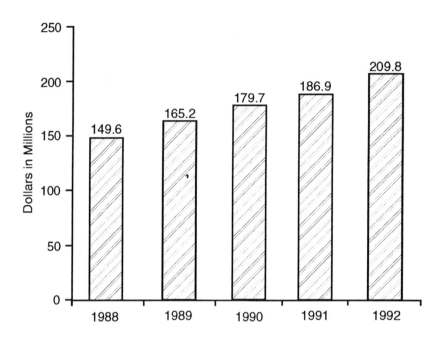

Source: Shorebank Corp. 1992 Annual Report.

ily housing. Of the 1992 loans, about $10.7 million was loaned in South Shore, another $9.3 million went to the Chicago neighborhood of Austin, where South Shore opened a branch in 1986, and the reminder was divided between three other Chicago neighborhoods.

Beyond that, Shorebank's The Neighborhood Institute developed over $6.1 million in commercial and residential property and City Lands developed $4.71 million in residential property in 1992.

As Shorebank Chairman Grzywinski pointed out in an article published in 1991, one of the bank's strengths has been identifying entrepreneurial local residents—many of them African-American married couples—with the ambition and character to become responsible rehabilitators and landlords of the numerous small apartment buildings that make up the bulk of South Shore's housing stock. While many of these so-called "ma and pa re-habbers" had never before received a bank loan, South Shore executives found them to be exceptionally committed to the success of their projects and good at re-paying their loans.

> One of our most successful housing entrepreneurs managed a dry-cleaning business on the north side in 1973. Urged on by an uncle who had fixed up buildings, he found a small apartment building in fair condition, bought it with money we lent him . . . fixed it up, rented it, and made regular payments on his loan. So we helped him buy a second building and a third. . . .
>
> We've found literally scores of such people. . . . They make up a body of small-business people that no market survey could possibly have identified.[9]

One challenging area for South Shore has been the bank's performance in small business lending. The bank cut its exposure to commercial loans— except those insured by the federal Small Business Administration (SBA)—in 1991 after experiencing high loan losses in that area.[10]

However, the bank's commercial loan portfolio grew by $5 million in 1992 for a total of $55 million. New lending included $10 million in SBA-guaranteed loans. Commercial loans in communities targeted for development totaled almost $3.2 million, including 14 such loans totaling $1.5 million in South Shore and one $90,000 loan in Austin, according to the annual report.

While the bank's goal of revitalizing the neighborhood's commercial strips has gone unfulfilled (an outcome the bank attributes to the lure of shopping malls), one particularly conspicuous success in commercial lending came in 1990, when the City Lands subsidiary opened the neighborhood's first new shopping center in decades. City Lands retains a 45 percent stake in the fully leased project, which features a major chain supermarket.

Shorebank Corp.'s Chicago Non-Bank Subsidiaries

City Lands Corp.

Shorebank's for-profit real estate development and management subsidiary, was formed to address the problem of finding an adequate number of developers willing to create a focused development strategy in South Shore. Its goal, according to Shorebank's Community Reinvestment Act (CRA) statement, is to "increase the number of rehabilitated residential and commercial properties available for rent or sale in South Shore and Austin."

Over its 15 years in business, City Lands Corp. had, by the end of 1992, developed 1,055 residential units and 129,000 square feet of commercial space in South Shore, valued at $68.48 million, according to the CRA statement. In addition, the company developed 481 housing units worth $30.2 million. By the end of 1992, City Lands managed 733 housing units in 30 buildings and one four-unit office building, according to Shorebank's annual report. City Lands generally owns the buildings along with limited equity partners or local community groups.

Among its more recent projects, the annual report states, "In 1992, City Lands put together a layered subsidy and equity finance package to renovate 115 apartment units in five buildings" and had begun renting the apartments at near-market rents in cooperation with a neighborhood coalition.

The Neighborhood Fund

Shorebank's venture capital unit was formed to help replace many of the local businesses that left the community when the racial composition of the community changed from predominantly white to mostly African-American during the 1960s. The unit, an SBA-licensed specialized small business investment corporation, was formed to assist socially and/or economically disadvantaged persons who want to start businesses in the area but lack the equity capital to qualify for financing from South Shore Bank.

Founded with an initial capitalization of $150,000 from Shorebank in 1978, The Neighborhood Fund had $2.18 million in capital as of the end of 1992; its portfolio included 16 companies, according the CRA statement.

The Neighborhood Institute

A nonprofit unit of Shorebank, The Neighborhood Institute (TNI) was formed to engage in a variety of community development, education, training, and employment programs utilizing the government and foundation grants that a for-profit institution, such as South Shore Bank, cannot legally accept.[11] The institute also owns a for-profit subsidiary called TNI Development Corp., which develops rental and cooperative housing for low-income people.

According to Shorebank's annual report, TNI referred 221 clients for employment; placed 154 clients in private-sector jobs; assisted the start-up of 140 new businesses; assisted 76 existing businesses, and rehabilitated 71 units of housing in 1992. Among its most recent projects, TNI "opened its third small business incubator, which houses Gallery 71, a summer arts enterprise program that employed 112 high school students," the annual report states.

In addition, TNI recently teamed up with a private developer to build 26 new single-family homes in the $90,000 price range, which has been called the largest single-family development on Chicago's Southeast side in 30 years.[12]

Shorebank Advisory Services

The consulting arm of Shorebank, Shorebank Advisory Services (SAS) was founded in 1988 to offer development banking and other economic development strategies to public and private organizations.

In 1992, Shorebank's annual report states, SAS projects included a feasibility study on forming a community development institution using "the proceeds of a lawsuit won on behalf of low-income utility customers;" a project to establish a development bank for Wayne County, Michigan; and development of a nine-month training program for directors of Los Angeles community organizations planning various commercial or industrial projects.

Development Projects Outside Chicago

Southern Development Bancorporation
In 1986 at the request of the Winthrop Rockefeller Foundation, Shorebank helped to set up the Southern Development Bancorporation, based on the model of South Shore Bank, to provide assistance to economically needy rural Arkansas. While separately owned and operated, Shorebank maintains close ties with Southern Development through a management advisory contract.

In 1988, Southern Development acquired Elk Horn Bank and Trust Co., an Arkadelphia-based bank with $55 million in assets. In addition to Elk Horn, the Southern Development operation includes a for-profit venture capital subsidiary called Southern Venture, a non-profit arm, called Arkansas Enterprise Group, which serves functions similar to Shorebank's Neighborhood Institute,[13] and a non-profit unit called the Good Faith Fund, which makes loans of $200 to $2,000 to small entrepreneurs.

According to Shorebank's annual report, the venture capital fund invested $1.9 million in 14 companies in 1992 and the Elk Horn Bank made $4.8 million in development-oriented loans.

Poland Initiative
Working with the congressionally chartered Polish-American Enterprise Fund since late 1989, Shorebank has helped to administer the group's Enterprise Credit Corp., which operates 13 loan windows at 10 banks across Poland. According to Shorebank's annual report, ECC made $28 million in loans during its first two years of operation, including $19.1 million disbursed in 1992.

Douglass Bank
In 1991, Shorebank began a five-year advisory contract to help recapitalize and restructure Kansas City–based Douglass Bank (named for Frederick Douglass), the oldest minority-owned bank west of the Mississippi. In 1992, Douglass, which has since received $3.35 million in new capital, turned a slim profit of $3,000, Shorebank states in its annual report.

Upper Peninsula Economic Development Initiative
Formed in 1992, Shorebank's initiative to spur economic development in Michigan's depressed Upper Peninsula, consists of three parts: a loan production office for South Shore Bank, the Northern Economic Initiatives (NEI)

Corp., a nonprofit organization designed to provide technical assistance to small businesses, and North Coast BIDCO (business and industrial development corporation), which provides equity capital and loans for job-creating enterprises.

NEI, formed from a business development program operated by Northern Michigan University, Marquette, is jointly controlled by the university and Shorebank. North Coast is s subsidiary of Shorebank financed with about $3.5 million from Shorebank and a $3 million loan from the State of Michigan. All or part of the loan can be converted to a grant, assuming the BIDCO meets targets for job creation and sales growth.[14]

North Coast's first deal was a $200,000 loan to Upper Peninsula Nursing, a Marquette-based home nursing company in late 1992. The woman-owned company planned to use the money to expand its operation to the eastern part of the Upper Peninsula, potentially creating 65 to 100 new jobs in the process.[15]

COULD A BANK LIKE SOUTH SHORE BANK WORK IN MY COMMUNITY?

Despite the impressive success of South Shore Bank in revitalizing its community while still earning a profit, there have been, surprisingly few attempts to reproduce the institution in other parts of the country.

Besides Southern Development Bancorporation, the only other recent success story is Brooklyn's Community Capital Bank, which opened its doors in January 1991 with the aim of providing needed capital to disadvantaged areas of New York City. Since that time, assets have grown to over $23 million, including $18 million in deposits. Loans and letters of credit totaled about $7 million, with about $6 million outstanding.

All of Community Capital Bank's loans have been for community development and all have been to commercial borrowers. About half of the loans have been to finance multi-family housing. In just under three years in business, Community Capital Bank has not only suffered no loan losses, but none of its loans have been delinquent.

The reasons why there are not more South Shore and Community Capital Banks are varied, but it is far from clear whether such institutions could work as successfully in all inner-city communities. This is particularly true for communities that have deteriorated farther than South Shore had by the early 1970s and in which incomes are lower.

In some cases, the problem is a simple lack of capital. In late 1991, for example, an effort to set up a similar institution in Washington, D.C., the Development Bank of Washington, was abandoned when the organizers failed to raise enough capital to open the doors.[16]

But despite the obstacles, and the fact that growth of community development banking has been limited so far, ideas abound for spreading the concept to more communities. And advocates of these ideas reside in powerful places.

For example, one vocal advocate of community development banking, the Southern Finance Project (SFP), issued a report in the summer of 1992 which calls for the creation of "public purpose banks" across the South to replace the numerous local savings and loan institutions that have disappeared in recent years. To do this, SFP suggests that the branches of failed thrifts be sold off as community development institutions.

In addition to providing capital to communities "hobbled" by the S&L crisis, the SFP said, such banks could help to revitalize communities by maintaining "extensive investments in local housing, community and industrial development, health and child care, agriculture, or environmental protection. Such institutions could operate on a for-profit or nonprofit basis.

And in January 1993, a coalition of community development organizations, including Community Capital Bank, put forward a series of proposals calling on the government to provide assistance for a broad array of community development lenders.

By far the most notable advocate of community development banks is President Bill Clinton, who, as governor of Arkansas, was involved with the establishment of Southern Development and, as a candidate, proposed federal assistance to establish 100 community development banks in the United States over time. Such banks would lend money in much the same fashion as South Shore bank, filling the "capital gaps" that plague cities and rural areas.

According to a campaign pamphlet, such a network of banks would:

> [P]rovide small loans to low income entrepreneurs and homeowners in
> the inner cities. These banks will also provide advice and assistance to
> entrepreneurs, invest in affordable housing, and help mobilize private
> lenders.[17]

In July 1993, President Clinton announced a plan to assist the development of community development financial institutions (CDFIs). Such institutions include not only banks like South Shore, but a variety of community development financial institutions. These include community development loan funds, community development credit unions, and "micro-enterprise" loan funds community development corporations, all of which have as their primary mission the extension of credit to "targeted populations" in impoverished communities.

In the proposal to Congress, Clinton suggested spending $382 million over four years to match dollar-for-dollar private sector money invested in such institutions. Aid would come in the form of grants, loans, or deposits.

Community development credit unions and banks could receive $5 million under the proposed program, while institutions like community development credit unions, would be eligible for up to $2 million in federal assistance.[18]

NOTES

1. Judy Pasternak, "Chicago's Shorebank Earns Interest as a Model for Rebirth, Renewal," *Los Angeles Times,* Feb. 22, 1993, part A, sec. 1.
2. Ronald Grzywinski, "The New Old-Fashioned Banking," *Harvard Business Review,* May–June 1991, pp. 87–98.
3. Ibid.
4. Elizabeth Leech, "Investing in the Community," *The Magazine of Bank Management,* Aug. 1992, p. 33.
5. J. Linn Allen, "Pride, Investment Help South Shore Fuel its Resurgence," *Chicago Tribune,* May 30, p. 1.
6. Paul Wiseman, "Investing in Inner City, Chicago Bank Redefines Role in Community," *USA Today,* Jan. 8, 1993, p 1B.
7. Joan Shapiro, "Community Development Banks," in Peter D. Kinder, Steven D. Lydenberg, Amy L. Domini, eds., *The Social Investment Almanac* (New York: Henry Holt Reference Books, 1992), p. 514.
8. Ibid.
9. Pasternak, "Chicago's Shorebank."
10. Leech, "Investing in the Community."
11. Pasternak, "Chicago's Shorebank."
12. Allen, "Pride, Investment."
13. Shapiro, "Community Development Banks."
14. "Shorebank Begins Northern Michigan Operations," *Responsive Investing News,* July 6, 1992, p. 4.
15. "South Shore's Michigan Operation Makes First Loan," *Responsive Investing News,* Oct. 12, 1992, p. 7.
16. "D.C. Development Bank Fails to Take Off," *Responsive Investing News,* Oct. 28, p. 3.
17. Bill Clinton, *Putting People First: A National Economic Strategy for America,* 1992.
18. Stella Dawson, "Clinton Unveils Plan to get Credit to Poor," *Reuter Business Report,* July 15, 1993; see also: "Clinton Announces Community Finance Bill," *CDCU Report,* July 1993.

9

Community Development Loan Funds and Credit Unions

Organizations interested in community development projects have a list of needs that are a nightmare to most bankers: they need to borrow relatively small amounts of money at low interest, for investment in low-income communities, for individuals or organizations that often have never received a loan before and, often, they need technical assistance or training in order to make the project work.

The task of providing basic financial services, such as checking and savings accounts to low-income communities, is yet another source of trouble. Poor people, after all, can't easily meet minimum deposit requirements. They certainly can't afford to pay the hefty fees that have become a major source of income for most financial institutions.

Because traditional banks and savings and loan institutions find it difficult to serve low-income communities at a profit, many poor people simply are forced to learn to live without basic financial services. Checks are cashed, for a fee, at check-cashing stores; small loans are made at the local pawn shop; expensive money orders are used to pay the rent.

In some communities, however, the labor-intensive job of providing financing for low-income housing and making small business loans has been championed by a fast-growing network of community development loan funds (CDLFs). Likewise, community development credit unions (CDCUs) have been successful at providing small consumer loans, checking accounts, savings accounts, and numerous other kinds of basic financial services to people who otherwise would have no access to them.

The managers of CDLFs and CDCUs have learned that, when inexpensive loans and financial services are made available by organizations willing to do the hard work required, good things happen, even in "bad" neighborhoods. Small businesses and home owners in formerly red-lined areas can and do pay back their loans; jobs are created; and the problems of poverty and homelessness are eased.

COMMUNITY DEVELOPMENT LOAN FUNDS

Half lender, half community development advocate, community development loan funds specialize in a wide variety of community development projects that, in most cases, could not otherwise receive financing.

Generally capitalized through numerous small investments made by individuals, foundations, churches, financial institutions, and others at zero interest or at below-market interest rates, CDLFs assist individuals, nonprofit organizations, and businesses with the aim of creating jobs, building affordable housing, or upgrading the kinds of services available to low-income communities. The types of loans made by CDLFs vary according to the communities they serve, but the broad goal of promoting community development remains the same wherever they operate. According to the National Association of Community Development Loan Funds, Philadelphia, the mission of community loan funds is threefold:

> All member funds of NACDLF intermediaries, forming a 'bridge' between a variety of investor/lenders and a variety of borrower/developers. A community development loan fund balances the needs of both investor and borrower and is accountable to both. NACDLF member funds are brokers who encourage those with capital to re-allocate or share its use with those who have little or none.
>
> NACDLF member funds are also, in every respect, disciplined lenders. . . . They place capital at risk, but expect and receive repayment of their loans in order to repay their own investors.
>
> . . . NACDLF member funds must also be advocates—for both social investing and community development.[1]

The NACDLF serves virtually all of the 40-plus CDLFs in the United States and Canada by offering technical assistance and training, acting as a national advocate for the movement, and by offering members access to inexpensive capital through its revolving loan fund. The organization also offers a peer-review process through which member funds are evaluated by a team of reviewers from other NACDLF member funds.

For the most part, CDLFs are designed to serve the credit needs in a specific geographic area, although a handful of funds operate with a national mandate, with the aim of financing worthy housing or business development projects wherever capital is needed. Service areas for CDLFs can be as small as one city, or as large as an entire state, or group of states in one region of the country, serving enormously varied types of communities, from large cities like New York, Chicago, and San Francisco to rural areas like Vermont, New Hampshire, and New Mexico.

Many of the CDLFs were set up to concentrate solely on creating low-income housing and the majority of CDLF loans are made in that area. However, across the country, CDLF financing has been used to support a wide variety of projects and enterprises, including: worker-owned cooperatives; micro-enterprises; nonprofit organizations; single-family mortgages; community land trusts; and agricultural production.

Compared with the slow movement toward creating new community development banks in the Unites States, the creation of new CDLFs seems explosive, even if the amount of capital raised is tiny by comparison. According to information provided by the NACDLF, there are 41 CDLFs qualified for membership in the organization. Of those funds, all but three were established since 1980 and the majority were formed since 1986.

Investments in CDLFs are not appropriate for pension funds, because such investments are risky and do not pay a market rate of return. However, the loan funds are increasingly gaining the attention of other kinds of institutional investors, such as foundations and religious organizations, that routinely make low-interest, socially targeted loans as part of their philanthropic or social mission. Such "program-related" and "social" investments provide a significant source of capital for the CDLF movement.

The newest CDLF, the Chicago Community Loan Fund, began lending money in the summer of 1992 when it made a $26,000 loan to rehabilitate a 64-unit apartment building in a depressed neighborhood in Chicago. Funded with an initial capitalization of $300,000, including money from the State of Illinois and a $200,000 investment from the Wieboldt Foundation, the fund's mission is to invest in housing, community services, and job creation in metropolitan Chicago.[2] As of the end of 1992, the fund's total capital had grown to $389,000, according to NACDLF data.

As of Dec. 31, 1992, the 41 member funds of the NACDLF were capitalized at a total of slightly more than $100 million, including about $17.25 million in equity, according to information provided by the organization (see Figure 9-1). The largest CDLF, the Low Income Housing Fund, a national fund based in San Francisco, had almost $12.5 million in capital as of Dec. 31, 1992. Roughly half of the CDLFs were capitalized at less than $1 million.

There were 1,356 loans and commitments on the books of the 41 NACDLF members as of year-end 1992, totaling roughly $66.7 million. At that time, the number of investors in CDLFs totaled 3,437 individuals, foundations, religious organizations, financial institutions, and others, according to the NACDLF.[3]

FIGURE 9-1   Capital Available to NACDLF Member Funds

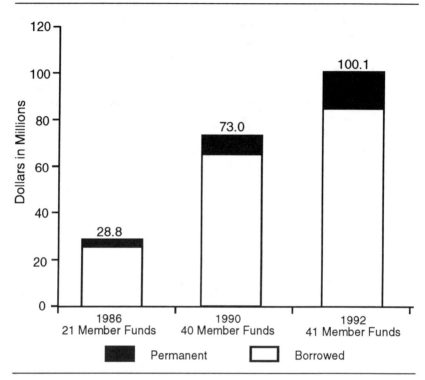

Source: National Association of Community Development Loan Funds.

According to a survey of NACDLF members published in 1991, individuals formed the largest source of money for CDLFs, accounting for 27 percent of the $73 million capital raised at that point. Religious organizations provided the second-largest source of capital (23 percent), followed by foundations (20 percent), governments (12 percent), financial institutions (11 percent), and all other sources, such as corporations, cultural/educational institutions, the NACDLF Central Fund, and the National Cooperative Bank Development Corp. (7.0 percent). (See Figure 9-2.)

A study of CDLFs by the Chicago-based Woodstock Institute in 1991 found that, despite their tiny size (the capitalization of all CDLFs totals less than half that of Chicago's South Shore Bank), such loan funds have made a significant contribution to the communities they serve. The institute found, the funds avoided significant losses by closely monitoring their lenders and providing technical assistance to help ensure that loans are repaid.

In total, the Woodstock study found, the funds had made more than 3,000 loans totaling $88 million through 1990. With that relatively small amount of money, the CDLFs, which at that time had a total capitalization of only $73 million, had created more than 10,000 units of housing, of which 96 percent were for low-income families. In addition, the study states, lending by CDLFs had created about 3,000 new jobs. Despite the seemingly risky nature of community development lending, losses amounted to only 1.3 percent of the total loans made.[4]

The study also found that 33 of the CDLFs had made loans to a total of 887 borrowers who had never before received a loan. CDLFs also made 484 loans to expand services available in the community they serve. Furthermore, the funds were able to use their capital to leverage more than $500 million in loans from other sources.

In terms of their impact on low-income populations, "$3 million in a community development loan fund can do more than $200 million in a traditional financial institution," asserted Kathryn Tholin, vice president of the Woodstock Institute and one of the authors of the study on CDLFs. In many cases, she said, the local CDLF is the only community development lender in the community.[5]

The Woodstock study found that sources of capital for CDLFs vary, according to the needs and philosophy of the organizers of each fund. Some funds, such as the Springfield, Massachusetts–based Institute for Community Economics fund, emphasize raising money from a wide variety of small investors, believing that this kind of capital raising helps to educate people about community development. Others raise funds only from institutions or from a variety of loan sources, including individuals.

In addition, the Woodstock Institute found, the types of loans offered by CDLF's vary widely, based on the needs of the communities they serve. Because specific economic needs vary from community to community, CDLFs have had to developed expertise in niche areas that have been neglected by banks and other lenders in their geographic area.

> For example, the New Hampshire Community Loan Fund (NHCLF) developed a very special expertise in organizing and financing mobile home cooperatives. . . .
> The [NHCLF] stepped into the vacuum [during the real estate boom of the 1980s] . . . to show mobile home owners how to organize as a cooperative that can allow them to become owners of the land.[6]

Through its efforts, the Woodstock report said, the NHCLF allowed numerous low-income families to avoid being displaced by developers of luxury housing.

FIGURE 9-2   NACDLF Member Fund Capital Sources, 1990

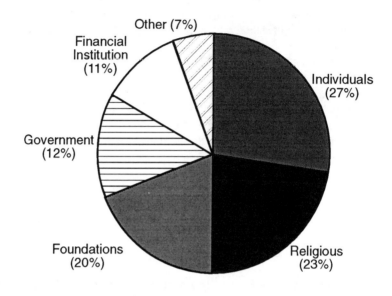

Source: National Association of Community Development Loan Funds.

As successful as CDLFs have been, the Woodstock Institute study suggests that the movement could do even more good if the funds received additional support from "policy makers and resource providers," such as banks, foundations, religious institutions, and state, local, and federal governments. Toward this end, the institute made a number of suggestions for ways the various types of mainstream institutions can do more to assist CDLFs. Among them:

✦ Banks, the institute said, can help CDLFs by providing loans in partnership with the loan funds in ways that allow each to play "an appropriate lending role." An example of this would be for the CDLF to provide construction financing or a short-term mortgage on a project, with the bank committing long-term financing afterward. In addition, the study suggests, banks can assist CDLFs through purchasing "seasoned" loans, providing lines of credit, contributing capital (either through a donation or a long-term, low interest loan), and donating money for technical assistance that CDLFs provide to their clients.

✦ Foundations can play a role in providing grant support for operations of the loan funds, whose work is expensive because of the labor-intensive nature of community development lending, and for specific development needs such as training of staff and strategic planning. In addition, foundations can help by providing permanent capital, making program-related investments, or other "creative" measures, such as providing loan guarantees or funding the loan loss reserve of CDLFs.

✦ Religious institutions can continue to provide capital to CDLFs by making loans and encouraging individual church members to make loans. In addition, churches can participate in the development of CDLFs by helping to recruit volunteers and by helping to plan the establishment of new CDLFs.

✦ State and local governments, which "share a common goal of community development" with CDLFs, can provide assistance through linked deposits in banks which, in turn, contribute a portion of the interest paid to the CDLF. Such an arrangement helps to finance the Chicago Community Loan Fund. In addition, governments can provide various tax incentives to encourage individuals and institutions to loan money to CDLFs and develop partnerships between the loan funds and state and local government agencies and departments.

✦ For the federal government, the institute suggests that it should allow mainstream lenders to use assistance to CDLFs as a method for fulfilling part of their requirements under the Community Reinvestment Act. The federal government can also: ensure that CDLFs are eligible for money under community development grant programs; provide tax incentives to encourage individuals and institutions to make loans to CDLFs; and "provide incentives and subsidies for community economic development projects" that can help to make projects financed by CDLFs more feasible, the Woodstock Institute suggests.

COMMUNITY DEVELOPMENT CREDIT UNIONS

Community development credit unions (CDCUs), like CDLFs, emphasize meeting the credit needs of their communities, and have received support, in the form of grants and equity capital, from foundations and religious institutions. However, CDCUs, which have a longer history than CDLFs, utilize a much more traditional and familiar structure.

Clifford Rosenthal, executive director of the National Federation of Community Development Credit Unions (NFCDCU), writes:

> Some CDCUs trace their roots back half a century. Many were formed during the civil rights and anti-poverty movements of the 1960s. During the last fifteen years, a number of CDCUs were organized as a response to redlining or bank branch closing.[7]

Like most credit unions, CDCUs are able to offer a range of traditional bank-like services, such as checking and savings accounts and consumer loans. Because of this, CDCUs serve a dual role in their communities, serving both as community development lenders and as providers of basic financial services to those who, otherwise, would not have access to them. Deposits in CDCUs, as in other kinds of credit unions, can be federally insured up to $100,000. However, because they are membership-owned and controlled non-profit organizations, depositors who are not members may not vote in credit union elections or borrow from the institutions.

CDCUs began soliciting non-member deposits from foundations and other organizations during the 1970s, but, "little money came in until the 1980s, when the social investment movement began to accelerate and expand. Today, such outside support is a major source of capital for CDCUs. As of 1992, such deposits totaled about $50 million out of about $400 million in total deposits in CDCUs.[8]

According the NFCDCU, there are currently about 300 CDCUs in the United States. The typical CDCU has assets of $1.7 million, although the largest such institutions have assets of more than $30 million and some smaller institutions have assets of $200,000 or less. Most CDCUs serve about 1,200 members, many of whom do not have depository accounts with any other financial institution.

The NFCDCU, based in New York, serves over 100 CDCUs in 35 states. In addition to providing training and management support for member organizations, the NFCDCU maintains a $6 million revolving loan fund to provide CDCUs with low-cost capital and has raised more than $4 million in low-cost deposits from groups such as foundations, churches, and banks through its capitalization program for CDCUs.

In 1991, the Chicago's Woodstock Institute released a comprehensive study of CDCUs. In it, the institute found that such institutions have been instrumental in helping many poor people leave the cash-only economy and gain access to basic financial services. Services offered by CDCUs vary depending on the size of the institution, but include: savings accounts, checking accounts, money orders, certificates of deposit, and even individual retirement accounts. In addition, Woodstock found, such institutions are a vital source of credit for people needing the kinds of small loans that banks often cannot make at a profit. According to the study:

Small loans to individuals are the key component of most community development credit union portfolios. The need for small loans arises from the continuing trend among commercial banks wanting to make all loans for less than $5,000 or even $10,000, as credit card purchases or advances. The problem is that many members of CDCUs do not make enough income or do not have a documented credit history to qualify for a credit card.[9]

Often, the institute found, CDCUs will specialize in one kind of lending that serves a specific community need. For example, the study cites the case of the St. Luke Credit Union which serves rural communities in eastern North Carolina by offering loans for members to add inside plumbing and bathrooms to their homes. The study also points to the Santa Cruz Credit Union in California, which focuses on providing small business loans.

In its report, Woodstock makes a number of suggestions for ways that institutions can help the CDCUs. As it does for community development loan funds, the institute suggests that banks, foundations, religious institutions, and state and local governments make deposits in and provide working capital for these institutions. In addition, the report recommends that churches encourage CDCU membership among their members and that state and local governments utilize CDCUs to package loans for state and local finance programs. Woodstock also suggests that state credit union leagues and community development organizations provide training and assistance to CDCUs.

The institute also suggests that the federal government ease regulations that make it difficult to charter new credit unions and expand existing ones, and provide special regulatory measures to ensure the soundness of CDCUs.

A GOOD-GUY LENDING POLITICAL AGENDA

In early 1993, a loose coalition of community development organizations, including the NACDLF, the NFCDCU, the Woodstock Institute, and Community Capital Bank, issued a position paper in which the organizations outlined their vision for accomplishing the Clinton Administration's stated goal of developing 100 or so new community development financial institutions around the country.

In the statement, the organizations called on the Clinton Administration to center its attention on fostering the growth of existing community development lenders, rather than simply starting new development banks from scratch. The network of existing community development lenders in the United States, the group stated, "offers a solid foundation" for achieving President Clinton's goal of establishing a network of 100 community development banks across the country. Such institutions, the group stated include the types of loan funds, credit unions and community development banks outlined in this chapter, as well as micro-enterprise funds—non-profit lenders organized to make very small loans to individuals—and other, unspecified kinds of institutions.

To accomplish its goal of fostering community development lending, the coalition suggested, the administration should create a "growth ladder" to assist existing institutions to grow and evolve. Under such a plan, the government would assist some of the larger institutions to evolve into "multi-service institutions," similar in scope to Chicago's South Shore Bank, Brooklyn's Community Capital Bank, or Elk Horn Bank and Trust in Arkansas. In turn, federal aid would also be used to "enable some micro-loan funds to evolve into [larger] loan funds or credit unions, [and] small loan funds and credit unions to grow larger."

Federal support, the group suggests, could come in the form of equity capital, grants, long-term deposits at below-market interest, training of "a new generation of directors, managers, and loan officers for community development lenders, and support for the work of providing technical assistance to those who borrow from such lenders."[10]

Many of the groups suggestions were eventually incorporated into the Clinton Administration's community development proposal, released in July 1993 (see Chapter 8).

NOTES

1. *Building the Foundation for Economic, Social and Political Justice,* National Association of Community Development Loan Funds, 1991, p. xii.
2. Press release from the Chicago Community Loan Fund, June 10, 1992.
3. Fax transmission from NACDLF.
4. Judy Stevens and Kathryn Tholin, "Lenders of First Resort: Community Development Loan Funds," Woodstock Institute, 1991, p. 31.
5. "Development Loan Funds Deserve Assistance: Woodstock Study," *Responsive Investing News,* Oct. 14, 1991, p. 2.
6. Ibid., note 4, p. 16
7. Clifford N. Rosenthal, "Community Development Credit Unions," *The Social Investment Almanac,* 1992, p. 531.
8. Ibid.
9. Kathryn Tholin and Jean Pogge, *Banking Services for the Poor: Community Development Credit Unions,* Woodstock Institute, p. 13.
10. *Principles of Community Development Lending & Proposals for Key Federal Support,* Association for Enterprise Opportunity et al., 1993.

10

Mainstream Banks

A DISAPPOINTING HISTORY

The sole reason that good-guy lenders, such as community development banks, loan funds, and credit unions exist and flourish in the United States today is that mainstream lenders—mainly the nation's banks and savings and loan associations—have failed to meet all of the credit needs of the communities they serve. If other banks had not given up on Chicago's South Shore community, for example, there would be no need for South Shore Bank. If poor people had adequate access to credit and banking services, there would be no niche for community development credit unions. If adequate funding for low-income housing and community development flowed from banks and savings and loans, there would be no need for loan funds to fill these needs.

In fairness, it is true that no ordinary bank could be expected to make most of the low-interest, high-risk loans that some alternative lending institutions have been willing to take on. But, in study after study, it has been made clear that most banks could do far more to serve low-income communities, even within the bounds of their traditional role. Sixteen years after the passage of the Community Reinvestment Act, red-lining (the practice of refusing to make loans in designated areas) still exists and minority loan applicants are still far more likely to be refused credit than whites with a similar income.

A study by the Federal Reserve Board in 1992 found that, according to data compiled under the Home Mortgage Disclosure Act (HMDA), African-Americans and Hispanics were two to three times as likely to be turned down for a mortgage in 1990 than white applicants, even when those applicants had similar incomes. Furthermore, a study released by the Federal Reserve Bank of Boston later that year found that, even when the HMDA data was controlled for such non-racial factors as credit history and the type of properties involved, a significant gap still exists between the mortgage acceptance rate of minorities and whites. The Boston report, which focused on the performance of Boston area institutions in 1990, found:

> The results of this study indicate that minority applicants, on average, do have greater debt burdens, higher loan-to-value ratios, and weaker credit histories and they are less likely to buy single-family homes than white applicants, and that these disadvantages do account for a large portion of the difference in denial rates. . . . But these factors do not wholly eliminate the disparity . . . even after controlling for financial, employment and neighborhood characteristics, black and Hispanic mortgage applicants in the Boston metropolitan area are roughly 60 percent more likely to be turned down than whites.[1]

A 1992 study of California banks by the National Community Reinvestment Network and the Greenlining Coalition found that, while less than 1 percent of U.S. banks and savings and loan institutions receive failing grades for their CRA compliance from federal regulators, the actual community investment performance of these institutions was disappointing. Among other things, the study, which also was based on 1990 HMDA data, found:

> No major California bank made loans to minorities at the same rate as they made loans to whites with similar incomes. And no major California bank made even one loan per branch to low-income African-Americans. Yet none of these banks received . . . a CRA rating indicating displeasure from either the Federal Reserve, [Federal Deposit Insurance Corp.], or the office of the Comptroller of the Currency.[2]

According to the California report, a survey of 6,668 CRA ratings granted by federal regulators nationwide between July 1990 and March 1992 found that 9 percent of all institutions received an "outstanding" grade, 80 percent were ranked "satisfactory," 9 percent were placed in the "needs to improve" category, and less than 1 percent were deemed to be in "substantial noncompliance" with CRA.

However, three California banks—Wells Fargo, Bank of America, and First Interstate—received outstanding grades despite the fact that they had made "less than one home loan per five branches to African-Americans earning $27,000 or less," according to the HMDA data, the report said.

Of course, not every bank can be a South Shore Bank. Like it or not, few financial institutions have community development as their primary mission. But that doesn't mean that some mainstream banks are not striving to make a difference in their communities. Amid all the bad news about the community reinvestment performance of major banks, there are success stories.

The following is a description of two innovative programs, both formed in 1989, which show that, with proper commitment, traditional banks can successfully begin to meet the credit needs of underprivileged communities while remaining true to their obligations to their shareholders and their duty to make loans prudently.

VERMONT NATIONAL BANK

The Socially Responsible Banking Fund at Vermont National Bank, Brattle-boro, was set up to allow depositors a chance to put their savings to work to make loans that meet certain social and ethical goals.

While the bank had, for some time, allowed customers of its trust department to make ethical decisions about the use of their money, the Socially Responsible Banking Fund was probably the first program in the country to apply social and ethical criteria in the use of regular bank deposits. Products available to depositors in the Socially Responsible Banking Fund include: savings accounts, personal and business checking accounts, money market accounts, certificates of deposit, individual retirement accounts, VISA Credit cards, trust services, and employee banking services.

Most of the bank's depositors are individuals in the local area, but, like South Shore Bank, the Vermont National fund seeks depositors from around the country. Among the fund's depositors are individuals, corporations, cities, counties, and school districts from all over the United States. Institutional customers include the city of Burlington, Vermont, which began depositing city accounts into the fund in 1992.

Depositors are attracted to the banking fund because, unlike other banks, Vermont national tells them up-front what kinds of projects and businesses their deposits will and will not support. The investment guidelines for the socially responsible banking fund state:

> In a world of limited resources, we choose to do business with those who, in our view, will use funds from the Socially Responsible Banking Fund to do the most good.
>
> We seek to lend to or invest in companies that make positive contributions to our natural environment, use or develop appropriate energy technologies, contribute significantly to the communities in which they operate, and treat their employees well.
>
> We will not lend or invest in companies that have negative records in these areas or that derive income from the manufacture of alcoholic beverages, tobacco products, or the sale of military weapons or weapons systems. Nor will we lend to or invest in companies that maintain more than minimal contact with South Africa.

Among the loans made by the Socially Responsible banking fund in 1992 were:

✦ Financing for organic vegetable farms and for the construction of greenhouses that extend the growing season for local farmers.

✦ Financing for Energy Recovery, a Brattleboro firm that draws methane gas from a local landfill and converts it into electricity for sale to a local utility company.

✦ A loan to World Learning Inc.'s School for International Training and another to finance the creation of Child's World Preschool, which leases space from a public elementary school.

✦ A line of credit for Rutland West Neighborhood Housing Services, which, in turn, helps lower-income people finance the purchase of a home.

✦ Financing for the creation of *Environmental Building News,* a Brattleboro-based newsletter on the use of environmentally sound building materials and practices for builders and architects.

FIGURE 10-1   VNB Socially Responsible Banking Fund Loan Portfolio (6/30/93)

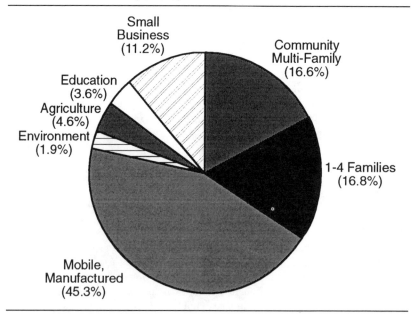

Small Business (11.2%)

Education (3.6%)

Agriculture (4.6%)

Environment (1.9%)

Community Multi-Family (16.6%)

1-4 Families (16.8%)

Mobile, Manufactured (45.3%)

Source: Vermont National Bank.

As of June 30, 1993, the assets of the Socially Responsible Banking Fund totaled $52.1 million, including 1,082 loans worth just under $52 million. The bank also owned a $50,000 stake in the Vermont Community Development Credit Union and about $101,000 worth of Federal Home Loan Bank stock. Of the fund's loan portfolio, about $41 million consisted of affordable housing loans, including $23.5 million for mobile and manufactured dwellings, $8.7 million in mortgages for 1–4-family homes, and $8.6 million for commercial multi-family housing. Other types of loans included those for agriculture, small businesses, environmental and conservation projects and a handful of educational loans (see Figure 10-1). The yield on the total loan portfolio of the Socially Responsible Banking Fund was 8.33 percent, the bank reports.

Deposits of $100,000 or less as of June 30, 1993 totaled $45.4 million. In addition, certificates of deposit of over $100,000 totaled another $2.6 million and repurchase agreements totaled $3.5 million.

BANK OF AMERICA AND BoA COMMUNITY DEVELOPMENT BANK

The Bank of America Community Development Bank is a wholly owned subsidiary of Bank of America designed to make loans to people and community development projects that otherwise would not get financing through traditional means. In the three years since it opened its doors, the bank, which operates branches in several California cities, in Phoenix, Arizona, and in Dallas, Texas, has made over $300 million in loans, most of which were backed by some sort of public sector guarantee, such as those offered by the federal Small Business Administration, or a guarantee from a foundation.

Among its recent projects, the BoA Community Development Bank funded a project to build 100 single-family homes priced at $92,000 to $115,000 in Brentwood, California.[3]

In 1992, according to information provided by the bank, BOA Community Development bank made $101 million in permanent and construction loans for low-income multi-family housing. The loans, which ranged in size between $300,000 and $17.7 million, financed the construction or renovation of 3,371 units of housing, in both urban and rural areas. In addition, the community development bank made just over $30 million in loans to small business assisted by the Small Business Administration or other government agencies. Of that amount, 39 percent went to women- and minority-owned enterprises. The small business loans ranged in size from $50,000 to $2.7 million, but 46 percent were for $100,000 or less.

The BOA Community Development Bank has received an "outstanding" rating for its compliance with the Community Reinvestment Act by the Federal Deposit Insurance Corp. and was recently named a Lender With a

Heart by the Farmers Home Administration for its work in making FHA-guaranteed loans in rural areas of California.

In addition to the activities of its community development bank, Bank of America has made other efforts to increase its lending activity in needy communities. According to the bank, its Community Reinvestment Act-related lending in California totaled about $2.1 billion in 1992, including $1.9 billion in housing loans. The Bank also made $239.6 million in CRA-related small business loans through a variety of programs and $3.7 million in CRA-related personal, auto, and home equity loans.

Among its other programs, in February 1993, Bank of America announced that it had established a $3 million fund to make predevelopment loans to nonprofit housing developers. The money, which was divided between three nonprofit housing organizations serving the western United States, will be used to finance site preparation, legal work, engineering studies, and other steps necessary before work on a construction project can begin.

Beneficiaries of the bank's Community Housing Fund program were: the Low Income Housing Fund, San Francisco, which received $1.5 million; the Rural Communities Assistance Corp., San Francisco, $1 million; and the Local Initiatives Support Corp., Los Angeles, $500,000. According to a statement issued by the bank at the time, the three groups will use the money "to provide pre-development loans to tenant groups and community-based nonprofits seeking to purchase federally insured multi-family housing" and to make loans for the "new construction and rehabilitation in urban and rural areas."

In April, 1992, when Bank of America merged with Security Pacific, the bank stated a goal of making a total of $12 billion in CRA-related home loans in low-income census tracts and through certain special programs over a 10-year period.

NOTES

1. Alicia Munnell, et al., *Mortgage Lending in Boston: Interpreting HMDA Data,* Federal Reserve Bank of Boston, 1992, p. 2.
2. *Inflated Grades and Dubious Performances: A Study of the National Implications of CRA Ratings and HMDA Data,* National Community Reinvestment Network and the Greenlining Coalition, 1992, p. 4.
3. Michael Liedtke, "BofA Community Loans Reach Out to Poor, Women," *Contra Costa Times,* March 22, 1993, p. 1D.

11

Some Money Managers Offering Responsive Investing Services

Most money managers will invest assets based on any criteria a client chooses, including any social criteria. Such firms, after all, make their living by satisfying their clients and, therefore, are more than willing to avoid making investments in South Africa–related companies or "sin" stocks, regardless of whether the management of the firm is enthusiastic about socially responsible investing. Money managers who *specialize* in social investing are more rare, but there currently exist several firms eager to help institutions that want to incorporate social values into their investment policy.

The following is a listing of some money management firms that have been active in pursuing institutional clients for various kinds of socially motivated investment products, along with a contact name and a telephone number. While not intended to constitute an exhaustive list, the sampling provides an indication of the kinds of investment services available to institutional investors who invest money based on social criteria or who wish to make economically targeted investments.

The information for the following list was compiled from The Social Investment Forum's annual directory of members, *The Social Investment Almanac* (Henry Holt, 1992), profiles published in *Pensions & Investments* magazine's annual directory of money management firms, articles in the press, and from the firms themselves.[1]

Ariel Capital Management is a Chicago-based money management firm that specializes in equities. The firm, which invests in small- and medium-sized corporationss, does not invest in companies that manufacture

229

weapons, are involved with nuclear power, or which do business in South Africa. The firm is also minority-owned.

In addition to serving individual accounts, the firm also serves as an investment advisor to the Calvert-Ariel Growth Fund and the Calvert-Ariel Appreciation fund, both distributed by Calvert Group, Bethesda, Maryland.

Contact: Mellody Hobson
(312) 726-0140

Baird Asset Management, Milwaukee, is the first investment advisor to specialize in economically targeted investments. The firm's investment programs are designed to provide "patient" capital investments in urban redevelopment, affordable housing, the improvement of local infrastructure, and other targeted projects, while providing a competitive, risk-adjusted return for the investor.

Baird Asset Management is a unit of Robert W. Baird & Co. Inc., a Milwaukee-based regional investment banking firm. Among its clients, Baird Asset was selected to be investment manager for the Commonwealth Diversified Trust.

Contact: Alton Bathrick
(414) 756-3815

Blairlogie Capital Management, with offices in Edinburgh, Scotland and Atlanta, was formed in late 1992 and is a unit of Pacific Financial Asset Management Corp. The firm offers clients the chance to invest in international equity portfolios with what the firm calls a "light green complexion."

According to its sales literature, Blairlogie offers actively managed portfolios based on Morgan Stanley Capital International's EAFE index, emerging markets accounts, emerging markets portfolios based on the IFC Investable Index, global large capitalization and small capitalization accounts, as well as regional portfolios concentrating on the stock markets of Europe and the Far East.

In order to decide where to invest, the firm first analyzes companies based on a variety of economic criteria to establish a "buy list." Blairlogie then applies a variety of ecological screens in order to pick the most environmentally responsible firms on that list.

Contacts: Darren W. DeVore, Atlanta
(404) 390-1799
Gavin Dobson, Edinburgh
(031) 529-0050

Christian Brothers Investment Services Inc., New York, is a registered investment advisory firm that serves Catholic institutional investors.

The firm manages two commingled trust funds, the Religious Communities Trust (RCT), which offers investors a choice of three short-term investment funds, and the Catholic United Investment Trust (CUIT). The CUIT includes a balanced fund (which invests in value-style equities and fixed income instruments) and a growth-oriented equity fund. In addition to the two trusts, Christian Brothers offers assistance for institutions that want to set up individually managed portfolios of $2 million or more.

The firm's social investment strategy emphasizes active engagement with corporations aimed at improving their social performance. Such activity includes active involvement in proxy voting, the sponsorship of shareholder resolutions, as well as dialogue and correspondence with the management of corporations represented in its portfolios.

Contact: Gerard J. Frendreis
(212) 490-0800

Commonwealth Capital Partners, Cambridge, Mass., is in the process of establishing the first commingled economically targeted investing portfolio for major institutional investors, the Commonwealth Diversified Trust. The company seeks to raise $500 million for investments in specially created securities designed to fund low-income housing, education, and training. Commitments must be made for three years.

The trust, which will be managed by Baird Asset Management, will seek investments of high credit quality, some of which may utilize guarantees and credit enhancements from state and federal agencies and the private sector. Investors will be able to designate 50 percent of their investment to be allocated to a designated state. The other half of the commitment will be allocated to investments in regions designated by other investors in the trust.

In 1992, the Wisconsin Investment board pledged $50 million to the trust, which will be allocated once other investors sign on.

Contact: David Sand
(617) 576-5858

Covenant Investment Management, based in Chicago, is a registered investment advisor that specializes in portfolios based on social criteria. Its products include the Covenant Portfolio, a growth and income-oriented mutual fund in which companies are screened for a variety of social issues. In addition, the company offers individually designed portfolios based on the requirements of individual clients.

The 36 "social screens" applied by the firm deal with community relations, treatment of customers, environmental conduct, employee and shareholder relations, and a variety of other social issues.

Formed in 1990, the firm had about $5 million under management as of August 1993.

Contact: Anthony J. Carfang
(312) 443-8472

Franklin Research & Development Corp., Boston, claims to be the largest and oldest investment advisory firm that exclusively manages socially screened portfolios. The firm, which manages just under $300 million, makes both conventional and economically targeted investments.

Social screening research is done in-house and part of the company's findings are published in its monthly newsletter, *INSIGHT.*

Contact: Patrick McVeigh
(617) 423-6655

Mellon Equity Associates, Pittsburgh, a unit of Mellon Bank Corp. with about $5 billion under management, offers actively managed equity, balanced, and tactical asset allocation portfolios. The firm has been managing South Africa–free portfolios since 1975, using the South Africa–free Standard & Poor's 500 stock index as its benchmark. In addition, the firm offers individualized portfolios screened based on other social issues, such as alcohol and tobacco or arms production.

Mellon Equity's investment approach is quantitative and based on bottom-up analysis.

Contact: Patricia K. Nichols
(412) 234-1394

Neuberger & Berman is a New York–based manager with about $25 billion under management as of January 1, 1993. The firm manages a variety of equity and fixed income portfolios.

For those wishing to invest with social criteria in mind, Neuberger & Berman designs accounts to fit the needs of individual clients, utilizing its own social research database through which it tracks the ethical and social performance of about 650 companies. The database includes information in seven major categories: product considerations; environmental impact; employment record; human rights; public health; corporate citizenship; and war and peace.

Contact: Robert McComsey
(212) 476-9000

NWQ Investment Management Co., Los Angeles, has been managing social investment portfolios since 1986. The company utilizes databases, as well as the input from interest groups, government departments, and others, and its own contacts with corporations to screen companies. Depending on the client's requirements, issues looked at include weapons manufacturing;

job discrimination; the environment; "sin" products; and the manufacture of contraceptive devices.

The firm, which has about $4.5 billion under management, manages active equity and balanced portfolios.

Contact: Karen McCue or James Owen
(213) 624-6700

Scudder, Stevens & Clark, based in New York, a money manager offering a wide variety of investment products, is the largest manager of social investment portfolios. About $4 billion of the firm's roughly $77 billion in assets under management are invested based on some kind of social criteria.

The firm's social investment approach, like its overall strategy, relies heavily on its proprietary, in-house research. In addition to a team of more than 45 analysts, the firm employs a separate team of social issue researchers. Individual portfolios are screened based on the needs of individual clients.

Contact: Edmund J. Thimme Jr.
(212) 326-6200

United States Trust Co. of Boston has been offering socially screened investment portfolios since 1974. Offering a range of equity, bond and balanced portfolios, US Trust employs a staff of five social issue researchers to develop a database of companies that meet the social criteria of the firm's clients. The firm also manages portfolios that are not socially screened.

Common screening criteria include: impact on the community and the environment; employee relations; and product safety. In addition, the company is also active in voting proxies and communicates regularly with corporate management regarding social and ethical concerns.

US Trust, which has about $3 billion in assets under management, offers individually managed portfolios as well as three commingled trust funds—equity and balanced funds for taxable investors and a balanced portfolio for pension and other retirement funds.

Contact: James McPartland
(617) 726-7367

NOTE

1. It is important to point out that inclusion on this list in no way constitutes a recommendation of any firm on the part of the authors or publisher. The needs and risk tolerance of individual institutions vary widely. Therefore, it is up to each organization to examine the investment products of each firm closely to determine whether they can be successfully incorporated into its portfolio.

Glossary

IMPORTANT ABBREVIATIONS AND ACRONYMS

ANC	African National Congress
ACTWU	Amalgamated Clothing and Textile Workers Union
AFL-CIO	American Federation of Labor-Congress of Industrial Organizations
BIT	Building Investment Trust of AFL-CIO
CalPERS	California Public Employees' Retirement System
CPA	Center for Policy Alternatives
CERES	Coalition for Environmentally Responsible Economies
CREF	College Retirement Equities Fund
CODESA	Congress for a Democratic South Africa
CRA	Community Reinvestment Act
DOL	Department of Labor
DSNI	Dudley Street Neighborhood Initiative
EBRI	Employee Benefits Research Institute
ETI	Economically Targeted Investing
ERISA	Employee Retirement Income Security Act of 1974
HIT	Housing Investment Trust of AFL-CIO
IFE	Institute for Fiduciary Education
ICCR	Interfaith Center on Corporate Responsibility
IRRC	Investor Responsibility Research Center

235

INC	Irish National Caucus
LIMAC	Local Initiatives Managed Assets Corporation
LISC	Local Initiatives Support Corporation
MASTERS	Massachusetts State Teachers' and Employees' Retirement System
NACDLF	National Association of Community Development Loan Funds
NCDI	National Community Development Initiative
NFCDCU	National Federation of Community Development Credit Unions
NYCERS	New York City Employees' Retirement System
PRI	Program-related Investing
SACC	South African Council of Churches
SEC	Securities and Exchange Commission
TIAA	Teachers Insurance and Annuity Association
TIAA-CREF	Teachers Insurance and Annuity Association– College Retirement Equities Fund
USA	United Shareholders Association

IMPORTANT TERMS

Apartheid: The system of forced racial separation in the Republic of South Africa.

Beneficiary: A person receiving or designated to received benefits of a trust or insurance policy, such as a person receiving benefits from a pension fund.

CERES Principles, formerly Valdez Principles: A code of environmental conduct for corporations developed by the Coalition for Environmentally Responsible Economies (CERES), Boston.

Community development bank: A bank for which community economic development is the primary mission.

Community development credit union: A credit union formed to serve low-income communities and to provide credit and basic financial services to people who, otherwise, might not have access to them.

Community development loan fund: A non-profit organization that makes loans, usually at low interest rates, for the purpose of promoting community and economic development. Typically such lending supports the creation of low-income housing, small business, and job creation.

Defined benefit plan: A traditional pension fund in which benefits paid to a retiree are based on factors such as age, length of service, and previous compensation, rather than on the size of an investment portfolio.

Defined contribution plan: A type of retirement plan in which benefits received by a retiree are determined by the size of the employee's investment account at the time of retirement. Defined contribution plans include 401(k) plans, profit sharing plans, and money purchase plans.

Divestment: The process of selling off the securities of corporations that do not meet certain ethical criteria. For example, many public pension funds have been forced to divest the stocks of corporations doing business in South Africa.

Economically targeted investing, or ETI: The investment of pension fund or other portfolio assets with the aim of providing benefits to the local economy while, at the same time, earning a competitive rate of return for the portfolio.

Emerging manager: Literally, any money management firm which is relatively young and lacks the assets under management generally required to be considered for pension fund accounts. The term is also widely used to refer to young, small women- and minority-owned firms.

Equity: An ownership interest in a company, such as the ownership of stock in the company.

Exclusive benefit rule: The rule requiring that all corporate pension funds be managed for the exclusive purpose of paying benefits to retirees and paying the reasonable costs of maintaining the fund.

Fiduciary: Someone who has the duty to act for the benefit of another person or group. For example, the trustees of a pension fund have a fiduciary duty to invest the fund's assets in the best interests of the fund's beneficiaries.

MacBride Principles: A code of conduct for corporations operating in Northern Ireland aimed at creating equal employment opportunities for Roman Catholics there.

Maquiladora: A foreign-owned factory in Mexico near the U.S. border. Under a special program, the corporations that assemble goods in maquiladoras are taxed only on the value added in Mexico when the goods are imported into the United States.

Minority manager: see **emerging manager**

Poison pill: An anti-takeover strategy in which existing shareholders are given the right to purchase additional shares of stock, or other securities, at a discount in the event of a takeover attempt.

Program-related investments (PRIs): Investments consistent with the philanthropic mission of a foundation. Under such arrangements, foundations accept a higher risk and/or lower investment return than could be earned elsewhere in order to make investments with a social purpose.

Proxy Statement: A statement sent to shareholders containing a proxy ballot describing resolutions to be voted on at the shareholder's meeting as well as candidates for the board of directors.

Prudent person rule; or, prudent man rule: The duty of a fiduciary to make only those investments that a prudent person would make when investing his or her own property, consistent with the goals of protecting the safety of the portfolio and meeting future financial obligations.

Sin stocks: Stocks of corporations that derive significant revenue from the production of alcoholic beverages, tobacco products, or gambling opportunities.

Social screening: The process of excluding corporations from an investment portfolio based on certain ethical criteria. For example, many religious organizations apply social screens in order to avoid sin stocks.

Statement of Principles, formerly, Sullivan Principles: A code of conduct for corporations operating in South Africa aimed at creating equal employment opportunities for the black majority there.

Sullivan Principles: see **Statement of Principles**

Valdez Principles: see **CERES Principles**

1

The CERES *Principles*
(*Formerly the* Valdez *Principles*)

INTRODUCTION

By adopting these Principles, we publicly affirm our belief that corporations have a responsibility for the environment, and must conduct all aspects of their business as responsible stewards of the environment by operating in a manner that protects the Earth. We believe that corporations must not compromise the ability of future generations to sustain themselves.

We will update our practices constantly in light of advances in technology and new understandings in health and environmental science. In collaboration with CERES, we will promote a dynamic process to ensure that the Principles are interpreted in a way that accommodates changing technologies and environmental realities. We intend to make consistent, measurable progress in implementing these Principles and to apply them to all aspects of our operations throughout the world.

Protection of the Biosphere

We will reduce and make continual progress toward eliminating the release of any substance that may cause environmental damage to the air, water, or the earth or its inhabitants. We will safeguard all habitats affected by our operations and will protect open spaces and wilderness, while preserving biodiversity.

Sustainable Use of Natural Resources

We will make sustainable use of renewable natural resources, such as water, soils and forests. We will conserve nonrenewable natural resources through efficient use and careful planning.

Reduction and Disposal of Wastes

We will reduce and where possible eliminate waste through source reduction and recycling. All waste will be handled and disposed of through safe and responsible methods.

Energy Conservation

We will conserve energy and improve the energy efficiency of our internal operations and of the goods and services we sell. We will make every effort to use environmentally safe and sustainable energy sources.

Risk Reduction

We will strive to minimize the environmental, health and safety risk to our employees and the communities in which we operate through safe technologies, facilities and operating procedures, and by being prepared for emergencies.

Safe Products and Services

We will reduce and where possible eliminate the use, manufacture or sale of products and services that cause environmental damage or health or safety hazards. We will inform our customers of the environmental impacts of our products or services and try to correct unsafe use.

Environmental Restoration

We will promptly and responsibility correct conditions we have caused that endanger health, safety or the environment. To the extent feasible, we will redress injuries we have caused to persons or damage we have caused to the environment and will restore the environment.

Informing the Public

We will inform in a timely manner everyone who may be affected by conditions caused by our company that might endanger health, safety or the environment. We will regularly seek advice and counsel through dialogue with persons in communities near our facilities. We will not take any action against employees for reporting dangerous incidents or conditions to management or to appropriate authorities.

Management Commitment

We will implement these Principles and sustain a process that ensures that the Board of Directors and Chief Executive Officer are fully informed about pertinent environmental issues and are fully responsible for environmental policy. In selecting our Board of Directors, we will consider demonstrated environmental commitment as a factor.

Audits and Reports

We will conduct an annual self-evaluation of our progress in implementing these Principles. We will support the timely creation of generally accepted environmental audit procedures. We will annually complete the CERES Report, which will be made available to the public.

DISCLAIMER

These Principles establish an environmental ethic with criteria by which investors and others can assess the environmental performance of companies. Companies that sign these Principles pledge to go voluntarily beyond the requirements of the law. These Principles are not intended to create new legal liabilities, expand existing rights or obligations, waive legal defenses, or otherwise affect the legal position of any signatory company, and are not intended to be used against a signatory in any legal proceeding for any purpose.

This amended version of the CERES Principles was adopted by the CERES Board of Directors on April 28, 1992.

CERES PRINCIPLES SIGNATORIES
(*as of August* 1993)

Ally Capital Corporation
Sausalito, CA

Equipment Finance
9/25/90

Atlantic Recycled Paper Company
Baltimore, MD

Recycled Paper
2/25/91

Aurora Press
Santa Fe, NM

Publishing
4/6/92

Aveda Corporation
Minneapolis, MN

Personal Care Products
11/22/89

B & B Publishing
Fontana, WI

Publishing
9/16/91

The Beamery, Inc.
Heiskell, TN

Timber Frame Homes
9/11/90

Bellcomb Technologies, Inc.
Minneapolis, MN

Structural Building Panels
10/31/90

Ben & Jerry's Homemade
Waterbury, VT

All-Natural Ice Cream
5/1/92

Bestmann Green Systems, Inc.
Boston, MA

Bioengineering
8/18/92

The Body Shop International
New York, London

Skin & Hair Care
3/30/93

C-A-P-D Consultants, Inc.
Decatur, GA

Environmental Consulting
5/24/93

Calvert Social Investment Fund
Bethesda, MD

Social Investing
3/19/91

Clivus Multrum, Inc.
Lawrence, MA

Waste Processing
10/10/90

Community Capital Bank
Brooklyn, NY

Banking
5/22/92

Consumers United Group
Washington, D.C.

Community Development,
Fundraising, Marketing, Insurance
6/9/92

Co-op America
Washington, D.C.

Social Investment
2/11/91

Council on Economic Priorities
New York, NY
Social Research
10/17/91

Coyote Found Candles, Inc.
Port Townsend, WA
Candles
7/17/92

Crib Diaper Service
Crystal, MN
Diaper Service
7/30/90

Cyclean, Inc.
Austin, TX
Asphalt Recycling
8/18/92

DEJA, Inc.
Tigard, OR
Recycled Footware
7/13/93

Domino's Pizza Distribution
Corporation
Ann Arbor, MI
Food Distribution
6/21/90

E Magazine
Norwalk, CT
Publishing
7/1/93

Earth Care Paper Company
Madison, WI
Recycled Paper
10/29/90

Earthrise Trading Company
Petaluma, CA
Nutritional Products
7/2/93

Eco-Invest Publishing, Ltd.
Vienna, Austria
Stock Research & Publishing
7/1/93

Eco-Logical Marketing
Phoenix, AZ
Marketing
5/26/92

Ecoprint
Silver Spring, MD
Printing
3/1/91

Environmental Risk & Loss
Control, Inc.
New York, NY
Consulting
5/4/93

Esalen Institute
Big Sur, CA
Education
6/9/92

Falcon Partners Management, L.P.
Boston, MA
Investment
1/11/92

First Affirmative Financial Network
Colorado Springs, CO
Social Investing
4/30/91

Franklin Research & Development
Corporation
Boston, MA
Social Investing
8/15/90

Geo. W. King Co. Baltimore, MD	Advertising 4/9/91
Global Environmental Technologies Allentown, PA	Water Purification 6/14/91
Greenworld Products Corporation Minneapolis, MN	Lawn & Garden 6/18/92
Hardwood Products Company Branscomb, CA	Lumber Manufacturing 7/18/90
Indian Foods Company Minneapolis, MN	Food Products 12/1/91
Intrigue Salon Marietta, GA	Personal Care 7/17/90
LecTec Corporation Minnetonka, MN	Medical Products 5/31/91
Lender Environmental Services, Inc. Dallas, TX	Computer Software 6/1/93
Louiseville & Jefferson County Metropolitan Sewer District Louisville, KY	Sanitation 8/15/90
MoneyMatters Corporation, Ltd. Sidney, Australia	Social Investing 3/8/92
Natural World, Inc. Stamford, CT	Household & Personal Care 6/5/93
Pacific Partners International Investments New York, NY	Investment 12/2/91
Paper Service, Ltd. Hinsdale, NH	Recycled Paper 8/9/93
Performance Computer Forms Lakeville, MN	Office Paper Products 6/30/92
Phoenix Heat Treating, Inc. Phoenix, AZ	Heat Treating 1/21/92
Progressive Asset Management Oakland, CA	Social Investing 2/1/91
Ringer Corporation Eden Prairie, MN	Lawn & Garden 3/31/92

Service Litho-Print Oshkosh, WI	Printing 7/22/91
Seventh Generation Colchester, VT	Mail Order Distribution 5/1/92
Smith & Hawken Mill Valley, CA	Mail Order Distribution 4/9/90
Stonyfield Farm Yogurt Londonderry, NH	Yogurt 5/1/90
Sullivan & Worcester Boston, MA	Legal Services 6/5/91
The Summit Group Minneapolis, MN	Marketing 6/3/92
Sun Company, Inc. Philadelphia, PA	Petroleum 2/10/93
The Timberland Company Hampton, NH	Outdoor Clothing 4/15/93
Tom's of Maine Kennebunk, ME	Natural Personal Care 4/22/92
United States Trust Company of Boston Boston, MA	Banking 5/21/93
VanCity Investment Service, Ltd. Vancouver, BC	Social Investing 6/27/90
Walnut Acres Penns Creek, PA	Organic Farming 2/28/91
The WATER Foundation Brainerd, MN	Radio Programming 7/31/92
Working Assets Funding Service San Francisco, CA	Social Investing 8/15/90

Code of Conduct
for Businesses Operating
in South Africa
(South African Council of Churches
Initiative; July, 1993)

INTRODUCTION

The apartheid system has historically burdened South Africa with gross economic distortions, stagnation, secrecy, severe discrimination, and natural devastation. It has deprived the country's workers, communities, and environment of the fundamental rights written into international conventions and upheld in other countries.

In order to reverse this crippling legacy and to improve the economic well-being of all South Africans, investment by both South African and multi-national companies needs to be reshaped in the image of an equitable, democratic and life-enhancing society.

It is out of this grave concern and motivation based on ethical religious considerations that the South African Council of Churches, meeting in conference on 8 July 1993, takes this initiative to introduce and support this code of conduct. The code outlines ways in which business can play a constructive and creative role in partnership with workers, communities and other members of civil society, to lay the economic foundations for a stable and prosperous South Africa.

While these standards are also expected to inform the policies of a democratically elected government, in the interim, they are designed to apply to companies operating in South Africa.

Source: Interfaith Center on Corporate Responsibility.

1. Equal Opportunity

Companies should insure that their operations are free from discrimination based on race, sex, religion, political opinion or physical handicap, and implement affirmative action programs designed to protect the equal rights and treatment of the historically disadvantaged.

2. Training and Education

Companies should develop and implement training and education programs to increase the productive capacities of their South African employees in consultation with the trade union movement.

3. Workers Rights

Companies should recognize representative unions and uphold their employees' rights to organize openly, bargain collectively, picket peacefully and strike without intimidation or harassment.

4. Working and Living Conditions

Companies should maintain safe and healthy work environment and strive to ensure that the working and living conditions they provide accord with relevant international conventions.

5. Job Creation and Security

Companies should strive to maintain productive employment opportunities and create new jobs for South Africans.

6. Community Relations

Companies should share information about their practices and projected plans with communities affected by their operations, and develop social responsibility programs in ongoing consideration with representative bodies in these communities.

7. Consumer Protection

Companies should inform consumers of any possible dangers associated with their products and cooperate with consumer protection and broader community organizations to develop and uphold appropriate product safety and quality standards.

8. Environmental Protection

Companies should utilize environmentally sound practices and technologies, disclose how and in what amounts they dispose of their waste products, and seek to minimize hazardous waste.

9. Empowerment of Black Businesses

Companies should strive to improve the development of black-owned South African businesses by purchasing from and sub-contracting to such firms.

10. Implementation

Companies should cooperate with monitors established to implement these standards by disclosing relevant information in a timely fashion.

Minority- and Women-Owned Money Management Firms

Abacus Financial Group Inc.
300 W. Washington St., Suite 1120
Chicago, IL 60606
(312) 553-9300   fax (312) 553-9308

	($ millions)
Total assets managed	50
Total tax-exempt assets	50

Abacus Financial Group Inc. is an active bond manager.

Advisers Capital Management Inc.
58 Pine St.
New York, NY 10005
(212) 248-8989   fax (212) 248-8109

	($ millions)
Total assets managed	1,365
Total tax-exempt assets	1,365

Advisers Capital Management Inc. is an active domestic and global bond and short-term manager.

Albritton Capital Management Co.
3 Ravinia Drive, Suite 1470
Atlanta, GA 30346
(404) 551-7560   fax (404) 551-7570

Source: Pensions and Investments, May 17, 1993. Reprinted with permission.

	($ millions)
Total assets managed	50
Total tax-exempt assets	15

Albritton Capital Management Co. is an active bond manager.

Alpha Capital Management Inc.
25505 W. Twelve Mile, Suite 4100
Southfield, MI 48034
(313) 827-3315   fax (313) 827-1268

	($ millions)
Total assets managed	45
Total tax-exempt assets	34

Alpha Capital Management Inc. is an active equity, active bond, and balanced manager.

Amerindo Investment Advisors Inc.
388 Market St., Suite 950
San Francisco, CA 94111
(415) 362-0292   fax (415) 362-0533

	($ millions)
Total assets managed	1,501
Total tax-exempt assets	1,501

Amerindo Investment Advisors Inc. is an active equity manager.

Amervest Co. Inc.
1875 Century Park East, Suite 1740
Los Angeles, CA 90067
(310) 552-7972   fax (310) 552-2665

	($ millions)
Total assets managed	250
Total tax-exempt assets	250

Amervest Co. Inc. is an active bond, balanced, short-term, and enhanced index manager.

Anderson Capital Management Inc.
220 Sansome St., Suite 400
San Francisco, CA 94104
(415) 433-5233   fax (415) 433-2737

	($ millions)
Total assets managed	86
Total tax-exempt assets	46

Anderson Capital Management Inc. is an active equity and convertibles manager.

Ariel Capital Management Inc.
307 N. Michigan Ave., Suite 500
Chicago, IL 60601
(312) 726-0140   fax (312) 726-7473

	($ millions)
Total assets managed	2,128
Total tax-exempt assets	1,665

Ariel Capital Management Inc. is an active equity manager.

Arnold Investment Counsel Inc.
700 N. Water St.
Milwaukee, WI 53202
(414) 271-2726   fax (414) 271-2809

	($ millions)
Total assets managed	125
Total tax-exempt assets	85

Arnold Investment Counsel Inc. is an active equity, active bond, balanced, and short-term manager.

Beal Investment Co.
366 Madison Ave., Fifth Floor
New York, NY 10017
(212) 983-4722   fax (212) 983-4539

	($ millions)
Total assets managed	205
Total tax-exempt assets	205

Beal Investment Co. is an active equity manager.

Bradford & Marzec Inc.
333 S. Hope St., Suite 4050
Los Angeles, CA 90071
(213) 687-9170   fax (213) 687-9189

	($ millions)
Total assets managed	1,727
Total tax-exempt assets	1,620

Bradford & Marzec Inc. is an active bond manager.

Cadinha & Co. Inc.
900 Fort Street Mall, Suite 1240
Honolulu, HI 96813
(808) 523-9488   fax (808) 526-9725

($ millions)

Total assets managed	346
Total tax-exempt assets	346

Cadinha & Co. Inc. is an active equity, active bond, and balanced manager.

Carr & Associates Inc.
P.O. Box 90, 300-2 Route 17
Lodi, NJ 07644
(201) 365-1920   fax (201) 365-2282

($ millions)

Total assets managed	16
Total tax-exempt assets	11

Carr & Associates Inc. is a convertibles manager.

Cashen Investment Advisors Inc.
5001 Spring Vally Road, Suite 824 East
Dallas, TX 75244
(214) 715-1860   fax (214) 715-1866

($ millions)

Total assets managed	498
Total tax-exempt assets	25

Cashen Investment Advisors Inc. is an active equity, active bond, balanced and cash manager.

Cattanach & Associates Ltd.
455 Sherman St., Suite 460
Denver, CO 80203
(303) 722-1595   fax (303) 722-1639

($ millions)

Total assets managed	41
Total tax-exempt assets	20

Cattanach & Associates Ltd. is a venture capital manager.

L.H. Chaing Investment Counsel
638 Lindero Canyon Road, Suite 327
Agoura, CA 91301
(805) 374-7774   fax (805) 374-7773

($ millions)

Total assets managed	61
Total tax-exempt assets	38

L.H. Chaing Investment Counsel is an active equity, active bond, balanced, passive international/global equity and bond, venture capital, and convertibles manager.

CIC Asset Management Inc.
707 Wilshire Blvd., Suite 5520
Los Angeles, CA 90017
(213) 629-0451   fax (213) 629-0901

	($ millions)
Total assets managed	122
Total tax-exempt assets	122

CIC Asset Management Inc. is an active equity manager.

Draper Computime Asset Management
34 Deer Path
Quogue, NY 11959
(516) 653-9158

	($ millions)
Total assets managed	86
Total tax-exempt assets	7

Draper Computime Asset Management is an active equity, short-term, TAA, and enhanced index manager.

Emerging Markets Investors Corp.
1001 19th St. N., 16th Floor
Arlington, VA 22209
(703) 243-8800   fax (703) 243-2266

	($ millions)
Total assets managed	1,075
Total tax-exempt assets	711

Emerging Markets Investors Corp. is an active international/global equity manager.

Evergreen Asset Management Inc.
1301 Fifth Ave., Suite 3634
Seattle, WA 98101
(206) 224-9914   fax (206) 382-0950

	($ millions)
Total assets managed	71
Total tax-exempt assets	71

Evergreen Asset Management Inc. is an active equity, bond, and short-term manager.

EverGreen Capital Management
10707 Pacific St., Suite 201
Omaha, NE 68114
(402) 392-1220   fax (402) 392-0863

	($ millions)
Total assets managed	56
Total tax-exempt assets	55

EverGreen Capital Management is an active equity and active bond manager.

Ewing Capital Inc.
727 15th St. N.W., Suite 700
Washington, DC 20005
(202) 737-1500   fax (202) 783-6392

	($ millions)
Total assets managed	37
Total tax-exempt assets	37

Ewing Capital Inc. is an active equity and balanced manager.

Ferguson Investment Consultants Inc.
528 Bellwood Ave.
North Tarrytown, NY 10591
(914) 631-7188   fax (914) 631-2621

	($ millions)
Total assets managed	10
Total tax-exempt assets	1

Ferguson Investment Consultants Inc. is an active domestic and international/global equity, active bond, and balanced manager.

Galleon Capital Management
5405 Morehouse Drive, Suite 327
San Diego, CA 92121
(619) 535-1144   fax (619) 535-0237

	($ millions)
Total assets managed	101
Total tax-exempt assets	84

Galleon Capital Management is an active equity and balanced manager.

Garner Asset Management Corp.
111 Center St., Suite 2110
Little Rock, AR 72201
(501) 688-2550   fax (501) 688-2538

	($ millions)
Total assets managed	219
Total tax-exempt assets	3

Garner Asset Management Corp. is an active bond manager.

GLOBALT Inc.
3060 Peachtree Road N.W., Suite 225
Atlanta, GA 30305
(404) 364-2188   fax (404) 364-2189

	($ millions)
Total assets managed	150
Total tax-exempt assets	85

GLOBALT Inc. is an active equity, active bond, and balanced manager.

GW Capital Inc.
10800 N.E. Eighth St., Suite 315
Bellevue, WA 98004
(206) 646-9336   fax (206) 646-5459

	($ millions)
Total assets managed	45
Total tax-exempt assets	45

GW Capital Inc. is an active equity, active bond, balanced, and convertibles manager.

Hamil & Holte Inc.
410 17th St., Suite 2460
Denver, CO 80202
(303) 820-3701   fax (303) 820-3705

	($ millions)
Total assets managed	45
Total tax-exempt assets	27

Hamil & Holte Inc. is an active equity, active bond, and balanced manager.

Hamilton Management Group Inc.
3775 NationsBank Plaza
Charlotte, NC 28280
(704) 358-9808   fax (704) 362-2150

	($ millions)
Total assets managed	90
Total tax-exempt assets	89

Hamilton Management Group Inc. is an active equity and balanced manager.

HCM Capital Management Inc.
P.O. Box 4342
Honolulu, HI 96812
(808) 841-3699   fax (808) 848-8636

	($ millions)
Total assets managed	220
Total tax-exempt assets	193

HCM Capital Management Inc. is an active bond manager.

Holt-Smith & Renk Inc.
4274 E. Towne Blvd., Essex Square, Suite 204
Madison, WI 53704
(608) 249-4488   fax (608) 249-7988

	($ millions)
Total assets managed	23
Total tax-exempt assets	10

Holt-Smith & Renk Inc. is an active equity, active bond, and balanced manager.

Howard and McInnes Inc.
820 Trustmark National Bank Building
Jackson, MS 39201
(601) 948-0952   fax (601) 948-5123

	($ millions)
Total assets managed	11
Total tax-exempt assets	2

Howard and McInnes Inc. is an active equity manager.

Investment Advisors of Key Biscayne Inc.
240 Crandon Blvd., Suite 200
Key Biscayne, FL 33149
(305) 361-7951   fax (305) 361-0517

	($ millions)
Total assets managed	10
Total tax-exempt assets	2

Investment Advisors of Key Biscayne Inc. is an active equity, active bond, balanced, and enhanced index manager.

Karpus Investment Management
5 Tobey Village Office Park
Rochester, NY 14534
(716) 586-4680   fax (716) 586-4315

	($ millions)
Total assets managed	200
Total tax-exempt assets	100

Karpus Investment Management is an active domestic and international/ global bond and short-term manager.

The Kenwood Group Inc.
77 W. Washington, Suite 1615
Chicago, IL 60602
(312) 368-1666   fax (312) 368-1769

	($ millions)
Total assets managed	45
Total tax-exempt assets	45

The Kenwood Group Inc. is an active equity manager.

Lakefront Capital Investors Inc.
1422 Euclid Ave., Suite 846
Cleveland, OH 44115
(216) 344-9200   fax (216) 344-9149

	($ millions)
Total assets managed	6
Total tax-exempt assets	6

Lakefront Capital Investors Inc. is an active equity manager.

The Lara Group
8000 Towers Crescent Drive, Suite 260
Vienna, VA 22182
(703) 827-2306

	($ millions)
Total assets managed	7
Total tax-exempt assets	4

The Lara Group is an active bond manager.

WR Lazard & Co.
14 Wall St.
New York, NY 10005
(212) 406-2700   fax (212) 587-9838

	($ millions)
Total assets managed	2,372
Total tax-exempt assets	2,372

WR Lazard Co. is an active and passive equity, active and passive bond, balanced, enhanced index, and short-term manager.

R.M. Leary & Co. Inc.
3300 E. First Ave., Suite 290
Denver, CO 80206
(303) 320-1063   fax (303) 320-6501

	($ millions)
Total assets managed	48
Total tax-exempt assets	39

R.M. Leary & Co. Inc. is a mutual fund manager.

Lee Capital Management
27520 Hawthorne Blvd., Suite 154
Rolling Hills Estates, CA 90274
(310) 541-9080   fax (310) 541-1017

	($ millions)
Total assets managed	18
Total tax-exempt assets	7

Lee Capital Management is an active bond manager.

Leshner Financial Services Inc.
312 Walnut St., Suite 2100
Cincinnati, OH 45202
(513) 629-2060   fax (513) 629-2082

	($ millions)
Total assets managed	215
Total tax-exempt assets	113

Leshner Financial Services Inc. is an active equity, active bond, balanced, short-term, and TAA manager.

Llama Asset Management Co.
1 McIlroy Plaza, Suite 302
Fayetteville, AR 72701
(501) 444-4080   fax (501) 444-4082

	($ millions)
Total assets managed	195
Total tax-exempt assets	85

Llama Asset Management Co. is an active bond manager.

LM Capital Management Inc.
5560 La Jolla Blvd., Suite E
La Jolla, CA 92037
(619) 459-8965   fax (619) 459-8968

	($ millions)
Total assets managed	207
Total tax-exempt assets	46

LM Capital Management Inc. is an active domestic and international/global bond and short-term manager.

Marathon Asset Management Co. Inc.
1250 Prospect St., Suite 300, P.O. Box 9117
La Jolla, CA 92037
(619) 456-8033   fax (619) 456-2513

	($ millions)
Total assets managed	116
Total tax-exempt assets	113

Marathon Asset Management Co. Inc. is an active equity, active bond, balanced, and short-term manager.

The Marshall Plan
31 Milk St.
Boston, MA 02109
(617) 482-4640   fax (617) 695-0499

	($ millions)
Total assets managed	59
Total tax-exempt assets	58

The Marshall Plan is an active equity manager.

North American Capital Management
8820 Delmar, P.O. Box 6728
Shawnee Mission, KS 66206
(913) 381-8401   fax (913) 381-8402

	($ millions)
Total assets managed	17
Total tax-exempt assets	7

North American Capital Management is an active equity manager.

Payden & Rygel
333 S. Grand Ave., 32nd Floor
Los Angeles, CA 90071
(213) 625-1900   fax (213) 625-1943

	($ millions)
Total assets managed	12,500
Total tax-exempt assets	9,500

Payden & Rygel is an active domestic and international/global bond, and short-term manager.

Pecksland Associates
537 Steamboat Road
Greenwich, CT 06830
(203) 661-4800   fax (203) 661-9730

	($ millions)
Total assets managed	115
Total tax-exempt assets	115

Pecksland Associates is an active domestic and international/global equity and bond, balanced, TAA, convertible, derivatives, arbitrage, and currencies manager.

Pena Investment Advisors Inc.
1200 17th St., Suite 1250
Denver, CO 80202
(303) 572-6888   fax (303) 572-6885

	($ millions)
Total assets managed	11
Total tax-exempt assets	11

Pena Investment Advisors Inc. is an active equity manager.

Phoenix Investment Management Co.
1 Citizens Plaza
Providence, RI 02903
(401) 331-6650   fax (401) 751-4575

	($ millions)
Total assets managed	339
Total tax-exempt assets	93

Phoenix Investment Management Co. is an active equity, active bond, balanced, and short-term manager.

Piedmont Capital Management Associates Inc.
800 Main St., Suite 200
Hilton Head, SC 29926
(803) 681-9023   fax (803) 681-9128

	($ millions)
Total assets managed	266
Total tax-exempt assets	42

Piedmont Capital Management Associates Inc. is an active equity, active bond, balanced, and short-term manager.

Progress Investment Management Co.
71 Stevenson St., Suite 1620
San Francisco, CA 94105
(415) 512-3480   fax (415) 512-3475

	($ millions)
Total assets managed	526 assigned to other firms
Total tax-exempt assets	526 assigned to other firms

Progress Investment Management Co. is a manager of managers, which offers active equity and active bond management.

The Quasar Group
751 Broad St., P.O. Box 1084
Newark, NJ 07102
(201) 802-9529   fax (201) 802-8529

	($ millions)
Total assets managed	290
Total tax-exempt assets	280

The Quasar Group is a quantitative and derivative strategies manager.

V.A. Reid & Associates Inc.
8 E. Hamilton St.
Baltimore, MD 21202
(410) 332-0893   fax (410) 332-0898

	($ millions)
Total assets managed	148
Total tax-exempt assets	148

V.A. Reid & Associates Inc. is an active bond and short-term manager.

RhumbLine Advisers
30 Rowes Warf, Suite 350
Boston, MA 02110
(617) 345-0434   fax (617) 345-0675

	($ millions)
Total assets managed	830
Total tax-exempt assets	830

RhumbLine Advisers is a passive domestic and international/global equity, enhanced index, and option enhanced index manager.

Rosenblum-Silverman-Sutton S.F. Inc.
1388 Sutter St., Suite 725
San Francisco, CA 94109
(415) 771-4500

	($ millions)
Total assets managed	200
Total tax-exempt assets	40

Rosenblum-Silverman-Sutton S.F. Inc. is an active equity, active bond, and balanced manager.

Sit Investment Associates Inc.
4600 Norwest Center, 90 S. Seventh St.
Minneapolis, MN 55402
(612) 332-3223   fax (612) 342-2018

	($ millions)
Total assets managed	4,683
Total tax-exempt assets	3,442

Sit Investment Associates Inc. is an active equity, active bond, and balanced manager.

Sit/Kim International Investment Associates Inc.
1285 Avenue of the Americas, 16th Floor
New York, NY 10019
(212) 713-8636   fax (212) 713-8670

	($ millions)
Total assets managed	189
Total tax-exempt assets	122

Sit/Kim International Investment Associates Inc. is an active international/global equity, and venture capital manager.

Smith, Grahm & Co.
3 Allen Center, 333 Clay St., Suite 4470
Houston, TX 77002
(713) 739-1113   fax (713) 739-8436

	($ millions)
Total assets managed	550
Total tax-exempt assets	550

Smith, Grahm & Co. is an active bond and short-term manager.

Stamco Inc.
1516 Second Ave., Suite 300
Seattle, WA 98101
(206) 340-1003   fax (206) 340-0843

	($ millions)
Total assets managed	320
Total tax-exempt assets	270

Stamco Inc. is a short-term manager.

Statistical Sciences Inc.
357 N. Canon Drive
Beverly Hills, CA 90210
(310) 275-5551   fax (310) 247-1943

	($ millions)
Total assets managed	375
Total tax-exempt assets	350

Statistical Sciences Inc. is an active equity, balanced, and market neutral manager.

Strategic Investment Partners Inc.

1001 19th St. N., 16th Floor
Arlington, VA 22209
(703) 243-4433   fax (703) 243-2266

	($ millions)
Total assets managed	internal = 25,
	assigned to other firms = 6,906
Total tax-exempt assets	internal = 25,
	assigned to other firms = 5,773

Strategic Investment Partners Inc. is a manager of managers which offers international/global equity and fixed income management.

Swarthmore Group Inc.

767 Third Ave.
New York, NY 10017
(212) 750-3200   fax (212) 750-3207

	($ millions)
Total assets managed	36
Total tax-exempt assets	36

Swarthmore Group Inc. is an active equity manager.

Taplin, Canida & Habacht

1001 S. Bayshore Drive, Suite 2100
Miami, FL 33131
(305) 379-2100   fax (305) 379-4452

	($ millions)
Total assets managed	465
Total tax-exempt assets	395

Taplin, Canida & Habacht is an active equity, active bond, and balanced manager.

Valenzuela Capital Management Inc.

1270 Ave. of the Americas, 12th Floor
New York, NY 10023
(212) 332-8590   fax (212) 332-8597

	($ millions)
Total assets managed	199
Total tax-exempt assets	199

Valenzuela Capital Management Inc. is an active equity manager.

Wagner Investment Management Inc.
410 17th St., Suite 840
Denver, CO 80202
(303) 892-0527   fax (303) 892-1337

	($ millions)
Total assets managed	236
Total tax-exempt assets	6

Wagner Investment Management Inc. is an active equity, active bond, balanced, short-term, and TAA manager.

Ward/M&C Asset Management Inc.
1100 Atlanta Financial Center
3343 Peachtree Road
Atlanta, GA 30326
(404) 262-0124   fax (404) 262-0105

	($ millions)
Total assets managed	30
Total tax-exempt assets	30

Ward/M&C Asset Management Inc. is an active equity, active bond, and balanced manager.

Wedgewood Capital Management Inc.
1350 I St., N.W., Suite 520
Washington, DC 20005
(202) 408-1550   fax (202) 408-1558

	($ millions)
Total assets managed	275
Total tax-exempt assets	275

Wedgewood Capital Management Inc. is an active bond and short-term manager.

Westwood Management Corp.
300 Crescent Court, Suite 1110
Dallas, TX 75201
(214) 871-6970   fax (214) 871-6979

	($ millions)
Total assets managed	703
Total tax-exempt assets	677

Westwood Management Corp. is an active equity, active bond, balanced, and short-term manager.

Woodford Capital Management Inc.
400 Madison Ave., Suite 1410
New York, NY 10017
(212) 758-2205   fax (212) 758-5147

	($ millions)
Total assets managed	75
Total tax-exempt assets	61

Woodford Capital Management Inc. is an active growth equity manager.

Zevenbergen Capital Inc.
601 Union St., Suite 2434
Seattle, WA 98101
(206) 682-8469   fax (206) 682-9625

	($ millions)
Total assets managed	215
Total tax-exempt assets	184

Zevenbergen Capital Inc. is an active equity manager.

4

Financial Professionals, Trade Organizations, and Information Sources

ACCION International
130 Prospect Street
Cambridge, Massachusetts 02139-9794
617-492-4930

Operates the Bridge Fund, a lending program for microenterprises in Central and South America.

Campaign for Human Development
1312 Massachusetts Avenue NW
Washington, D.C. 20005
212-659-6650

Operates the Economic Development Loan Program, funded by the nation's Catholic bishops, which provides loans and loan guarantees to worker- and community-owned businesses in low-income areas.

CANNICOR
P.O. Box. 6819
San Francisco, California 94101
415-885-5102

Affiliated with the Interfaith Center on Corporate Responsibility, conducts research on the banking industry, including a useful 1992 study on mortgage lending in American cities.

Center for Corporate Social Responsibility
1001 Pennsylvania Avenue
Washington, D.C. 20004-2599
202-624-2430

Organization for members of the American Council of Life Insurance and the Health Insurance Association of America; encourages corporate community involvement, philanthropy, volunteerism, and social investing.

Christian Brothers Investment Services
675 Third Avenue, 31st Floor
New York, New York 10017
212- 490-0800

Investment advisor and manager for Catholic institutional investors.

Council on Economic Priorities
30 Irving Place
New York, New York 10003
800-822-6435

Ecumenical Development Cooperative Society
155 N. Michigan Avenue, Suite 627
Chicago, Illinois, 60601
312-938-3056

Franklin Research & Development Company
711 Atlantic Avenue, Fifth Floor
Boston, Massachusetts 02111
617-423-6655

Interfaith Center on Corporate Responsibility
475 Riverside Drive, Room 566
New York, New York 10115
212-870-2295

Investor Responsibility Research Center
1755 Massachusetts Avenue NW
Washington, D.C. 20036
202-939-6500

Kinder, Lydenberg, Domini & Company
7 Dana Street
Cambridge, Massachusetts 02138
617-547-7479

National Association of Community Development Loan Funds
P.O. Box 40085
Philadelphia, Pennsylvania 19106-5085
215-923-4754

Organization of funds that lend capital borrowed from social investors to residents, community development organizations and others in areas often bypassed by conventional lenders.

National Bankers Association
122 C Street NW, Suite 300
Washington, D.C. 20005
202-682-4200

Association of women- and minority-owned banks.

National Cooperative Bank
1630 Connecticut Avenue NW
Washington, D.C. 20009-1004
202-745-4600

Intermediary that develops financial services and offers technical support for cooperatively owned businesses.

National Federation of Community Development Credit Unions
59 John Street, Eighth Floor
New York, New York 10038
800-437-8711 or 212-513-7191

Provides technical assistance and support to member credit unions.

Social Investment Forum
430 First Avenue North, Suite 290
Minneapolis, Minnesota 55401
612-333-8338

Woodstock Institute
407 South Dearborn
Chicago, Illinois 60605
312-427-8070

Advocate of community investing, has published numerous studies on the Community Reinvestment Act and the financial industry's relationship with communities.

PUBLICATIONS/INFORMATION SOURCES

Business and Society Review
2513 Old Kings Highway North, Suite 107
Darien, Connecticut 06820

Magazine of opinion, commentary, and general interest articles.

Business Ethics Magazine
1107 Hazeltine Boulevard, Suite 530
Chaska, Minnesota 55318
612-448-8864

Magazine of general interest articles.

Catalyst
P.O. Box 1308
Montpelier, Vermont 05601
802-223-7943

Quarterly newsletter on alternative investments, with emphasis on small businesses, worker-owned companies, non-profits, and emerging technology.

Chronicle of Philanthropy
1255 23rd Street NW
Washington, D.C. 20037
202-466-1200

Newspaper covering the non-profit sector.

Clean Yield
Box 1880
Greenboro Bend, Vermont 05842
802-533-7178

General interest social investing newsletter, with tips on stocks to watch.

Co-op America Quarterly
A Socially Responsible Financial Planning Guide
Co-op America
2100 M Street NW, Suite 403
Washington, D.C. 20063
800-424-2667 or 202-872-5307

Information about social investing opportunities and services.

The Corporate Examiner
Interfaith Center on Corporate Responsibility
475 Riverside Drive, Room 566
New York, New York 10115
212-870-2293

Information on shareholder activism and corporate dialogue.

Directory of Socially Responsible Investments
666 Broadway, 5th Floor
New York, New York 10012
212-529-5300

Franklin's Insight
Franklin's Insight: Investing for a Better World
711 Atlantic Avenue, 5th Floor
Boston, Massachusetts 02111
617-423-6655

Good Money
P.O. Box 363 B
Calais State Road
Worcester, Vermont 05682
800-223-3911

National Boycott Newsletter
6506 28th Avenue, NE
Seattle, Washington 98115
206-523-0421

COMMUNITY DEVELOPMENT BANKS

Ameritrust Development Bank
840 Halle Building
1228 Euclid Avenue
Cleveland, Ohio 441115-1831
216-861-6984

Blackfeet National Bank
P.O. Box 730
Browning, Montana 59417
406-338-7000

Community Capital Bank
P.O. Box 404920
Brooklyn, New York 11240
718-768-9344 or 800-827-6699

Elk Horn Bank and Trust
P.O. Box 248
Arkadelphia, Arkansas 71923
501-246-5811

South Shore Bank
71st and Jeffery Boulevard
Chicago, Illinois 60649-2096
312-288-7017 or 800-669-7725

OTHER BANKING INSTITUTIONS

First Trade Union Savings Bank
10 Drydock Avenue
Boston, Massachusetts 02205-9063
617-482-4000

Owned by trade unions.

Self-Help Credit Union
Center for Community Self-Help
413 East Chapel Hill Street
Durham, North Carolina 27701
919-683-3016

Vermont National Bank
P.O. Box 804-C
Brattleboro, Vermont 05301
802-257-7151 or 800-544-7108, extension 2414

Women's World Banking
140 East 40th Street, Suite 607
New York, New York 10016
212-953-2390

5

Community Development Loan Funds

ANAWIM Fund of the Midwest
517 W. 7th Street
P.O. Box 4022
Davenport, Iowa 52808
319-324-6632

Association for Regional Agriculture Building the Local Economy (ARABLE)
715 Lincoln Street
Eugene, Oregon 97401
503-485-7630

Berakah Alternative Investment Fund
925 S. Mason, Suite 131
Katy, Texas 7754
713-392-3838

Boston Community Loan Fund
30 Germania Street
Boston, Massachusetts 02130
617-522-6768

Source: National Association of Community Development Loan Funds.

Capital District Community Loan Fund
340 First Street
Albany, New York 12206
518-436-8586

Cascadia Revolving Fund
175 Yesler, Suite 414
Seattle, Washington 98104
206-447-9226

Chicago Community Loan Fund
343 South Dearborn, Suite 1001
Chicago, Illinois 60604
312-922-1350

Common Wealth Revolving Loan Fund
1221 Elm Street
Youngstown, Ohio 44505
216-744-2667

Community Loan Fund of Southwest Pennsylvania
48 South 14th Street
Pittsburgh, Pennsylvania 15203
412-381-9965

Cooperative Fund of New England
108 Kenyon Street
Hartford, Connecticut 06105
203-523-4305

Cornerstone-Homesource Loan Fund
P.O. Box 6842
Cincinnati, Ohio 45206
513-651-1505

Delaware Valley Community Reinvestment Fund
924 Cherry Street, 3rd Floor
Philadelphia, Pennsylvania 19107
215-925-1130

Federation for Appalachian Housing Enterprises
Drawer B
Berea, Kentucky 40403
606-986-2321

FORGE
Route 6, Box 134-1
Tahlequah, Oklahoma 74464
918-456-1615

Fund for an OPEN Society
311 S. Juniper Street, Suite 400
Phildelphia, Pennsylvania 19107
215-735-6915

Greater New Haven Community Loan Fund
5 Elm Street
New Haven, Connecticut 06510
203-789-8690

Human/Economic Appalachian Development Corporation Revolving Loan Fund
P.O. Box 504
Berea, Kentucky 40403
606-986-3283

Illinois Facilities Fund
300 West Adams Street
Chicago, Illinois 60606-5101
312-629-0060

Industrial Cooperative Association Revolving Loan Fund
20 Park Plaza, Suite 1127
Boston, Massachusetts 02116
617-338-0010

Institute for Community Economics Revolving Loan Fund
57 School Street
Springfield, Massachusetts 01105-1331
413-746-8660

Jubilee Community Loan Fund
55 Tree Haven Road
Buffalo, New York 14215
716-836-6355

Lakota Fund
P.O. Box 340
Kyle, South Dakota 57752
605-455-2500

Leviticus 25:23 Alternative Fund
299 North Highland Avenue
Ossining, New York 10562
914-941-9422

Low Income Housing Fund
605 Market Street, Suite 709
San Francisco, California 94105
415-777-9804

Maine Community Loan Fund
300 St. John Street
P.O. Box 931
Portland, Maine 04104-0931
207-767-4755

McAuley Housing Fund
1650 Farnum Street
Omaha, Nebraska 68102
402-346-6000, ext. 344

McAuley Institute
8300 Colesville Road, Suite 310
Silver Spring, Maryland 20910
301-588-8110

Michigan Housing Trust Fund
3401 East Saginaw, Suite 212
Lansing, Michigan 48912
517-336-9919

MICRO Industry Credit Rural Organization
802 East 46th Street
Tucson, Arizona 85713
602-622-3553

Montreal Community Loan Association
914 Rachel East Street
Montreal, Quebec, Canada H2J 2J1
514-525-6628

New Hampshire Community Loan Fund
Box 666
Concord, New Hampshire 03302-0666
603-224-6669

New Jersey Community Loan Fund
P.O. Box 1655
Trenton, New Jersey 08607
609-989-7766

New Mexico Community Development Loan Fund
P.O. Box 705
Albuquerque, New Mexico 87103
505-243-3196

Non-Profit Facilities Fund
12 West 31st Street
New York, New York 10001
212-868-6710

Northcountry Cooperative Development Fund
2129-A Riverside Avenue
Minneapolis, Minnesota 55454
612-371-0325

Northern California Community Loan Fund
14 Precita Avenue
San Francisco, California 94110
415-285-3909

Rural Community Assistance Corporation
2125 19th Street, Suite 203
Sacramento, California 95818
916-447-2854

Self-Help Ventures Fund
413 East Chapel Hill Street
Durham, North Carolina 27701
919-683-3016

Southeastern Reinvestment Ventures, Inc.
159 Ralph McGill Boulevard, N.E., Room 505
Atlanta, Georgia 30308
404-659-0002, ext. 3240

Vermont Community Loan Fund
P.O. Box 827
Montpelier, Vermont 05601
802-223-1448

Washington Area Community Investment Fund
2201 P Street NW
Washington, D.C. 20037
202-462-4727

Worcester Community Loan Fund
P.O. Box 271, Mid Town Mall
Worcester, Massachusetts 01614
508-799-6106

Index

290 / INDEX

Start-up capital, 75, 130
State
  insurance pools, 16
  pension funds, 10, 12, 27, 93, 122
  pension systems, 92
State of Conneccticut Trust Funds, 81-82
State of New York Mortgage Authority (SONYMA), 73-75
State of Wisconsin Investment Board, 76-77
Statement of Principles, 24, 25, 30, 33, 43, 98
State-wide pension funds, 22
Stock(s), 12, 56, 84
  see Company, Corporate, Preferred, Sin, Tobacco, Value
  owner(s), 174
  ownership, 128
Stockholders, 173
Students for Business Ethics, 162
Subcontractors, 92
Sullivan Principles for Fair Employment in South Africa, 24, 43, 155, 157, 173, 176, 177
Sunset provision, 99
Supreme Court, 189
Sustainable development, 102

T

Taft-Hartley
  Act, 113
  assets, 116, 129
  funds, 115, 116, 118, 120, 125, 129, 131
  trusts, 125, 165
Takeover, 84
  see Anti-takeover, Poison pill
  attempt, 85
Tangible assets, 107
Targeted investing, 67
  portfolio, 71
Targeted investments, 7, 9-11, 14, 16
  see Economically
Tax incentives, 219
Tax Reform Act of 1986, 105
Tax withholding, 138
  see Federal
Teacher's Fund, 74, 75
Teachers Insurance and Annuity Association (TIAA), 57, 145

College Retirement Equities Fund, 43, 57, 164
Technical assistance, 216, 218
Texas Teachers Retirement Fund, 166
Third World factories, 122
TIAA, see Teachers
Tobacco, 39-43, 49-55, 58, 98, 99, 162, 163, 172, 184-185
  Control Resource Center, 53
  Divestment Project, 41, 52, 53, 163
  stocks, 54
Transaction costs, 161
Transitional Executive Council, 153, 159
Treasury/Treasuries, 80, 193
  certificates, 191
  notes, 80
Trustees, 3, 6, 83, 157
  see Labor, Pension fund

U

ULLICO, see Union Labor Life
Underwriting, 192
  requirements, 78
UNICEF, 185
Union(s), 40, 49, 113-134
  see Community, Credit, Labor
  funds, 120
  Labor Life Insurance Company (ULLICO), 117, 118
  Mortgage Account, 117
  pension funds, 5, 22, 47, 68, 114
Union-affiliated funds, 116, 129
Unitarian Universalist Association, 197
United Food and Commercial Workers, 123
United Mine Workers of America, 121, 122
United Nations, 153, 185, 186
United Shareholders Association (USA), 47, 52, 53
Universities, 153-170
Upper Peninsula Economic Development Initiative, 209-210
Urban Development Action Grant, 149
Urban Investment Program, 135
U.S. Agency for International Development, 106
U.S. Department of Agriculture (USDA), 149